MELBOURNE

Edited by John Borthwick and David McGonigal
Designed by Ken Gilroy and Brian Hutchinson
Directed by Hans Hoefer
Produced by Geoffrey Eu
Photographed by Paul Steel and Others

APA PUBLICATIONS

MELBOURNE

First Edition

Printed in Singapore by Höfer Press Pte Ltd

ABOUT THIS BOOK

Like most good journeys, it happened at short notice. When Apa Publications' Editorial Director Geoffrey Eu proposed to prolific Australian travel writers **John Borthwick** and **David McGonigal** that their next trip could take them down the path to producing a book on Melbourne, they signed on immediately. This promised to be no literary cruise, but a production itinerary "chock-a-block" with research, writing, commissioning and photography.

The ground to be travelled was clear: there would be tours through boulevards, alleys and galleries of Melbourne, historical journeys covering Melbourne's Gold Rush youth to its elegant present, and discoveries of the magic of Melbourne.

Both writers were well qualified for the task. John Borthwick had combined for most of the 1980s the multiple roles of travel writer, photographer and adventure travel tour leader. He had worked also in Melbourne radio for several years and knew the city's ambience and excitement well. In addition, he was an "old APA hand," having previously written six chapters of *Insight Guide: Australia*.

David McGonigal is an inveterate traveller—his adventures include a four year motorcycle odyssey around the world which took him across Asia to Tibet, Nepal, Afghanistan, and Turkey as well as everywhere in Europe and North America. McGonigal has also made frequent trips in and out of Melbourne which have given him an appreciation of the unique character of the city (and an indelible knowledge of the Tullamarine freeway from the airport to downtown). McGonigal has also spent time exploring Melbourne's hinterlands which he has covered in his book *Wilderness Australia*. A keen photographer, many of his images appear in this book.

Borthwick and McGonigal worked closely with the person they dubbed "our electromagnetic man in Singapore," **Geoffrey Eu**. Via telephone, fax and floppy disc they steered the book on its tight course, constantly swapping information, copy, photographs and page layouts.

Cityguide: Melbourne, like other Apa publications, is dedicated to providing informative and relevant text and vivid photography to enhance a traveller's journeys through interesting places. The internationally-acclaimed guides are the brainchild of **Hans Hoefer**, a German designer trained in the Bahaus tradition. Hoefer, who established Apa in Singapore in 1970, has directed and designed some 100 travel books. Many of these have enjoyed numerous reprints and have been translated to other languages, including Spanish, French, Chinese, Italian and German.

Joining Borthwick and McGonigal on the production trail were two other experts in travel book production, **Ken Gilroy** and **Brian Hutchinson**, the namesakes of Hutchinson Gilroy Design of Northbridge, Sydney. In addition to designing a wide range of books for adults and children, Gilroy is a successful painter who exhibits regularly—and sells well—in Australian galleries. He undertook the multiple tasks of photo selection, copyfitting the text and designing the book layout.

Borthwick

McGonigal

Gilroy

Hutchinson

Brian Hutchinson co-ordinated the project, keeping in touch with the writers of each section and with photographers, scheduling all aspects of the work to ensure that deadlines were met. A former executive of an adventure travel company, Hutchinson is not only an astoundingly organised person but he has the rare ability to impart this to the wildest and woolliest of writers and photographers so deadlines were met and photographic shot lists accomplished with apparent ease.

Melbourne, southern belle of Australia's mainland capitals, is a city of mixed ethnicity, a robust history and sports fanatics. To explore its nuances, the project editors turned to some of Australia's best journalists and writers.

Liz Porter spent three years in Europe as a correspondent for Melbourne's (and Australia's) most prestigious daily newspaper, *The Age*. Long an admirer of the city's gracious architecture, Porter penned an appreciative essay on that subject, then explored, notebook in hand, the suburbs of Carlton, Fitzroy, St. Kilda, Prahran, Toorak and the heart of the city. Not content with such a varied geography and ethnography, Porter then indulged her *bon vivant* self by heartily sampling the food, booze and music possibilities of Melbourne.

Freelance writer **Helen Elliott** contributed her thoughts on many aspects of Melbourne, including its local heroes, things to do, festivals and museums. In addition, she explored day trips to the east and to the vineyards north of the city.

David Loh is a Melbourne poet, freelance writer and teacher, who knows well the city's exit routes. To him fell the enviable task of researching the joys of excursions to the southern, western and northern hinterlands of Melbourne.

Simon Hunter combines the life of a city journalist with escapology into Melbourne's non-urban attractions. He enthusiastically absconded to write about the great outdoors, Port Phillip Bay and skiing resorts near Melbourne.

Glenn A. Baker is officially "Rock Brain of the Universe," having won the title against all international (and presumably, intergalactic) comers on three occasions. The author of seven books and the compiler/annotator of more than 200 record albums, Baker also has a national weekly FM radio program. There is no-one in Australia better able to comment on the music scene.

Stephen Pepper, who compiled the comprehensive Travel Tips, knows Melbourne well. He is a meticulous researcher.

Martin Blake, who provided an aficionado's-eye view of Melbourne sport, and of course Australian Rules football, brings to his coverage the informed fanaticism and one-eyed insight which true sports lovers everywhere will recognise.

To add that final polish which is a feature of the *Insight Guides*, **Sally Kaufman's** sub-editorial skills were invaluable.

The wonderfully evocative photography of *Melbourne* is mainly the work of **Paul Steel.**

—APA PUBLICATIONS

Porter

Loh

Pepper

VIRES ACQUIRIT EUNDO

ABOUT MELBOURNE

IN AND AROUND

OUTDOORS

TRAVEL TIPS

National Mutual
PATRICKS

500
46

MARVELLOUS MELBOURNE

Melbourne—dear old dowager of the south sitting on the banks of a river which flows upside-down (with the mud on top)? Or, town of innovation, planning and panache? In its architecture, climate and manners Melbourne (which was never a convict settlement) has a more European atmosphere than any other Australian city, and vies with Sydney (not Canberra) for the reputation as the nation's "true" capital. With a reputation for fine restaurants, better music, more theatres, progressive social legislation and being inhabited by people who actually *talk* to each other, Australia's second largest city (2.83 million people) is a place of quality for both the visitor and the permanent resident.

It is also home to such quintessentially *non*-European cultural advances as Foster's Lager, Vegemite, Dame Nellie Melba and "Edna Everage" and bands such as Men at Work and the Little River Band. It holds the world record for attendance at a cricket match crowd (90,800 people), has Australia's richest horse-race (the Melbourne Cup), and is the fashion capital of "Oz." The list goes on.

Such pre-eminence wasn't always the way. When John Batman sailed over from Tasmania in 1835 to found a settlement on the shores of Port Phillip, he did so by "buying" around 240,000 hectares (592,800 acres) of land from the local Dutigalla Aborigines for a swag of blankets, knives and axes. The British government officials in Sydney denounced the deal as chicanery, and instead claimed that it was *their* land—never mind the Aborigines. The behaviour of both parties set the tone for future real estate protocol in Melbourne and elsewhere in Australia. Earlier versions of Melbourne history have recently been amended to admit that John Batman was far from the model outdoorsman painted by the city's publicists of last century. Victoria's State Historian has discovered evidence to show that Australian-born Batman was a criminal transported from Sydney to Tasmania in 1821, who "spent much of his time boozing and whoring," and "had a serious alcohol problem and advanced syphilis, and died aged 38." So, while Melbourne was not a convict settlement, it wasn't squeaky-clean either.

Melbourne soon got over these hiccups, and with the discovery of gold in 1851 at Ballarat, was inundated by fortune-seekers from Europe, California and China. For young Melbourne, this was at first a near disaster, because every man with dreams of avarice departed for the diggings. In the first week of 1852 only three of the 35 foreign ships anchored in Melbourne had full crews, and shipping was so crippled by desertions that the government had to pass harsh laws to discourage the trend. Even Lola Montez came to

Preceding pages: long the commercial heart of Australia, Melbourne is (after Sydney) the nation's second largest city; Port Melbourne is a major hub for shipping trade across Bass Strait, the Tasman and the world; rowing and picnicking on the Yarra are true Melbourne traditions; St. Kilda Pier has been restored to its former glory as a place for that morning or afternoon promenade. Left, a burst of outdoor exuberance.

Melbourne in 1855 to dance her suggestive "Spider Dance."

Despite such highlights Melbourne has long been considered the more conservative of Australia's cities. Very early in its history "The Melbourne Club" was founded, to be a "Club [based] upon the London principles, amongst the gentlemen of Melbourne"; to this day it is seen as the training ground (along with elite private schools like Melbourne and Geelong Grammars) for the leaders of Australia's conservative political parties. Despite this tendency towards the orthodox, Victoria has frequently been in the forefront of social progress in Australia, with such advances as the "eight hour day" for workers in 1856, the introduction of the secret ballot in that same year, and the Factory Act of 1873 which improved conditions for female factory workers.

Australia's first Stock Exchange (1861), telephone exchange (1880), electric lamps (1882), cable trams (1885) and other advances, including the first "test tube" baby (1980), all occurred in Melbourne. The establishment of a solid manufacturing and mining industry have kept Victoria's unemployment rate the lowest in the country.

Citizens of other cities may scoff at Melbourne's brown river. Melbourne doesn't care. The city on the Yarra has given Australia its best daily newspaper (*The Age*, established in 1854, and still going strong), its most important sporting event (the Melbourne Cup, first run in 1861), the first Australian Impressionists (1880s), the only horse to become a national hero, Phar Lap (died 1932), and that legend in her own hatbox, Dame Edna Everage (a.k.a. Barry Humphries), who made her social debut in 1955 and is still delivering matronising remarks about us all.

Melbourne can claim to just about have it all, either at home or on the doorstep. *Cityguide: Melbourne* covers the city, and much more, including a selection of trips out of town to major points of interest for the traveller.

Right, a newspaper vendor outside Flinders Street station: peddling hope to the masses.

WIN $16,000 TODAY

150 Years of Settlement

John Batman was a "currency lad"—one born of European parents in Australia, as opposed to being a transported convict. He was also an alcoholic and a lecher. It remains one of the paradoxes of history that it was to this man that the honour of founding Melbourne fell. As every Victorian schoolchild knows, it was Batman who uttered those prophetic, albeit utterly dull words: "This will be a place for a village." Honour aside, within four years he was dead (as a result of his own excesses) and never saw what became of his village.

It seems odd now to realise that venerable Melbourne was first established as an outpost of Tasmania. There had been some exploration of the Victorian coastline as early as 1802 when John Murray became the first white man to enter Port Phillip Bay. Murray gave a glowing account of the area, but after the 1824 expedition from Sydney to Western Port by Hume and Hovell, when a settlement was tried and abandoned, the Port Phillip District fell out of favour.

Ten years later there was no suitable land left in Tasmania to grant to free settlers, and Edward Henty and his family left to settle on the Victorian mainland in what is now Portland. Encouraged by the success of this settlement, a company was formed in Tasmania with a charter drawn up by a lawyer, John Gellibrand, to settle in Port Phillip.

The company's forward scout, John Batman made a treaty with the Aborigines of the Dutigalla tribe, thereby claiming that the company now owned 240,000 hectares (592,800 acres) of land on the shores of Port Phillip and stretching far inland. The Aborigines received, for the place they called "Bararing"—and which the white men somehow transcribed as "Bearbrass"—30 tomahawks, 40 blankets, 100 knives, 200 handkerchiefs, some flour and a promise of future payments. Of course, the whole thing was illegal; but as soon as the treaty was signed shareholders crossed from Tasmania. By the time the administration in Sydney heard about this illegal settlement the population was over 2,000. It was impossible to arrest them all.

John Gellibrand noted in his journal on Jan. 31,1836, that the "settlement consists of about a dozen huts built with turf on the left bank of the River Yarra Yarra." Shortly after, the name "Bearbrass" was replaced by "Melbourne," after the British Prime Minister of that name. By 1838 Melbourne boasted "... ten brick houses ... some large ... and six are of two storeys with underground cellars." In the meantime, Robert Hoddle (a man with "geometry in his soul," according to eminent Australian historian Charles Manning Clarke) was already in his element, planning a spacious, gridded, modern city.

NED KELLY, THE BUSHRANGER.

Gold fever: When the first Governor, Charles La Trobe, arrived to administer the district in 1839, he found that already the inhabitants were quite different from those of Sydney. Not only was Melbourne the place for the most junior colonial officials, unlike Sydney where the senior officials lived, but the farms were small and worked by the farmers themselves rather than by convicts. The feeling against convict labour was so strong that the citizens of Melbourne had a policy of never allowing transported convicts into their settlement. By 1841 Port Phillip already considered itself an independent community, but it did not officially become so until 1851. Until then it remained part of the colony of New South Wales and was administered, much to its chagrin, from Sydney, by absentee rulers. Then in 1851, the year in which Victoria held its first Legislative Council meeting, something happened that was to alter the face of Melbourne, and Australia, forever—Edward Hargraves discovered gold at Ophir, near Bathurst, NSW.

Immediately, a prize of 200 pounds was offered to anyone finding gold in Victoria. Some suggest that it was offered simply to try to keep the workmen in the southern colony. But there was no need for a prize. It could have been won many times over in that same miraculous year when gold was discovered in Victoria at Bendigo, Ballarat, Castlemaine, Warrandyte and a score of other places. Within two months of becoming officially independent, Victoria was producing more gold than any other place on earth. The effects of sudden great wealth are not always as agreeable as the fantasies; and if elements of Victorian and Melbourne society had been brutish up until the discovery of gold, those qualities were intensified during the 1850s and 1860s. It is difficult, now, to imagine the chaos. The population increased at a fantastic rate: in 1850 there were 77,500 people in the colony. By the following year the number of migrants was 95,000, and by 1860 the population had reached 140,000.

Manning Clarke has detailed the lawless confusion of those early goldrush years, the canvas towns that sprang up and the impossibility of finding anyone to do the everyday work in a place where "Jack was as good as his master" (and, according to Jack, frequently better). Even Governor La Trobe had to groom and feed his own horse. Melbourne was said to be as chaotic as Calcutta in 1853—the year in which Melbourne University was established. As an index of the "mania of the times," more people were noted as going insane in Melbourne than in any other city of the civilised world. Into this miserable, frightening place poured thousands more hopefuls wanting to "make their pile." Civilisation seemed to collapse under the weight of the barbaric influx. Even the older inhabitants became tainted. One wag inserted a notice into the daily newspaper, *The Argus*: "Wanted: Civility from the people of Melbourne towards any New Arrival who may ask them a necessary question."

These were the years of "topsy-turvydom" and only those endowed with a gift of foresight, like Friedrich Engels, could see that what was happening on the Australian goldfields would turn the world upside down. In 1854 there took place on the Ballarat goldfields one of the the most far-reaching actions in Australian history. The event became known as "The Eureka Stockade." (See feature in "Ballarat" chapter.) Several hundred miners—from Britain, America, Greece, Germany and Italy—tired of the iniquities of the government's administration, built a fort and barricaded themselves in, preparing to stand siege. They didn't stand a chance against the 300 soldiers who attacked in the night.

Preceding pages: mail day in mid-19th century Melbourne. Opposite page: left, Melbourne's founder John Batman; right, bushranger Ned Kelly. Above, Collins Street, 1870.

Social change: The Eureka miners did eventually win most of the points of grievance on their charter; but in spite of this, there were great implications for the direction of Australian society in the suppression of their movement. Manning Clarke interprets this moment as the time when the "foundations for conservatism" in Australia were laid. The genuine democratic spirit of the miners, and the beginnings of the cultivation of an Australian sentiment had been overcome by the force of the colonial bourgeoisie. This bourgeoisie continued thereafter to educate the working class in their own values and laid a firm foundation for that conservatism which is the traditional complexion of Melbourne in particular.

The real winners in the battle for wealth on the gold-fields had been this bourgeoisie, the shopkeepers and the bankers whose values

the artist S. T. Gill satirized when he drew them as "Mr Money Bags." At Eureka the dream of those miners of a just and egalitarian future had fallen onto barren ground. The task for the bourgeoisie was now to win political power—or at least equality of power—from the landed gentry and the heads of the colonial bureaucracy; to tame and convert the people to their own values, and to create institutions where they could enjoy politically and socially what they already enjoyed economically.

The colonial bourgeoisie believed it was possible to achieve material progress, promote equality of opportunity and abolish the privileges of birth while remaining loyal subjects of her Majesty. The preponderance of the notion that Melbourne would be a respectable, proper and prosperous city was established in those years immediately after the Eureka Stockade. The visible evidence was the flourishing of suburbia with successful individuals erecting mansions in faithful imitations of what was in vogue in the mother country. Egalitarianism of an odd sort was a also a reality, with a worker sometimes ending up as owner of the mansion he had once laboured on. More probably, he would live in a version of his master's mansion, with the same iron-lace edgings, plaster urns and stained glass windows—all copied exactly but in smaller proportions. Those years saw the beginnings of over a century of the belief that an imported civilisation was of greater value and worth than any created in the new colony. Even the ornamental trees and shrubs which the colonists planted in their gardens were imported from England. For "Melbourne Englishmen," life was permeated by a dual attachment and loyalty.

Those gilded years from the 1860s were ones of amazing prosperity for Melbourne.

As the commercial centre and most important port of Australia, it easily wrested the title of financial capital from Sydney. Despite the problems of such tremendous growth Melbourne saw itself as one of the proudest, progressive cities in the world. The village had become a metropolis. Nothing seemed able to impede its progress—even the criticisms some of the less Philistine Melburnians made of its garish tendencies in architecture went unheeded.

The network of roads, river craft and trains improved communications rapidly, and the electric telegraph, overseas cables, telephone, electric lights and rapid printing presses spread the benevolent influences of civilisation—*British* civilisation—throughout the Australian colonies. Importantly too, a Bill had been passed providing "free, secular and compulsory education" for all children between the ages of six and 13. The need for such education was great, not only in Melbourne, but all over Australia. But, worthy as the Bill was, it was extremely difficult to implement. Tied to this were the inevitable class problems, with the rapid development of a private schools system for the "better classes" becoming an entrenched Melbourne feature. Melbourne Grammar, Geelong Grammar, Scotch College and Presbyterian Ladies College were all rapidly established as places to educate the sons (and, as an afterthought, the daughters) of well-to-do Christian gentlemen.

It seemed that nothing could impede Melbourne's prosperous progress. But behind this "progress" there was a riot of land speculation that revolutionised values and transformed patterns of land use. Money was in the air. As one woman wrote, these were times when Melburnians gloried in being "rich and dishonest and mercenary and vulgar." Land deals fetched spectacular sums. The upper-classes wanted even more pleasure and titillation; the working-classes had never had it so good with the development of secondary industry and shorter hours, creature comforts, a social life and entertainments. In these years of boom, Melbourne was, indeed, the "working man's paradise."

In 1887 the Victorian Parliament spent 250,000 pounds on the Great Centennial Exhibition of 1888. Nothing was too much in

Left, a refurbished main street of the Gold Rush era in Sovereign Hill, reflecting the trans-Pacific origins of some of the diggers. Above, Victorian Parliament House in the 19th century.

such fanciful times. There were seals in an aquarium, paintings on loan from famous overseas galleries, the sensuous "new" music of Wagner played to men and women lolling on soft cushions, or a trip up in the hydraulic lift to survey all Melbourne from the great dome of the Exhibition Buildings—all followed by tea at one of the many dainty tea pavillions. Money and its display was the spirit of the times. As Clarke says, "The money-changers had begun to set the tone of public life in Australia."

Of course it couldn't last. The irresponsible years of land boom had to be paid for, and in the 1890s they were repaid with interest in the most severe depression Australia has ever suffered. Not only was there depression but appalling droughts and violent strikes. In 1888 there had already been the collapse of the land boom and the beginnings of public unease in Melbourne. In 1892 there had been a run on the banks in Sydney, and the Melbourne business world looked on with great anxiety. In March 1892 the directors of Australian Deposit and Mortage Bank closed their doors. That year the Colonial Investment Company failed. Thousands of small depositors in banks and land companies were ruined. In the whole of Australia only 10 banks survived the depression and those in Victoria were the worst hit. It was the beginning of her decline in financial dominance. Men who had been seen as pillars of bourgeoisie rectitude were indicted on criminal charges. Prominent sharebrokers committed suicide rather than face charges. But, as usual, it was the poor who suffered most, and in the working class districts of Melbourne there was "stark staring poverty."

The Aussie identity: Yet, in Australia, in the minds and imaginations of the artists and writers there was a vision of something new. The Sydney writer Henry Lawson identified this need for a real Australian civilisation, not a second rate imported one; in Melbourne, the painters Condor, McCubbin, Roberts and others were making similar attempts at a vernacular rendering of what they saw. Melbourne composer Percy Grainger was attempting the same in his music. They focussed attention on the perceptions, history and pleasures of an emerging and authentic Australian cultural identity. While the idealism of the 1880s had vanished, the sturdier reflection upon the need for a type of nationalism was emerging. In 1901, in a country largely recovered from the depression of the 1890s, a Federation of the six Australian colonies was achieved: independence—of a timid kind—from Mother England had been won.

Federation, and Melbourne, still recovering its tentative self-respect after the lessons of the 1890s, was declared Australia's temporary capital (and remained so until Canberra was founded in 1927). The first Federal parliament opened in Melbourne's Royal Exhibition Buildings. In 1906 the Melbourne Symphony Orchestra was formed. In 1908 the first full adult suffrage was achieved when the vote was granted to women. In 1908 Flinders Street Railway station was built and in 1909 the Saturday Half Holiday Act was proclaimed. Melbourne was steady, harmonious and progressive and continued in this dignified fashion all through the straitened war years of 1914 to 1918.

In the 1920s the Melbourne tramway system was electrified and the first traffic lights were installed. Culturally conscious Melburnians saw Anna Pavlova dance in their city and heard their own Helen Mitchell, the famed Dame Nellie Melba, sing at their Town Hall. Melbourne University Press was founded in 1928—and the gangster "Squizzy" Taylor was gunned down in Carlton. The gaiety and superficiality of the 1920s continued feverishly until 1929 when there was a relapse into economic depression. Pleasure, it seemed, was extracting its payment.

The Great Depression of the 1930s was not as terrible as that of the late 1890s but was still severe. It appears that the wealthier suburbs of Toorak and South Yarra escaped its ravages and partied as blithely as ever, without seeming to be aware of the grim poverty in neighbouring suburbs. Melburnians saw the splendid Phar Lap win the Melbourne Cup in 1930, but many were out of work and some had no homes. Unemployment peaked at over 30 percent in 1932 and many workers were put on sustenance pay—"susso"—labouring on the Yarra Boulevard, St. Kilda Road and the Shrine of Remembrance. "Susso" workers received 25 shillings a week for a single man. The dole was worth 14 shillings for a man and wife with an extra seven shillings for each child.

Left, cable trams in Collins Street (early 1900s). Above, these grand buildings, constructed for the International Exhibition of 1880, housed the first Australian Federal Parliament.

George Johnston and Alan Marshall, two Melbourne writers, wrote eloquently of those years. In his novel *My Brother Jack*, Johnston tells how the Victorian Government "unlocked the defence department warehouses, and out of the mothballs they took the old surplus greatcoats and tunics and they dyed them a dull black ... and issued them out as a charity to keep the workless warm. So that as the unemployed grew in number the black army coats became a kind of badge of adversity, a stigma of suffering." By 1933 Melbourne's population had passed the one million mark and economic conditions were slowly beginning to improve. In the same year Captain Cook's cottage was brought from England and rebuilt in the Fitzroy gardens, and in the following year the Shrine of Remembrance was opened before a record crowd of 317,000 people.

Melbourne in those years was dominated by the presence of one fascinating man, Sidney Myer. Myer was born of Jewish parents in Russia in 1878 and migrated to Melbourne in 1894. He prospered as a merchant and by 1930 the Myer store in Bourke Street was renowned throughout the state. Myer issued shares to his staff, but cut their (and his own) wages in 1931 so that no staff need suffer retrenchment. He made an example by selling Australian-made goods, enlarging his own premises, donating over 20,000 pounds to the Yarra Boulevard scheme and holding a vast Christmas Dinner for the unemployed in 1930. His life was marked by philanthropy, and love for, and encouragement of, the arts and education. The name Sidney Myer has become an inspiring part of Melbourne tradition, and the Myer store today still retains some of this peculiar mystique even though it is no longer owned by the Myer family.

After World War II Melbourne sustained her fastest period of growth since the gold rush, with a constantly expanding industrial production drawing a huge influx of migrants. Perhaps Melbourne's finest moment in this century commenced on Nov. 22, 1956, when the Duke of Edinburgh opened the Melbourne Olympic Games. Still known as "the friendly games," the '56 Olympics seem in retrospect a gathering of innocents. Steroids, terrorism, boycotts and "shamateurism" were nowhere in the language of the press reports. Also, they were Australia's finest sporting hour, as the small host nation came in third in the final tally behind the USSR and USA.

Enlightened years: By 1961 Melbourne's population was over two million and Monash University was opened. Six years later, a third university, La Trobe, was inaugurated. The 1960s were progressive years, but two events make particularly pertinent comments about Melbourne. Hotels, which, by law had been forced to shut at 6 p.m., producing the barbarous "six o'clock swill"—during which men would force down vast quantities of beer after work and before closing time—were permitted in 1966 to stay open until 10 p.m. The power of conservative and Church lobbies to effect legislation was beginning to decline. More significantly, in 1967 public outcry was so great at the hanging at Pentridge Gaol of Ronald Ryan (the last man to go to the gallows in Australia) that capital punishment was abolished in Victoria. Two steps for civilisation, almost 150 turbulent years after Batman had first bargained with the Aborigines for their land on the muddy Yarra Yarra.

This new enlightenment continued during the early years of the 1970s when Melbourne was the most vocal place in Australia in its opposition to the Vietnam War. The Peace Rallies and marches, led by that inspired humanitarian and very public Melbourne politician, Dr Jim Cairns, were unlike anything Melbourne had ever seen.

In Melbourne too, as in most other large cities worldwide, there was a tremendous change in the inner-city areas as people realised the disadvantages of living far away from the city centre. The former working-class areas of South Melbourne, Albert Park, Carlton, Fitzroy and North Melbourne all became very desirable places in which to live for the newly affluent middle-classes. Older residents watched with amusement, shock and then immense irony as their formerly very much declasse suburbs became chic, as working people's cottages became transformed into middle-class villas. The old Australian dream of one's own home on a quarter acre block seemed very backward as everyone wanted a trendy villa with a postage stamp-sized garden in Carlton. In the late 1980s these suburbs are very much the domain of the upwardly mobile with considerable cash.

Left, cricket on the green of Melbourne Grammar School. Above, the flame at Melbourne's Shrine of Remembrance for those who have died in war.

Some working class areas were altered in a different way. In the late '70s there was a great influx of refugees from Vietnam and Cambodia. The Vietnamese have found Melbourne very welcoming, but in such an initially alien culture they have naturally tended to congregate in one area. In the inner suburbs of Collingwood, Richmond and particularly in Fitzroy there is a remarkable Indo-Chinese/Australian culture. Victoria Street, Richmond has become known as Little Saigon, and a walk in this thriving area will demonstrate why. With the shops, the signs, the language, and the people all comfortably going about their daily lives in this transported world, there is no indication that one is in a suburb of an Australian city.

However, despite the new political awareness and the social progress of the '70s it was during this time that many of Melbourne's loveliest buildings were destroyed to make way for the new towering complexes. Collins Street, once the most glamourous street in Australia, lost much of its charm as the town planners thoughtlessly swept Melbourne into the new age. It has taken Melburnians until the 1980s to realise the damage that was done, and to begin to protest and attempt to protect what is left.

As the hopeful '70s gave way to the materialistic, anxious '80s Melbourne celebrated 150 years of growth in 1985. It also saw, after decades of talk and planning, the implementation of an inner city underground rail network in conjunction with other transport facilities—the Met. Perhaps the next decade will see the covering of the remarkably ugly railway yards at Flinders Street, a topic which has been on the tongues of politicians for 50 years.

One hundred years ago Melbourne was Australia's premier city, but time has taken the edge off that. However, Melbourne has always had drive and energy and there are many diverse interest groups working together with a common aim—to reposition Melbourne once again as one of the great cities in this part of the world.

Right, Parliament House at the top of Collins Street is one of Melbourne's most imposing structures.

PARLIAMENT
OF
VICTORIA

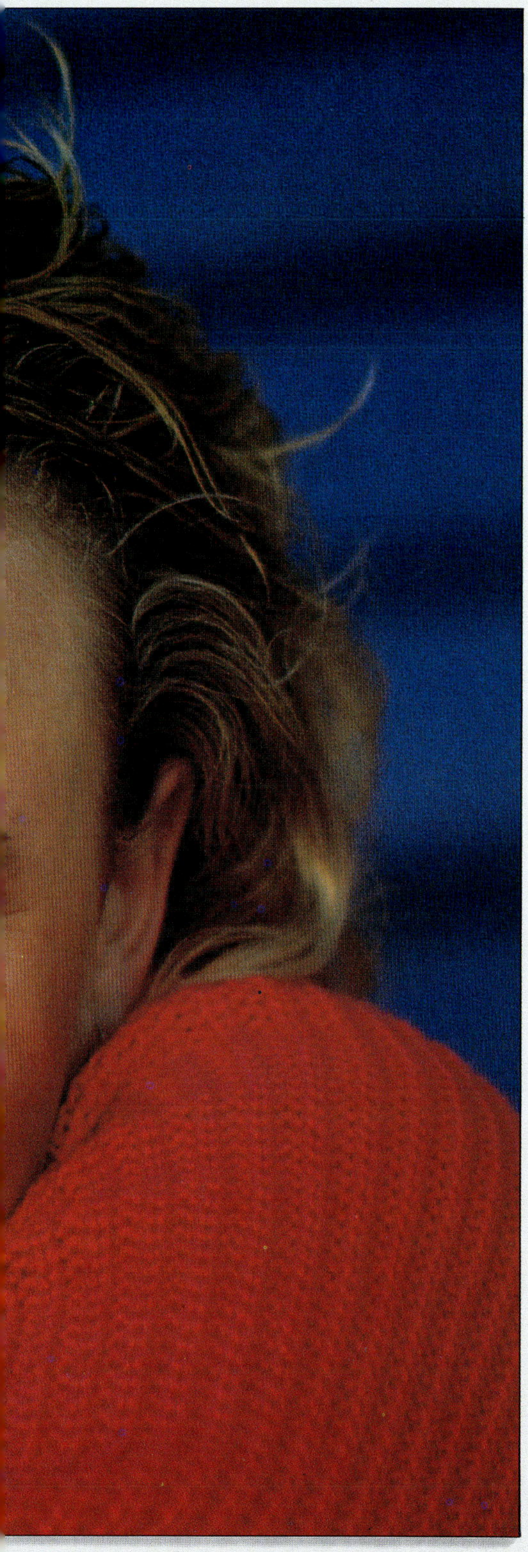

MELBURNIANS

"Piss-elegant and nervously smug"—is how one visitor saw Melburnians in the late 1940s. In 1956 Ava Gardner, here to film *On The Beach,* pushed Melbourne into world headlines with her comment that it was the ideal place in which to make a film about the end of the world. Poor, maligned Melbourne! In the late 20th century Melbourne shrugs off these barbs, confident of the fact that it is now a genuinely cosmopolitan city, and has sufficient grace, dignity and charm to politely freeze out (or, alternatively, buy and sell) such critics.

While Sydney grew haphazardly by fitting into the line of its coast, Melbourne was carefully plotted in the clear, hard light of town planner Robert Hoddle's calculations. Melburnians have reason to be grateful to his foresight: as a result of those magnificent wide streets which he laid out in the age of the horse and carriage, Melbourne remains, in the era of the automobile, one of the few great cities that is still eminently liveable. In Melbourne, life remains comfortable because it is still possible to exist on a human scale.

The Melbourne character: People seem to reflect their cities in character, and Melburnians certainly reflect theirs. Given the spaciousness everywhere evident in Melbourne, the grave charm apparent in many of its fine Victorian buildings and the general appearance of solidity and permanency, there is little wonder that Melburnians take themselves seriously. Old-fashioned virtues of reliability and rectitude seem utterly appropriate to Melbourne—even if one critic did rephrase it as "sodden rectitude."

It is perhaps this sense of solidity—as well as its many deciduous trees—which place Melbourne and its inhabitants apart from every other Australian city. Melburnians, it is often noted, have a unique sense of culture. In a country which has often been branded notoriously "anti-intellectual" they are not afraid to be seen as cultivated. As a result, their achievements are considerable. Film producer, columnist and broadcaster

Philip Adams summarises Melbourne's contribution: "Australia's film industry began here (Melbourne) and was rekindled here, even though it was Sydney that built the studios. Australia's first school of indigenous paintings was born in one of Melbourne's suburbs, even though it was Sydney that built the commercial galleries. While Sydney is the more theatrical city, it was Melbourne that produced Ray Lawler, Barry Humphries, David Williamson and Jack Hibberd. You could say that Sydney markets what Melbourne creates."

It's always hazardous to categorise the people of an entire city or country but there

is an atmosphere in Melbourne which is unique. Melburnians, with their reticence, self-consciousness and sense of "doing the right thing" often seem to lack the spontaneity of Sydneysiders, the relaxation of Brisbanites and the openness of, well, "Perthlings." They are probably more akin to Europeans, perhaps most of all in their devotion to cultivated pastimes—conversation, good food, music. Yet, for all these urban pursuits, Melburnians are a suburban people. Victoria is not lightly called "the Garden State," and Victorians often see their garden as epitomising their home. They value "home" and "family," the foundations of solid, middle-class suburbia. Both suburbia and intelligentsia seem to co-exist quite nicely, if largely separately, in Melbourne.

In such a sprawling, almost centreless city, it is impossible to focus on one single thing that defines Melbourne and Melburnians. It was founded by that paradox, John Batman—"the syphilitic son of a saltpetre snatcher"—and has progressed just as paradoxically. Melbourne is, at once, the home of Australia's most radical campus, Monash University, and also the bastion of the nation's "Establishment."

Visitors are often amused, and occasion-

ally repelled, by the fact that in Melbourne one is frequently asked "What school did you attend?" rather than "What do you do for a living?" In such circles the preferred reply is "Melbourne Grammar" ("Grammar" to the initiated), "Geelong Grammar" or "Scotch College." It is *de rigueur* to go from these schools to "The Shop," Melbourne University. The newer universities—La Trobe and Monash—simply don't rate. The Old Boy Network has always been an important feature of "society" in Melbourne, and is still thriving. Intricately bound to and fostered by a system of private schools, exclusive clubs and "old" money (as "old" as money can be in young Melbourne, and some of it not acquired as genteelly as its inheritors might like to pretend), this Establishment accepts its role as the power base for conservative politics in Australia. Perhaps those "piss-elegant and nervously smug" Melburnians still exist, tucked away in the bowels of exclusive establishments such as the Melbourne Club—originally established for rich pastoralists on their visits to town—where, even today, Jews, Catholics and women *still* need not apply.

Apart from such anachronisms as the Melbourne Club, the greater city of Melbourne has never stood still. From its ordered beginnings, through the gold rushes and then the depressions, through the serene, dull years of the 1950s and early 1960s it has now re-emerged with enthusiasm. Despite the weather ("four seasons in one day" is a common plaint) Melburnians are able to pursue the good life in a wide variety of ways. Setting aside the obvious factor of sport (Melbourne has always been a great sporting city), the "good life" is most apparent in the extraordinary diversity and richness of cultures in Melbourne.

Preceding pages: a sunny Melbourne smile. Left and above, the many faces of Melbourne.

The last haven: Traditionally a landing place for new arrivals, immigrants from Britain, Ireland and Scotland—particularly Scotland (Melbourne has a profound Presbyterian streak)—formed Melbourne's original European stock. This century, they were followed by large scale immigration from northern and southern Europe, Malta, Lebanon and Turkey. Most of this took place after World War II: often whole villages—particularly from Greece—came looking for a better way of life. Even before World War II there was a huge Jewish population in Melbourne, and Melbourne owes its position as the fashion centre of Australia to those Jewish families who started the great ragtrade businesses in Flinders Lane.

Survivors of the holocaust saw Melbourne as the last haven, the place farthest from Europe, and so vastly different that an absolutely new life could begin. Melbourne has, per capita, the largest percentage of holocaust survivors of any city in the world. Their determination to begin again, bringing what was best in their culture with them, has left its mark on the city.

There are some 35,000 Jews in Melbourne, many of whom migrated from eastern and central Europe, and more recently from South Africa, to the calmer climes of Caulfield, Elwood and Doncaster. When large numbers of Jewish settlers arrived in Melbourne in the late 1930s, "culture" was still looked upon with suspicion by the "average" Australian. The new arrivals, who regarded artistic activity as an everyday aspect of life, forced Melbourne into a cultural adulthood. Yossel Bergner, a Polish painter, began to paint the urban Aborigines, to depict them with the discriminating eye of a Social Realist, as opposed to a 19th century sentimentalist, and a new school of painting

began to emerge. Writers such as Judah Waten began a similar process in literature. The eastern European refugees generated a demand for fine chamber music, and Musica Viva—dedicated to the promotion of, and tours by, classical musicians—soon became an integral part of Melbourne's newly flourishing and cohesive musical life. Other Melburnians suddenly had an insight into what a deeply-lived, unassuming culture meant, and began to absorb these values into their own lives.

If the Jewish community has had a deep cultural influence on Melburnians, the Greek community has been equally influential, although in a different direction. Melbourne is the third largest Greek city in the world, after Athens and Thessaloniki, with a Greek-born or descended population of 800,000. This extraordinary growth has occurred since 1945—there were only 10,000 Greeks in Melbourne prior to that time. Greek villages were the main sources of immigrants, so these new arrivals were often uneducated (unlike many of the Jewish immigrants), yet all left with the same courage and came for one uniting reason—to begin a better life. Language and religious differences originally set these newcomers apart; but now, into the second and third generations, there have been some unpredictable and fascinating developments. Melbourne Greeks have fiercely maintained their "Greekness" and now, when in Greece itself many young people no longer know their traditional national dances, young Melbourne Greeks treasure and nourish their heritage. There are still remnants of the old patriarchial society which existed in the villages, but also bilingual schools, newspapers and theatres. The "Greekness" of Melbourne is accepted, simply, as Melbourne.

With the leavening which Melbourne

gained from the Jewish and Greek communities, as well as an energetic Italian community (of some 230,000 people), it was a cosmopolitan city well prepared for the influx of Asian immigration which has burgeoned since the mid-1970s. Vietnamese came in large numbers and now almost 40,000 of them live in such suburbs as Springvale, Richmond and Footscray. Melburnians, be they Polish, Turkish, Chinese, Cambodian or Tasmanian by descent live harmoniously enough with one another, even while certain areas around the city centre (such as Richmond, Footscray and Brunswick) seem to have become vivid enclaves—but not ghettos—of particular cultures. Melburnians have had to learn to change from their Anglo clanishness (not to mention their mutton, peas and potatoes!) and to be more tolerant of other cultures. Overall, it has been a successful and certainly enriching interchange.

Sports mad: Of course Melburnians wouldn't be Melburnians without their two great sporting fixations—the Melbourne Cup and Australian Rules Football. The city-wide fevers—"metropsychosis" isn't too strong a term—which rage around both "The Cup" and "the footy" defy class boundaries, which are otherwise still quite strong in Melbourne. Melburnians from the more affluent suburbs—predominantly those in the east—mix with those from less affluent western and northern areas in order to follow the same football team, or to punt on the same horses. Of course, whether one watches the game from the Members Stand or "the paddock", or whether one takes one's champagne breakfast to the course in the Rolls-Royce or by train makes its own telling point about this so-called egalitarian society. Yet paradoxically, Melburnians also have a strident group who are devotedly anti-football. Each year, at Grand Final time, it gives an award to the figure in public life who has been the most disdainful of the game throughout the winter months.

Melburnians are a confident lot: that shows in their trams. Where else in the world is there such a vast network devoted to such a useful, ludicrous vehicle? It says everything about Melbourne and its inhabitants—conventional, practical, a bit rattley, but endearingly individual.

Street performances range from unofficial sidewalk sonatas (left) to a scheduled choreography of tram and hand (above).

BUILT TO ENDURE

"Paris of the Antipodes," "Chicago of the South" or simply "Marvellous Melbourne"? These were stock descriptions for Melbourne of 1880s, a city which had grown, in little over 40 years, from a muddy village to one of the great cities of the Victorian age. Melbourne was a typical product of an era that revelled in monumental public buildings, exuberantly ornate private villas and splendidly expansive parks and gardens.

In 1837, under the direction of the Governor of New South Wales, Sir Richard Bourke and planner Robert Hoddle, central Melbourne had been laid out on a grand grid of north-south and east-west streets, some a generous 30 metres (100 feet) across. The unrelenting geometry of their plan reflected the attitude of these truely Victorian Empire builders to the landscape's physical contours; that is, Nature must yield to Man.

By the 1850s and 1860s Melbourne could boast imposing public edifices like the Treasury Building in Spring Street, the Royal Mint in William Street (now the Civil Marriage Registry) and the State Library, all now recognised as among the world's richest examples of Victoriana. The Treasury Building, the design of which is generally acknowledged as the work of John James Clark, a 19-year-old junior draughtsman in the Department of Public Works, was immediately proclaimed by newspapers as "Melbourne's most elegant building," a title which, in the opinion of many, it is yet to relinquish. Its superb facade displays the work of the highly skilled European craftsmen attracted to Melbourne by the gold rush. It was, moreover, the city's first building in the Italian Renaissance style (copied from 16th century Italian flat-fronted palaces) which was to become such a significant feature of Melbourne's architecture.

However, while Melbourne's architectural aspirations may have appeared Italianate, its cultural priorities and yardsticks remained steadfastly British. The highest compliment that could be paid to Melbourne's Theatre Royal, built in 1842, was that one could see Italian opera "in a style worthy of the English metropolis itself"; while the new Melbourne Club, opened in 1858, aspired to be worthy—both architecturally and ideologically—of a place on London's St. James Street. Carlton, the site for the dreaming spires of Melbourne University, founded in 1854, was laid out using London's Bloomsbury as a model. Melbourne also proudly emulated the example of British cities by expanding her suburbs as quickly as possible, with progress measured by the numbers of elegant mansions being built in the new wealthy enclaves of Richmond, South Yarra, Hawthorn and Kew. Here the rich could achieve the Victorian ideal of *rus in urbe* ("the country in the city") in the privacy of their own gardens.

Grand gardens: But the general population was not forgotten. Melbourne, like all the great cities of Victoria's Empire, had to have huge parks, with bandstands and displays of rare and exotic horticultural specimens from all over the world. Around 1870, a disused quarry was transformed into the Fitzroy Gardens (on Wellington Parade) by the Scot James Sinclair, who had designed estates for the Russian nobility in the Crimea. Meanwhile, the brilliant landscape designer William Guilfoyle had turned the former bed of one section of the Yarra into the Royal Botanic Gardens, now regarded as one of the finest examples of Victorian landscaping in the world—and among the most beautiful gardens in Australia. Director of the gardens from 1874-1909, Guilfoyle (in partnership with the government botanist Baron Ferdinand Von Mueller) was responsible for the huge range of botanical specimens and created a jewel hailed by Sir Arthur Conan Doyle as "absolutely the most beautiful place I have ever seen." In 1904, well before most of the plants had reached their current mature splendour, the visiting Polish pianist Paderweski said Guilfoyle had achieved with trees what a pianist tries to do with music.

The genius of Guilfoyle is seen, above all, in cunning placements of plants which lead the stroller's eyes to a special view. Thus, the Canary Island palms placed among the shrub *coprosma*, or mirrorleaf, on six headlands in the main lake, draw the eye towards a church spire in the distance. The elegant white tower of Government House is framed by a skyline of mature trees and an arucaria transplanted by the designer for this very purpose. People enjoying the garden city of Melbourne today have Guilfoyle and Von Mueller to thank—along with Governor La Trobe, who saved Royal Park, Princes Park and the Carlton Gardens from being swallowed up by land developers eager to accommodate a population almost tripled by the 1850s gold rush.

After the 1850s, Melburnians boasted that their city had everything that London or Paris could offer, except seas of slums. But in 1880 and 1881, when the whole world brought its wares to Melbourne's first great International Exhibition, they could truly claim a reputation as a great city of the world. London's 1851 Great Exhibition, in the Crystal Palace, had set the pattern for regular displays of homage to the Victorian ideal of industrial progress. When Melbourne's turn came, the city fathers were determined both to build a venue appropriate to the splendour of the occasion and to outdo Sydney, which had hastily thrown together Australia's first international exhibition the year before. The Exhibition Buildings in Nicholson Street, Carlton and the surrounding Exhibition Gardens, are the result of these ambitions.

The Victorian Parliament voted 100,000 pounds for the building and site and commissioned architects Joseph Reed and Frederick Barnes (designers of the Melbourne Town Hall, Trades Hall and ten city banks) who came up with the largest construction in Australasia, a huge, confidently domed stucco palace that was later to be the venue for the meeting of the first Australian Federal Parliament in 1901. The foundation stone had been laid in February 1879 with a shovel made of 22 ounces of 18-carat gold. The 246,000-pound building that went up over it during the next 15 months maintained this spirit of opulence with its 150-metre (495-foot) facade, 8.8 hectares (21.7 acres) of floor space and 66-metre (218-foot) dome, which, contemporaries preened, was larger than London's St. Paul's Cathedral.

Two lakes were sunk in its gardens and a large decorative stucco fountain built, while the Garden Committee planted cedars, planes, pittosporums, willows and bluegums, now gloriously mature, but then mere saplings which earned the blushing committee members rounds of public ridicule. In-

Preceding pages: eloquent European-style iron lacework. Opposite page: left, Flinders Street station in the era of "Tin Lizzie" and horse-drawn carriages; right, the former Alexander Club. Above, facade of the "Gothic Revival" Olderfleet Building.

side this monument to optimism and confidence, Austrian glassware was displayed alongside English vases, a German billiard saloon, a 12-metre (40-foot) high German Imperial tent, a miniature Taj Mahal, American lawn movers, automatic door-closing devices, an early typewriter, and the latest in 1880s state-of-the-art corsetry! Visitors were entertained with two concerts a day, which included excerpts from the latest Wagner opera.

Good times: 1880s Melbourne certainly knew how to party. Even suburban subdivision sales were done in style, with autioneers putting on special trains and free champagne

visited the exhibition, filing past displays from 93 different countries, including Anton von Werner's life-size painting of Bismarck addressing the Reichstag. There were symphony concerts and recitals by a 5,000-voice choir.

Indeed, the city felt it had plenty to celebrate. On Jan. 20, 1888, two million pounds worth of stock had been traded on the Melbourne Stock Exchange and the city had electric light, telephones, a well established rail system and a new tramway system. Melburnians could also experience the novel sensation of riding in the new hydraulic passenger lifts, a technological prerequi-

lunches for potential buyers. Building boomed accordingly, with the number of dwellings in Melbourne almost doubling between 1880 (when there were 52,181) and 1890 (93,161). The city's celebrations of Queen Victoria's jubilee in 1887, were marked, contemporary visitors noted, by "an enthusiasm not excelled in any part of the Empire." The next year the Victorian Government spent 250,000 pounds (10 times the original estimate) on the second great Melbourne international exhibition, held to commemorate the centenary of British settlement in Australia. Over two million people

site for the multi-storey red-brick Gothic revival delights of west Collins Street (see box) and the Grand Hotel (now the Windsor Hotel) in Spring Street, built for a staggering 110,000 pounds and decorated for an extravagant 30,000 pounds. The new Australia Building, at the corner of Elizabeth Street and Flinders Lane, was to be a soaring 12-storey high, the tallest building in Australia, and surpassed only by the fledgling skyscrapers of Chicago and New York. Here was the architectural proof that Melbourne was the trade, business and pleasure capital of Australia. And the citizens behaved accordingly. "The Melbourne man is always on the lookout for business," wrote an 1883 observer, "the Sydney man waits for business to come to him. The one is always in a hurry, the other takes life more easily. And as it is with business, so it is with pleasure."

The legacy of the four decades of prosperity between the discovery of gold in Victoria in 1851 and the end of the land boom in 1891 (which precipitated the great crash of 1892-93) was a truly extraordinary range of domestic architecture. There was something for every taste, from the cool elegance of superb mansions like Como, Illawarra and Government House, to the florid Italianate

grandeur of houses like Benvenuta in Drummond Street, Carlton or Labassa in Manor Grove, Caulfield or the graceful uniformity of whole suburbs of terraced houses with iron-laced verandahs. Cast-iron made in local foundries, along with stucco male and female faces, urns and flowers, decorated both the modest workers' cottages of Fitzroy and Collingwood and the mansions of Toorak and South Yarra.

Exquisite pockets of Victorian housing survive all over Melbourne, including South and East Melbourne, Fitzroy and Carlton. Gems include Tasma Terrace (the headquarters of the National Trust) in Parliament Place, and terraces in Powlett Street, East Melbourne and St. Vincent's Place, South Melbourne. But the best surviving large expanse of Victorian terrace housing is at Parkville, where the action of conservationists has avoided the worst excesses of well-meaning amateur renovators (and not-so-well-meaning developers who, in the 1960s, were trying to sell the idea of South Parkville as a slum in need of clearance). Houses at the top end of Gatehouse Street are notable for their heavy baroque detailing, while Morrah Street, the south end of Park Drive (especially "Wardlow" at Number 114) and the delightful Fitzgibbon Street reward inspection. Home builders of the time could buy cast cement decoration (whether heads, fruit or flowers) "off the shelf"; Parkville residents were clearly enthusiastic shoppers.

By 1920, this Victorian style was being condemned as symptomatic of a time when, as the 1926 Australian Encyclopedia put it, "taste was at a low ebb and cheap ornament popular." The move away from the style had begun even earlier. With the 1890s depression, the use of iron decreased, to be replaced by the terracotta and timber characteristic of Australian housing of the Edwardian era. This local adaptation of the "Queen Anne" style tempered with Art Nouveau elements, produced the picturesque Australian style known as "Federation."

Suburbs like Camberwell, Elwood and St. Kilda are full of fine example of these red-brick, red-tiled fantasies, with their white painted ornamental timber work, candle-snuffer spires, octagonal towers, multiple chimneys and polygonal bay windows. The roof was the Federation house's crowning glory, with the architect's imagination the only limitation. Some decorative roof finials display dragons and other mythical beasts, while others have Australian motifs: waratahs, gum nuts or kangaroos. Inside, the houses were as homely as their gingerbread house-style exteriors suggested, with their window seats and art-nouveau stained-glass windows.

Left, Melbourne's pride is its lush, rolling parks. Above, the spires of separate centuries.

ARCHITECTURAL STYLES

Gothic Revival: The architectural movement known as International Gothic Revival, inspired by the medieval churches of Europe, did not hit Australia until the mid to late 19th century, a good half century after it flowered in England. In Melbourne the style produced many fine churches such as St. Patrick's Cathedral (1860) and St. John's, Toorak (1861), both designed by William Wardell, Wesley Church in Lonsdale Street and St. Paul's Cathedral. The application of this style in the commercial area, funded by land boom money, has been immortalised in the gloriously exotic business buildings at the western end of Collins Street.

In 1882, William Wardell designed a Venetian-flavoured Gothic bank and office building, now the ANZ Bank, on the corner of Queens and Collins streets. The kind of building which, according to the architect Granville Wilson, "needs to be seen fronting a canal," it has a 20 metre by 18 metre (60 feet by 59 feet) banking chamber, with a nine metre (30 foot) high hand-painted ceiling decorated in a profusion of gold leaf.

Next door, the former Stock Exchange Building (now also the ANZ), finished in 1890 at a cost of 200,000 pounds is another Gothic extravaganza.

Labassa: Labassa in Caulfield (which, unfortunately, is open to the public only four or five times per year) is an outstanding example of the opulence of building in boomtime suburban Melbourne. Designed by the German architect John Augustus Bernard Koch, Labassa was commissioned by Alexander Roberton, who had made his fortune through mining interests and the famous Cobb & Co stagecoach line.

Exterior delights include caryatids at the main entrance, sculptured female figures thought to be copied from the famous Villa Knoop in Bremen, Germany, and bays, like those in the New Louvre in Paris. Inside, the Entrance Hall has a superb stencilled and hand-painted ceiling.

Rippon Lea: (Hotham Road, Elsternwick) Designed by architects Reed and Barnes (of Exhibition Building fame) as a private Xanadu for Sir Frederick Sargood, who named the property after his mother Emma Rippon, this polychrome brick work mansion is the last great Australian suburban property from the Victorian era to remain intact. Most of its interior, however, has undergone substantial renovation over the years.

Work began on a 15-room house in 1868, but the house grew with Sir Frederick's family, ending up with 33 rooms in 1903. Later a ballroom in the 1920s Grand Hotel style was added. The mansion's main drive sweeps towards an 1800s vintage porte cochere, a shelter for carriages depositing elegantly-clad guests at the Sargoods' famous "at homes" and balls. The entrance features stained-glass panels depicting English historical figures like Sir Francis Drake and the Duke of Marlborough, along with richly-scrolled plaster friezes with leaf and flower motifs. The stairway leads up to a large stained-glass window, featuring panels of kingfish, owl, leaf and pomegranate fruit patterns. The gardens, Sir Frederick's pride, joy and passion, had grown to 17 hectares (42 acres) by the turn of the century, a paradise of conservatories, ferneries and orchards with an ornamental lake fed by a huge spring.

Como House: Como House (Como Avenue, South Yarra) is a fine example of the kind of gracious living possible in Melbourne less than 20 years after white settlement was first established on the banks of the Yarra. The first sections of the house were built in 1846 for the lawyer and later judge, Edward Eyre Williams, on a hill sloping down to a riverside "billabong" which reminded him of Italy's Lake Como. During the early 1850s the house changed hands twice, until the architect John Brown bought it in 1854 and transformed it into an elegant Georgian-style mansion, adding wrought-iron railings and gates imported from Scotland and hirimg Baron von Mueller (of the Botanic Gardens) to direct the planting of its gardens.

Later famous for the lavish entertainment he provided in his mansion, Brown suffered a reversal of fortune and was forced to sell Como in 1864 to Charles Henry Armytage. The Armytages added a wing without altering the house's classic design and turned the house into a centre of Melbourne social life again.

Left, awe-inspiring view of St. Patrick's Cathedral. Above, Como House in South Yarra epitomises the grand ambitions of 19th century captains of industry and their architects.

One of Melbourne's—and Australia's—first local heroines, coloratura soprano Dame Nellie Melba, was born plain Helen Mitchell on 19 May, 1861, in the inner Melbourne suburb of Richmond. Later, to honour her home city she took "Melba" as her stage name, and went on to reign at London's Covent Garden from 1892 to 1926. Bernard Shaw described her voice as having "super-human beauty"; Sarah Bernhardt heard it as a "voice of pure crystal"; but more recently, Australian social critic Max Harris has called her "the all-Australian world champion bitch ...about as lovable as the Bubonic Plague." She died in February, 1931, and is buried near the home she built at Coldstream, east of Melbourne. Before this final curtain she made so many "final appearances" on stage that you'll often hear Australians refer to someone who keeps on re-appearing, or never quite leaving, as having had "more farewells (or comebacks) than Dame Nellie Melba."

Cultural comic: Once, at an Old Boy's dinner at Melbourne's most intensely "Establishment" school, Melbourne Grammar, a young man was observed to be solemnly cutting his tie into pieces and dropping them into his soup. This was, of course, Barry Humphries, a born eccentric who, over the years, has blossomed into international fame as the "Housewife Superstar" Dame Edna Everage, late of Moonie Ponds, or as Sir Les Patterson, Australia's monstrous "Cultural Ambassador." Humphries, born in 1934, began his career as one of the leading wags at Melbourne University in the 1950s. Academic pursuits quickly gave way to the need to create havoc both inside and outside the hallowed cloisters of this most prim university. The outrageous Humphries and his madness lurched into the streets, restaurants and trams, until every student of the time carried a swag of Humphries anecdotes with which to impress his peers. With its easily characterised (and readily satirised) gladiola filled suburban gardens, Ducks-on-the-Wall taste, and the essential blandness of its people, Melbourne became the butt for the Dame Edna joke which carried Humphries away—and on to his brilliant career on the world stage.

Left, Helen Mitchell, who changed her name to Nellie Melba in honour of her home town.

A writers' writer: Perhaps it was those same qualities in Melbourne which caused Germaine Greer to move to Sydney. Greer was born in Melbourne in January 1939. A convent girl, who, from the age of 11 was educated entirely on scholarships, in 1956 she too, went to Melbourne University but her activities were a great deal more serious than Humphries'. She maintains that the education she received in the English Department at Melbourne was "the best I was going to get for the rest of my life," with her fellow students all "sharp, passionate and hard-working." She was already an anarchist (but didn't know why until she went to Sydney University in 1959), spoke four languages fluently—a rare thing for an Australian even now—and held all night "anti-seminars" in her loft opposite the university. Incredible as it may seem now, the good Melbourne convent girl still found swearing "common," a prejudice that was not to dissolve until she got to Sydney. After that it was England, a PhD and *The Female Eunuch.* The rest, as they say, is history.

Australia's original Liberal: In those apparently serene and prosperous years from December 1949, until January 1966, Australia was led by the conservative statesman, Robert Menzies. Menzies exuded every appearance of being born and bred Melbourne "Establishment," but he was in fact the third son of a small town shopkeeper. Educated at State schools and in law at Melbourne University, Menzies was called to the bar in 1918. In 1934 he became Member of the House of Representatives for the safe conservative Melbourne suburban electorate of Kooyong. Immediately appointed Commonwealth Attorney General and Minister for Industry, by 1939 Menzies was Prime

Minister, from which position he won the dubious sobriquet of "Pig-Iron Bob" for having sold Australian pig-iron to a re-arming Japan for weapons manufacture.

His government failed in the war-time elections of 1940, but Menzies was a master tactician, and in the early post-war years he pulled together the disparate anti-Labour forces and formed the new Liberal Party, who, under his leadership, won a tumultuous victory in the 1949 elections. Middle-class Australia felt safe behind the image of patriarch-cum-statesman which this portly Anglophile projected, and the Liberals settled in for 23 years of continuous rule, with Menzies as Prime Minister for 18 of them. He retired, encrusted in knighthoods, leaving an adolescent Australia still clinging to the political, military and economic skirts of Mother England (though there was an ever-increasing tendency to turn towards Uncle Sam).

A pioneer and a politician: In today's politics—and on the other side of the fence—is Barry Jones, Minister for Science, Customs and Small Business in the Labor Government. Jones is a fascinating character, an intellectual and social visionary. His philosophies are expounded in serious, provocative works, especially *Sleepers Awake!* in which he urges Australians to look to the future in a clear-sighted and technologically informed manner—neither of which are hallmarks of the Australian *modus operandi*.

Jones was born in Geelong in 1932 and was educated at Melbourne University. He was a public servant, teacher, lecturer and a solicitor before becoming Federal Member for Lalor in 1977. With his encyclopaedic knowledge, he was Australian Quiz Champion from 1960 to 1968, although he shudders when reminded of this. His passionate concerns are penal reform and the urgent need to educate the Australian public about science and technology—"the end product of science is omniscience, knowledge," he says—have seen him blaze unusual trails. He pioneered "talk back" radio and produced *Encounter*, one of the first intellectual television programmes in the 1960s, which was responsible for bringing Arthur Koestler, Malcolm Muggeridge and Ralph Nader—among others—to Australia. Barry Jones once said "Australia must be one of the very few countries in the world, other than South Africa, where terms like "intellectual" and "academic" and "theoretical" are all regarded as terms of abuse." Perhaps his greatest achievement has been to establish The Commission for the Future, an organisation which is attempting to plot an intelligent course for Australian society well into the 21st century. Jones believes that there is a single characteristic common to most of history's great leaders: a preparedness "to go against the mainstream—not just to be a team player, not just to be part of the gang."

A powerful publisher: "The Dirty Digger" is what his enemies call the most powerful media baron in the world, Rupert Murdoch. His somewhat coy self-description is "a newsman and a publisher". Murdoch, now an American citizen, was born in 1931, into a powerful Melbourne family. His father, Sir Keith Murdoch, built the *Herald* and *Weekly Times* group into the largest media empire in Australia. Educated at fashionable Geelong Grammar, he was said to be "shy, academically slow, and athletically inept." He also became known for his left-wing views, which earned him the name "Red Rupert"—

a title which no one has called him for years. In the 1950s he inherited from his father substantial holdings in News Ltd. Adelaide and many other publishing concerns. From this base he systematically, and brilliantly set about building his media empire in Australia, Britain and the United States. Views on the merits of his various publications vary widely (from "deplorable" to "what's the girl on page three like?"): bumper stickers appeared years ago in Australia declaring "Murdoch is Bad News." He created in 1964 Australia's first national newspaper *The Australian*, and operates simultaneously some of the world's most *and* least respected newspapers.

Investigative medicine: Melbourne's first *in vitro* fertilisation (IVF) baby, Candice Reed, was born at the Queen Victoria Medical Centre in 1980. Since then, the work of the IVF team has brought it to the cutting edge of the legal, social and ethical issues related to human fertility science. The team has produced the world's first frozen embryo baby, donor egg baby, and IVF twins, triplets and quadruplets. In 1988 the team made history again when a woman bore the baby of her sister fertilized by donor sperm. Some 12,000 patients pass through the IVF program each year, resulting in 100 pregnancies. The team's research and refinement of its IVF reproduction techniques continues under Carl Wood, professor of Obstetrics and Gynaecology at Melbourne's Monash University. Wood, the leader of the *in vitro* fertilisation team, declares that he "was always attracted to the Sherlock Holmes side of medicine." After 10 years of research into childbirth in London and at the Rockerfeller Institute, he learned that there were 200,000 couples in Australia desperate for children and unable to adopt them. Of his work in fertility enhancement, he says he has not been sustained by any belief in either science or religion, but by "the faith of the IVF patients." The stress that the work has brought shows on his face, and some of his friends believe he has pushed himself perilously close to self destruction. At the height of the debate about the ethics of IVF procedures, he was accused of "tampering with creation." Wood simply says, "It's a hell of a struggle to introduce something new, but it's not impossible."

Top performers in their chosen fields: comedian Barry Humphries (left) and media boss Rupert Murdoch (right).

ON THE FIELD

Melburnians are a hardy bunch. For them, culture is not just a night at the theatre or the art gallery. It can.be a day at the football or the races or the cricket—more often than not in the midst of a heatwave or in torrential rain. By necessity, the Melbourne sports lover is equipped with a special type of resilience: he or she will, for instance, have a very tough backside, fashioned from years of braving the uncompromising wooden benches at the famous Melbourne Cricket Ground.

In the height of summer, when the temperature pushes toward, and sometimes beyond "the century" (37.7 degrees Celsius), thousands of Melburnians make the annual pilgrimage to this magnificent stadium, smother themselves with sunscreen, and cheer on the Australian cricket team and its international rivals. The crowds which gather to watch the locals face the Poms (England), Windies (West Indies), Kiwis (New Zealand), Indians, Pakistanis or Sri Lankans can be astonishing. When the Australians met the flamboyant West Indians on the second day of the deciding fifth Test match in 1961, a world record 90,800 people jammed into the M.C.G. Crowds of around 80,000 are commonplace.

This sporting obsession has deep roots: the 1892 Melbourne Cup attracted a crowd of 67,000, a figure made more remarkable by the fact that the population of Melbourne at the time was less than half a million.

The folk of Melbourne engage in a myriad of sporting pastimes, but from the tourist's point of view, football, cricket, racing and tennis are the biggest attractions. The city's obsession with sport has left it with some of the best facilities the world can offer, and mostly within easy access of the central business district.

Bowled over: Cricket is played at the M.C.G., just a short walk from the city, throughout the summer, from November to February. It is a game of quaint traditions, subtle touches and occasional nerve-tingling tension, invented by the English in the 18th century and transplanted to Australia not long after European settlement. In the commercially-oriented 1980s, two distinct forms of the game have developed: the traditional five-day Test matches, and the new one day "limited-overs" game. Test cricket, in which players still wear traditional white clothing, remains, for the cricket purist, the *real* game. In the sporting sense it is a remarkable event, in that there is no guarantee of a result, even after five days of toil. To lose, a team (of 11 players) has to be bowled out twice. It is an odd game, and that, perhaps, is its attraction. Few other sports could produce such unpredictable results, and it has often been said that patience is as much a virtue of the good cricketer as any other factor.

The M.C.G., which served as the main stadium for the 1956 Olympic Games, has a long Test cricket history. It hosted the very first Test match in 1877, when the upstart colonial gentlemen of Australia defeated England by 45 runs. One hundred years later cricket's oldest and fiercest rivals gathered on the same site for the Centenary Test of 1977. Remarkably, Australia won by precisely the same margin: 45 runs. The parallel is typical of the quirky stories which abound in the annals of Test cricket.

Cricketers are cult figures in Australia. The greatest of them all, Sir Donald Bradman, was an international hero who could not walk the streets of any cricketing nation without being mobbed. He dominated world cricket from the late 1920s to the late 1940s. In his last Test match, at The Oval in London in 1948, Bradman needed to make just four runs to complete his career with an average of 100 runs per innings. He was bowled out before he had scored (that's a "duck" in cricket parlance), but his average of 99.94 has never been approached, even by modern-day superstars. When Bradman was at his peak, Test match attendances boomed. His Melbourne Test appearances of the 1936-37 summer attracted 350,000 people over its five days, a record that almost certainly will never be broken.

For the tourist, the limited-overs/one-day cricket match is the more attractive event. This is a commercial form of the traditional game—a bastardised version, if you believe the critics—which nevertheless, has proved to be hugely successful in Australia in the 1980s. It is without question the more popular form of the game among spectators. One-day cricket is attractive to the non-cricketing viewer because it has a guaranteed result, with the teams having one innings each, it is completed relatively quickly, and almost always provides an exciting finish.

Hot to trot: Melbourne has a passion for horse racing that is unmatched in any other Australian city, and it is a love that goes back as far as the birth of the settlement itself. Less than three years after Melbourne was founded, a group of men formed the first turf club, the forerunner of today's Victorian Racing Club. They inaugurated the Melbourne Cup, the premier horse race of the southern hemisphere and one of the most famous in the world. Melbourne's first race meeting was held in 1838 under humble conditions. A series of bullock carts served as grandstands, and bets were taken and paid out in bottles of rum. Legend has it that one successful punter imbibed so freely of his winnings that he tumbled into the Yarra River and drowned.

The months of October and November in Melbourne are dominated by horse racing. This is the "Sport of Kings," where the winners stalls are frequented by Australia and Asia's business tycoons, occasionally royalty and even oil barons from the Middle East. All of Melbourne's major race tracks—Flemington, Caulfield, Moonee Valley and Sandown—are within close range of the city centre and although they operate throughout the year it is the Spring season that provides the main impetus. The highlight of the racing calendar is the Melbourne Cup, a $1.65 million handicap run over two miles (3.2 kilometres/1.9 miles)) at Flemington on the first Tuesday of November. Apart from its rich tradition—it was first run in 1861—the fascination of the race comes through its handicap format, which provides outsiders with the opportunity to get up and beat horses with blue chip breeding.

Preceding pages: a penny-farthing bicycle race at the Melbourne Cricket Ground. Left, the whole country comes to a halt for the Melbourne Cup. Above, a tale of two styles—Melbourne perfected Australian Rules football but the Sydney Swans introduced the cheergirls.

Indeed, the cup has a history of producing upset winners, although two champions are generally singled out. One was Carbine, who made his way past 38 other runners to win the 1890 Melbourne Cup in record time, and was greeted with a reception that is still regarded as the most tumultuous in the race's history. Even then, the Melbourne Cup was worth a fortune: Carbine's owner won more than 10,000 pounds. The other great champion was Phar Lap, who won the 1930 Cup. Foaled in New Zealand, Phar Lap was a phenomenal horse who eventually died in 1932 while his owner was engaged in a barnstorming tour of the United States. The story of this heroic galloper was captured in the Australian film, *Phar Lap*.

The drama of his 1930 victory is etched into Australian turf history. On the Saturday before the Melbourne Cup the champion was due to race at Flemington. As his young strapper led him up a back alley near the course, a gun appeared from the window of a passing vehicle and several shots were fired at the horse. Fortunately the shots were wide, and Phar Lap survived to win that afternoon. The following day he was secretly whisked away to a stable near Geelong, an hour's drive from Melbourne, and guarded around the clock by the strapper and a police constable. Even then, Phar Lap almost never made it to Flemington. When his owners set out to drive him back to Melbourne for the Cup, their vehicle refused to start. The champion arrived at the course just 40 minutes before the race. Despite these tribulations, once it came down to the race itself he was never in danger of losing.

With Flemington's rose-lined home straight and 80,000 people out for the day—Melbourne Cup Day is a public holiday in Victoria—the great race is a wonderful social occasion for the whole city. Outrageous dress sense and champagne parties make it far more than a horse race: it is literally "the race that stops Australia."

Centre court: Tennis is another major spectator sport in Melbourne. The game's archives show that the first tennis match was played in Australia on an asphalt court at the Melbourne Cricket Club in 1878. Since then, the nation has produced some of the game's great champions—"Rocket" Rod Laver, Lew Hoad, Ken Rosewall, Yvonne Cawley (nee Goolagong), Margaret Court and Pat Cash. Where cricket and football are the sports of the masses, tennis attracts a slightly more upmarket audience, and it is played in summer when thousands of its followers bask in the sunshine, often clad in bathing suits.

The highlight of the tennis season is the Australian Open Championships in early January. The Open is part of tennis's Grand Slam—along with the French, US and Wimbledon titles—and thereby attracts the best players in the world. Traditionally, Melbourne has been the home of the Australian Open, firstly on the grass courts of the old Kooyong Stadium, and since 1988 at the plush, new National Tennis Centre, which ranks among the best sports stadiums in the world. The Centre has a unique remote-control roof that can be closed in the event of inclement weather, and is within walking distance of the city, just across the railway from the M.C.G.

Aerial ping-pong: In winter, it is time for Australian's unique brand of football to go on show. The game of Australian Rules Football—a.k.a. "Aussie Rules," "Rules," or simply "the footie"—was invented in Melbourne in the mid-19th century and to this day, it is Melbourne which retains the most intense love for the code. Australian Rules is a uniquely antipodean sport that has flourished despite various critics who have lampooned its violent nature and the almost blind faith of its followers. As far back as 1891, one author had this to say about the colony's new game: "Without wishing to give offence to any one, I may remark that it is a game which commends itself to barbarous races." In 1968 they were still saying rude things. One James Murray thought "Australian Rules football might best be described as a game devised for padded cells, played in the open air." Such observations have had no effect on its popularity. In Melbourne, its birthplace, Aussie Rules rules.

The first game was played between Scotch College and The Melbourne Church of England Grammar School on a paddock close to the site of the code's present home, the Melbourne Cricket Ground, on August 7, 1858. It was conceived as a recreational game to help hefty cricketers maintain fitness in the winter, but has developed into a highly skilled and professional game in its own right. Like cricket, it has its quaint touches that are part of its mystique—such as the fact that the cursed oblong ball has a fickle bounce and a single bounce can decide the fate of a club.

Left, felled or just sleeping? Above, patterns of play in lawn bowls.

There were 40 men to a team in that first game, but today there are only 20 a side, with goal posts 6.4 metres (21 feet) apart. To the unitiated there might appear to be no rules, but in fact there are numerous penalties and restrictions on the contestants; they just don't get in the way of the action. Certainly, it is an intensely physical game, and no place

25
35

for the faint-hearted. There is no padding and the injured are merely carried from the arena and replaced by fresh warriors.

The game has produced some wonderfully earthy and tough Australian characters, like Richmond's strongman of the 1940s, Jack ("Captain Blood") Dyer, Ron Barassi, who once played on after he broke a collarbone, and latterday heroes like Hawthorn's Dermott Brereton, who has a peculiar habit of changing into radiant lime green boots at half-time. The heroes come and go, always replaced by new ones. The Victorian Football League's popularity is based on the fierce rivalry which has existed between the various Melbourne suburbs since the settlement's early years. The near-wars between famous old clubs like Carlon and Collingwood were legendary, and those rivalries have never died, even in the modern era of interstate clubs. V.F.L. games are played on Friday, Saturday and Sundays throughout the winter. The three main grounds are the M.C.G., V.F.L. Park at Waverley, and Princes Park in Carlton.

More than three million people watch the V.F.L. games each winter (the season runs from April to September) and 100,000 attend the M.C.G. Grand Final alone. In 1970, a record 131,000 saw Carlton defeat Collingwood for the premiership. Top players are paid in the vicinity of $100,000 a year and clubs need up to $5 million per season to field a team. It is a unique game which bears no direct resemblance to other football codes such as rugby or soccer, although there is a similarity to Gaelic football. Even the first-time spectator cannot fail to be caught up in the excitement of a Melbourne September, when the finals are played. The atmosphere at the M.C.G., in those electric moments before the first bounce of the Grand Final, has to be experienced to be believed.

Dribble fever: Another emerging spectator sport in Melbourne is basketball, the game invented in America as an off-season exercise for its footballers. The sport experienced unprecedented growth in Australia after the formation of a national league in 1979, and by the mid-80s had established itself as a multi-million dollar operation with more than half a million spectators per year. Melbourne has more basketballers and more stadiums than any other capital city and fields four of the 13 teams competing in the National Basketball League. Games are played at the 7,000-seat Sports and Entertainment Centre on weekends throughout winter.

Left and right, Melbourne's sporting passion, Aussie Rules, is characterised by spectacular marking (catching).

Melbourne's multi-cultural population has ensured that soccer is a major spectator sport in the city. Major games are played at Olympic Park, alongside the Sports and Entertainment Centre—again, just a short walk from the city. Like basketball, soccer has experienced significant growth since a national league was formed.

For those with the time to travel out of town, one of Melbourne's great annual sporting events is the Bells Beach Surfing Classic, held each Easter in the long point surf waves near Torquay, a little more than an hour's drive west of Melbourne. The Bells contest, first held in 1962, is the world's longest-running pro surfing contest, and has become a lucrative affair with the best international surfers competing for points towards the world crown.

YARRA EMPRESS
Coca-Cola
RIVER

FAIRWAY
AT ALL TIMES
TRAM STOP
SPOLETO
FESTIVAL
VILLAGE CENTRE

DAVID WANG
ONLY
Port Melbourne 111
288

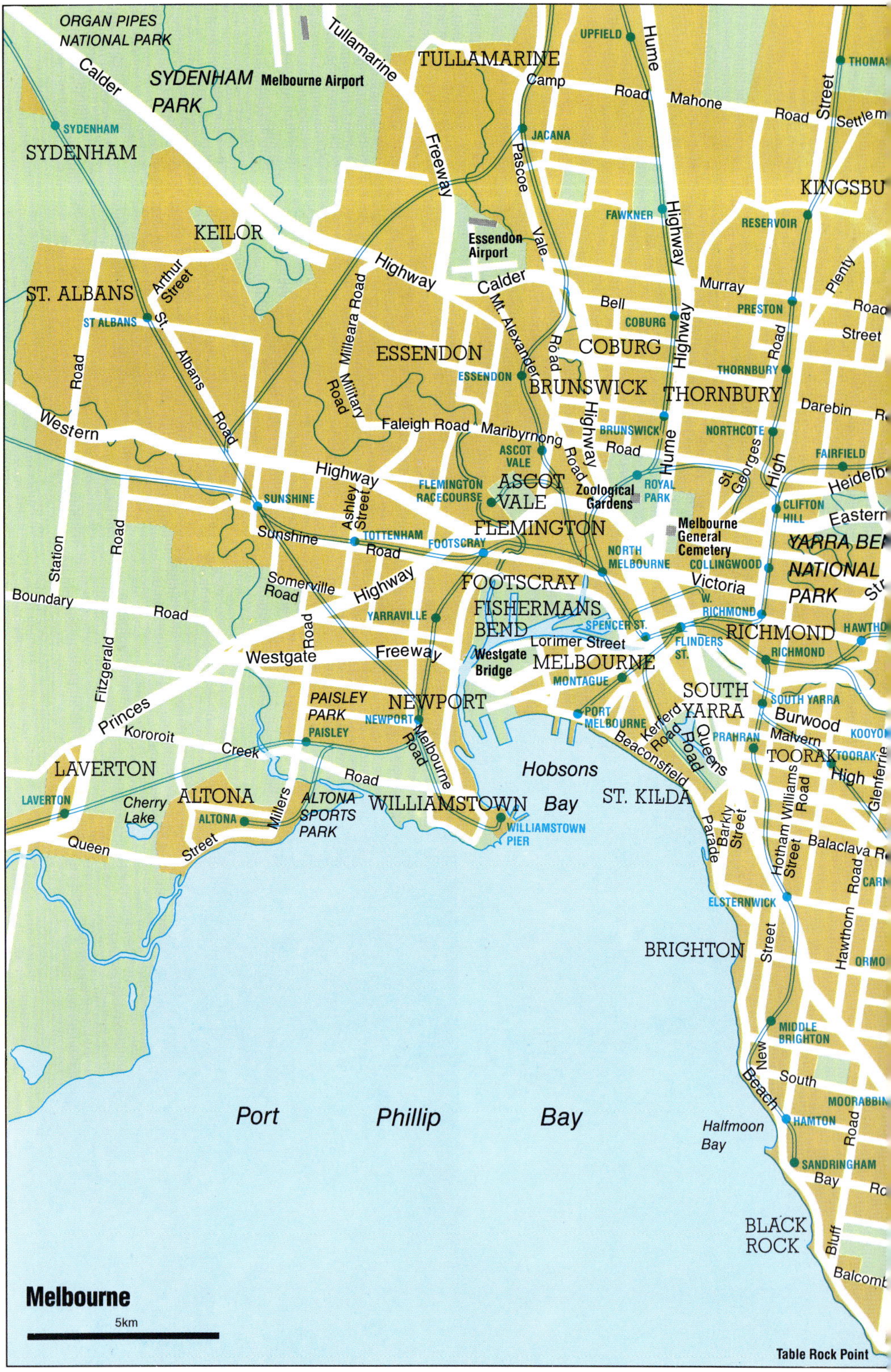
ORGAN PIPES NATIONAL PARK
Calder
SYDENHAM PARK
Melbourne Airport
Tullamarine
TULLAMARINE
Camp
Road
Mahone
Road
Street
Settlem
UPFIELD
Hume
THOMAS
SYDENHAM
SYDENHAM
JACANA
Pascoe
Vale
Freeway
KINGSBU
KEILOR
Essendon Airport
FAWKNER
Highway
RESERVOIR
Plenty
Highway
Calder
Murray
Road
ST. ALBANS
Arthur Street
ST ALBANS
St. Albans Road
Milleara Road
Mt. Alexander
Road
Bell
COBURG
Highway
PRESTON
Street
ESSENDON
COBURG
Road
Road
ESSENDON
Military Road
BRUNSWICK
THORNBURY
THORNBURY
Darebin
Western
Highway
Faleigh Road
Maribyrnong
Road
BRUNSWICK
NORTHCOTE
Hume
Road
ASCOT VALE
Road
St. Georges
High
FAIRFIELD
Heidelb
Highway
Ashley Street
FLEMINGTON RACECOURSE
ASCOT VALE
Zoological Gardens
ROYAL PARK
CLIFTON HILL
Eastern
SUNSHINE
Sunshine
Road
TOTTENHAM
FOOTSCRAY
FLEMINGTON
Melbourne General Cemetery
YARRA BE
NATIONAL PARK
Station
Road
NORTH MELBOURNE
COLLINGWOOD
Somerville Road
Highway
FOOTSCRAY
Victoria
Boundary
Road
YARRAVILLE
FISHERMANS BEND
SPENCER ST.
W. RICHMOND
RICHMOND
HAWTHO
Lorimer Street
FLINDERS ST.
Westgate
Road
Freeway
Westgate Bridge
MELBOURNE
RICHMOND
Fitzgerald
MONTAGUE
SOUTH YARRA
Princes
PAISLEY PARK
NEWPORT
NEWPORT
SOUTH YARRA
Burwood
Kororoit
PAISLEY
PORT MELBOURNE
Kerferd Road
Queens Road
Malvern
KOOYO
Creek
Melbourne Road
Beaconsfield
PRAHRAN
TOORAK
TOORAK
High
LAVERTON
Road
Hobsons
Glenferrie
LAVERTON
Cherry Lake
ALTONA
Millers
ALTONA SPORTS PARK
WILLIAMSTOWN
Bay
ST. KILDA
Williams Road
ALTONA
WILLIAMSTOWN PIER
Barkly Street
Queen
Street
Parade
Hotham Street
Balaclava R
Road
CARN
ELSTERNWICK
BRIGHTON
Street
Hawthorn
ORMO
MIDDLE BRIGHTON
New
South
Beach
MOORABBIN
Port
Phillip
Bay
Halfmoon Bay
HAMTON
Road
SANDRINGHAM
Bay
Rc
BLACK ROCK
Bluff
Balcomb
Melbourne
5km
Table Rock Point

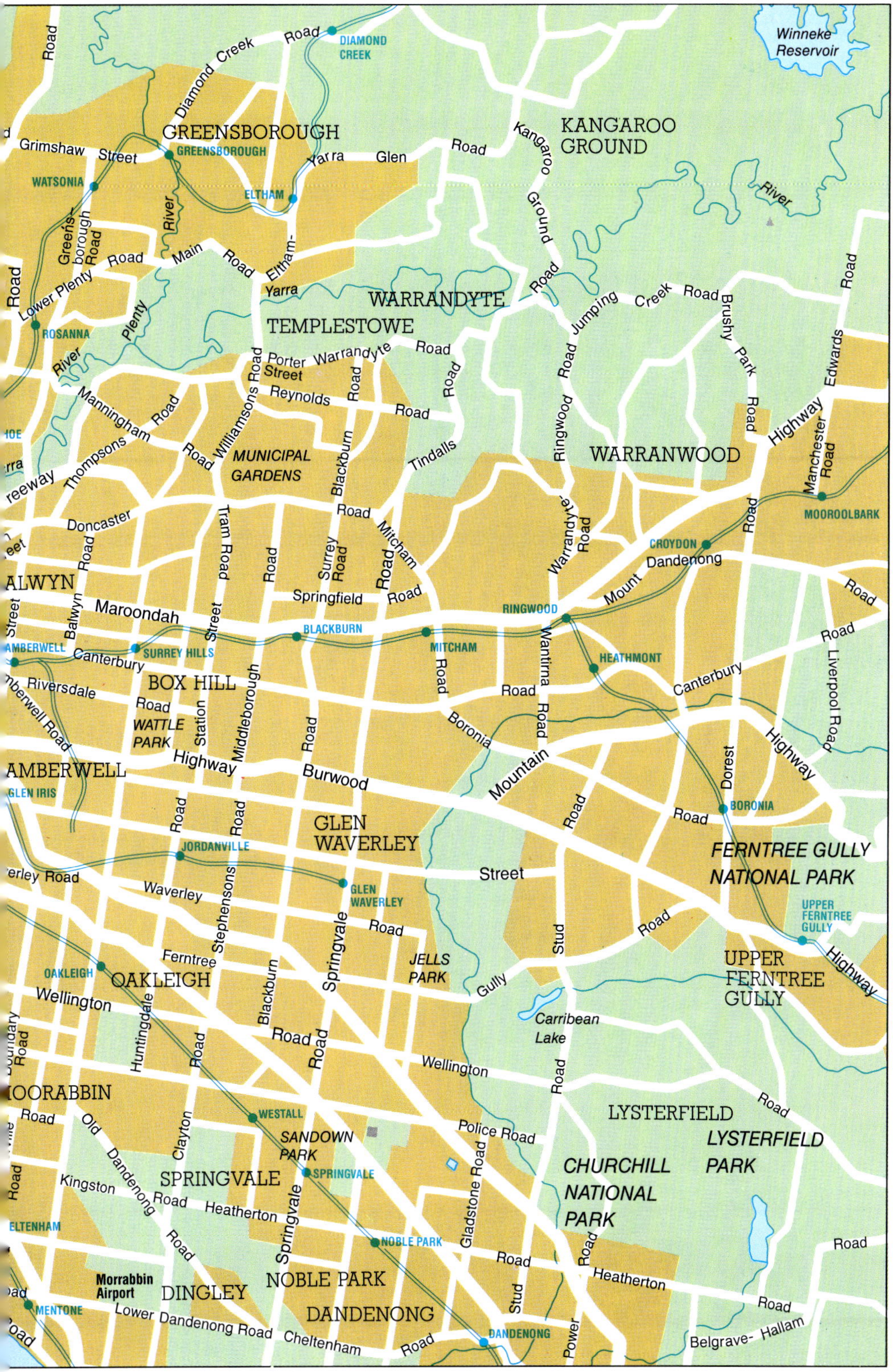

Winneke Reservoir
DIAMOND CREEK
KANGAROO GROUND
GREENSBOROUGH
WATSONIA
ELTHAM
ROSANNA
WARRANDYTE
TEMPLESTOWE
MUNICIPAL GARDENS
WARRANWOOD
MOOROOLBARK
CROYDON
RINGWOOD
BLACKBURN
MITCHAM
HEATHMONT
SURREY HILLS
BOX HILL
WATTLE PARK
AMBERWELL
GLEN IRIS
BORONIA
GLEN WAVERLEY
JORDANVILLE
FERNTREE GULLY NATIONAL PARK
UPPER FERNTREE GULLY
OAKLEIGH
JELLS PARK
Carribean Lake
LYSTERFIELD
LYSTERFIELD PARK
CHURCHILL NATIONAL PARK
WESTALL
SANDOWN PARK
SPRINGVALE
NOBLE PARK
DANDENONG
DINGLEY
Morrabbin Airport
MENTONE
ELTENHAM
IOORABBIN
Diamond Creek Road
Grimshaw Street
Kangaroo Ground Road
Yarra Glen Road
Main Road
Eltham-Yarra Road
Lower Plenty Road
Plenty River
Jumping Creek Road
Brushy Park Road
Edwards Road
Porter Street
Warrandyte Road
Reynolds Road
Manningham Road
Williamsons Road
Blackburn Road
Tindalls Road
Ringwood Warrandyte Road
Manchester Road
Thompsons Road
Doncaster Road
Tram Road
Mitcham Road
Surrey Road
Springfield Road
Maroondah Highway
Mount Dandenong Road
Balwyn Road
Station Street
Middleborough Road
Canterbury Road
Riversdale Road
Wantirna Road
Boronia Road
Liverpool Road
Burwood Highway
Mountain Highway
Dorest Road
Waverley Road
Stephensons Road
Springvale Road
Ferntree Gully Road
Stud Road
Wellington Road
Huntingdale Road
Police Road
Gladstone Road
Clayton Road
Old Dandenong Road
Kingston Road
Heatherton Road
Lower Dandenong Road
Cheltenham Road
Power Road
Belgrave-Hallam Road

The scene is Brunswick Street, Fitzroy. The event is the street party which opens the Spoleto Fringe Festival, the annual accompaniment to that mainstream showcase for artists and theatre companies from America, Europe and Australia, the Spoleto Festival of the Arts. The opening parade of cavorting dancers, musicians, actors and artists from Melbourne's lively local comedy and music scene culminates in this boisterous public celebration. Rap dancers bop with tap dancers and cabarettists in preposterous hats, bands play on the pavement and revellers cheer on competitors in the annual waiters' race—two cappucinos to be borne aloft along the track from Black Cat at No. 252 to Rhumbaralla at No. 342.

Yes, this is the city that is supposed to be quiet, sedate and . . . sometimes . . . boring. Even Melburnians have to plead guilty to perpetuating such ghastly slanders, which may have been appropriate in the pre-multicultural, pre-weekend shopping, pre-all night liquor licence days of the past, but which no longer match the vibrant cosmopolitan feel of contemporary Melbourne.

A character in a Martin Boyd novel set early this century remarks that "Melbourne on a Sunday is like a Quaker meeting without the Holy Ghost." Intriguingly, one still hears this repeated—although a Melbourne Sunday now means throngs of people shopping in Brunswick Street or the Victoria Markets and bon vivants sipping champagne and listening to a *diva* sing Puccini in Mietta's salon. Meanwhile, down in St. Kilda's Acland Street, Scheherezade cafe is full of men in cloth caps gossiping in Yiddish, while crowds three deep agonise between strudel and kugelhoupf.

Nevertheless, Melburnians on holiday in Sydney still nod and shrug passively when the harbourside city's taxi drivers commiserate as they drive them to the airport for homeward flights. Citizens of Melbourne also happily quote their city's most famous comic export, Barry Humphries (a.k.a. "Dame Edna Everage"), with "Melbourne is unique from the spiritual point of view. It's the only place on earth where the visitor from abroad can close his eyes and wonder if there really is life before death."

OK. So self-deprecation can certainly be an important ingredient in comedy, and nobody likes the opposite habit of blowing one's own horn. But Melburnians seem to carry it too far. Or could it all be a joke? After all, the city, is, more or less, solely responsible for the explosion of excellent home-grown Australian comedy over the last 15 years—from The Last Laugh theatre restaurant, TV's Comedy Company, and Rod Quantock and the other members of "Oznost" who starred at the 1988 Edinburgh Festival, to groups like "Wogs Out Of Work" and "The Hot Bagels," with their routines

Preceding pages: a single scull is a rapid but exotic way to view the Yarra; from sandstone to neon glow, Collins Street is a gallery of the city's history; map of Melbourne. Left, not everyone has respect for the classics.

about growing up Italian, Greek or Jewish.

Melburnians not only help perpetuate the hackneyed comparisons with Sydney, they sometimes turn it to their own advantage, hinting—for instance—that Melburnians go to restaurants to dine, while superficial Sydneysiders go to be seen. Who are they kidding? Melbourne is the city where the European custom of the weekend promenade is practised with a vengeance, and where well-dressed people drive right across town just to sip cocktails and watch each other eat pumpkin gnocchi. And, Flinders Lane's vast mosaic-floored food temple, Rosati, sells more Moet & Chandon than any other restaurant in Australia. (Rosati and its sister restaurant, the cathedral-like Pieroni, in Toorak Road, South Yarra, are the two high tech/classical giants in a veritable forest of Italianate glitterati eating-meeting houses that have sprung up in Melbourne over the last few years.)

Appearances to the contrary, however, food is just as important as the waiters' haircuts in these and other stylish eateries, like Cafe di Stasio and Acland Street's Caffe Maximus. In truth, the only significant behavioural difference between Melbourne and Sydney diners is that, overall, Melbourne gourmets have better restaurants to visit. So, more Melburnians can go out to dine *and* be seen than those Sydneysiders who might have to settle for just being seen.

A great many of Melbourne's charms—notably the fact that you can have a great deal of fun in the city—remain a secret that Melburnians hug to themselves. The locals know that their city offers the attractions of many worlds in one, from the Mediterranean images of the glistening expanse of yachts off St. Kilda Beach, to the middle European Jewish atmosphere of Acland Street, the Greek flavour of Lonsdale Street, the Via Veneto pulse of Lygon Street, Carlton, and the Asian aromas of Chinatown and the Vietnamese areas of Richmond.

But if Melburnians wish to keep all this under their hats, who are outsiders to argue? They can still get in on the act as Melbourne goes its merry way, feasting on the cuisine of a dozen nations, drinking wine in the sun and eating fish at Jean Jacques By the Sea, promenading along Lygon Street, St. Kilda Pier or through the Botanical Gardens, and rocking away until the wee hours in the city's dance clubs.

It is impossible to give the "last word" on the great variety of things to do, see and eat around Melbourne. What follows in this section is a representative but not exclusive sampling of the city's and region's attractions. Strongly recommended are the free publications of the Victorian Tourist Commission available from Victours head office (230 Collins St., Melbourne [03] 619 9444), or regional, interstate and international offices. For excursions beyond the city, ask for *Victoria. Your Motoring Holiday Planner* and *Vintage Victoria. Your Wine and Food Guide*.

Right, the gravity-free atmosphere on Port Phillip Bay.

HEART OF THE CITY

In the 1930s, Swanston Street was one of Melbourne's most gracious thoroughfares. Now one of the major north-south routes through the city and the main processional route for the Anzac Day and Moomba parades, its "golden mile" has degenerated—to the regret of proud Melburnians—into a succession of sex cinemas, tacky cafes and down-market shops.

Fortunately, the uplifting view down to St. Kilda Road and the Shrine of Rememberance remains, as do various buildings which evoke the past dignity and splendour of the street. Swanston Street's first landmark is **Flinders Street Station**, the design of which (the subject of an 1899 competition) features a dome similar to that of Paris's Church of the Sorbonne. Across the intersection from the station stands **St. Paul's Cathedral**, with its Vienna-influenced spires. A block further up Swanston, at the corner of Collins Street, is the Reed and Barnes-designed **Melbourne Town Hall** (1867-1870), a monument to post-Gold Rush prosperity and confidence.

The Town Hall faces a building which evokes Manhattan, the 1930s Gothic perpendicular of Marcus Barlow's **Manchester Unity Building**, a construction along the lines of the American Radiator Company building in New York or the famous Chicago Tribune Building. The clean lines of the **Century Building** (1938-9) on the corner of Little Collins Street are also Barlow's architectural vision. Between the two stands Walter Burley Griffin's **Capitol Theatre**, with its elaborately designed ceiling.

The architectural banality of the next few blocks of Swanston Street is finally relieved at Latrobe Street, with the Corinthian porticos of the **State Library**. Joseph Reed (of Reed and Barnes, designers of so many of Melbourne's public buildings) began his career by winning the 1854 competition for the library, which in fact is most celebrated for a later addition, the 1913 concrete dome over the Reading Room—at the time the largest construction of its kind in the southern hemisphere. One block further up Swanston, the beautifully refurbished **City Baths** (1903), with their twin cupolas and fussy Edwardian detailing, are still in use.

From Flinders Street Station to the Public Library and the St. Kilda Road synagogue, Melbourne's public buildings are a dome buff's delight, although the city skyline is no longer dominated, as it was in pre-high rise days, by the domes of the Exhibition Buildings and the Williams Street Law Courts. The Renaissance-style dome, with a circular gallery and libraries underneath it, is the most striking feature of the **Law Courts**, an architectural tribute to the Four Courts in Dublin. A dome was also part of the original plan for Parliament House in Spring Street, which nevertheless remains immensely stately for all its domelessness.

The centre of Melbourne is home both to the classical perfection of the **Elizabeth Street Post Office**, in which the three orders of architectural columns—Doric, Ionic and Corinthian—are used in succeeding stories, as they are in Rome's Colosseum—and also in the Hollywood-meets-Arabian-Nights fantasy of the old **Forum Theatre** (1920), now a religious revival centre, with its tower topped by a beaten copper Saracenic dome. Both buildings are typical of this city of contrasts, in which the shops and restaurants of Little Bourke Street's Chinatown rub back walls with the cafes and cake shops of "Little Greece" in adjoining Lonsdale Street.

The Victorian State Government is encouraging the conservation of **Chinatown**—the area between Bourke, Lonsdale, Swanston and Spring streets—which became a centre for the

Left, the Rialto Tower is Melbourne's tallest building.

outcast Chinese in the Gold Rush days of the 1850s. The opium dens, brothels, bars, lodging houses, herbalists and cabinet makers that packed the area in the 1880s have now been replaced by Chinese restaurants, food stores (which still sell herbs) and shops full of handicrafts, furniture, martial arts supplies and jewellery. But the old streetscape, with its low-rise 19th century brick buildings, narrow allotments and tiny lanes, has remained largely free of the post-World War II development which ravaged the face of Swanston Street. In fact, Melbourne's and Sydney's Chinatowns are the only two substantial survivors of the many which once existed around Australia, while Melbourne's can claim the honour of being the only area of continuous Chinese settlement in Australia.

A walk under the Facing Heaven Archway to the **Museum of Chinese Australian History**, housed in an 1890s Victorian warehouse in Cohen Place, is a good first stop in Chinatown before a stroll along Little Bourke Street, past the Po Hong Trading Co. Building (formerly the Chinese Mission Church, 1884), the Oriental Gourmet Building (1887-8) next door at 112, The Chinese Mission Church at 119, the Chinese Uniting Church (1873) at 196 and the Num Pon Soon Building (1861) at 200.

Meanwhile, at 209 Lonsdale St., only a few steps away from the great lions on the Chinatown gateways in Little Bourke Street, **Salapatas Brothers** is thronged with local Greek people picking up airmail copies of last weekend's Athens newspapers. The shop stocks Melbourne's four local Greek language publications and a range of Athens papers and magazines (including Greek *Playboy*) that would rival the booths on Athens' Syntagma Square. Anyone who wants a whole team of friendly advisors to help in choosing a Greek souvenir or music tape should go on Wednesday, the day the papers

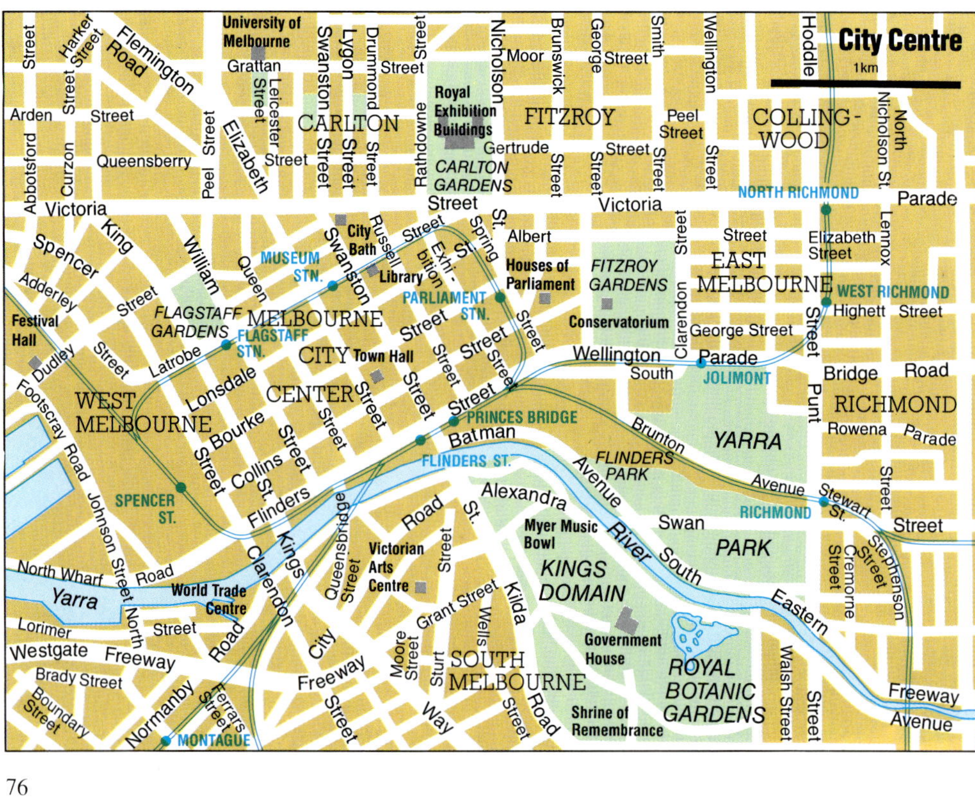

come in. Greek cafes, selling mouth-wateringly gooey cakes, dominate the Lonsdale Street strip, although two Chinese restaurants nestle uneasily between shops selling jewellery, Greek language videos and CDs . . . and Greek bridal head-dresses.

The walk from Lonsdale Street to the so-called "Paris end" of Collins Street may be short. But the gulf between the style and dress of the respective shopkeepers and their customers couldn't be larger. The eastern hilly end of Collins Street was originally likened to Paris because of its spreading plane trees and elegant old buildings, many of which have now been redeveloped, that is, torn down. The old outdoor cafes have been replaced by more practical all-weather solutions, like the Collins Place courtyard, at the **Regent Hotel** complex (25 Collins St.), where singers entertain lunchtime crowds who are sheltered from the notoriously unpredictable Melbourne weather by a glassed-in roof high overhead. Meanwhile, glass-walled semi-circular lifts glide up and down, taking people up to the hotel foyer. The complex contains the Kino cinema and a host of luxury shops, including Frou Frou, where women in urgent need of one more pair of French designer silk knickers can shop for them on Sundays.

Further down the street, one can rest up after the rigours of inspecting items like a $14,000 Louis Vuitton steamer trunk, with a drink in the Collins Chase shopping centre at the **Hyatt on Collins** (123 Collins St.). Here, under a glassed-in conservatory roof four stories high, Collins Street cafe society sits amongst giant palms, bathed in the pinkish glow generated by the imported Verona marble, while the splashing of a huge fountain tries to drown the sound of money talking.

The grand old style of Collins Street lives on at **Le Louvre** (No. 74) with its two special frocks displayed in a window that eschews any further new-fangled ideas of window-dressing,

Left, the gingerbread exterior of the Public Baths in Swanston Street. Right, a Chinatown dragon.

while curtained doors intimidate all but the bravest browser. Its owner, "Luxury Lil" Wightman, was importing Paris labels to Melbourne when the people working at nearby Jaeger, Dunhill and Cartier were still in nappies. "I've been here for ever," she sighs. "And this is still the most beautiful street in Australia. We used to get the carriage trade, when people would be dropped off in their limousines. And the best-dressed women in Australia still fly in to be fitted out for their whole wardrobe."

The hats-and-gloves era, when Collins Street was full of well-dressed women strolling up and down, is over. But busy 1980s women still make a beeline for the Paris end when they need to buy a special dress. There they can choose from Le Louvre's range of Chloe, Mila Schoen, Jean Muir and Andre Laug, or they can go to **Georges** or **The Shop of Shops**. From the eastern end of Collins Street it's a 10-minute walk—or a few minutes on a tram—to the Gothic Revival glories of the ANZ Bank, at the corner of Collins Street and Queen Street and the Rialto Building, now redeveloped into the hotel **Menzies at Rialto**, built in a grandiloquent style which has been described as "the quintessential expression of Melbourne's imperial delusions." The **Olderfleet Buildings** next door now house the Victorian Ministry of Planning and Environment, which has a bookshop full of material on Melbourne's architectural heritage.

For an instant insight into Melbourne's history, try the **Melbourne Heritage Walk**. A do-it-yourself venture, accomplished with a pamphlet available from the Melbourne Town Hall or the Victorian Tourist Commission (230 Collins St), the walk offers a glimpse of the way things were, comparing old photos in the booklet to present day locations. The journey starts at Town Hall, and takes in Collins, Queen, Bourke, Little Bourke and Spring streets, before finishing at Flinders Street Station.

Live Theatre

On any night in Melbourne, theatre goers can choose between more than a dozen plays and up to 15 comedy/cabaret shows. The new plush theatres at The Arts Centre in St. Kilda Road are the city's pride and joy, while other venues include the long-established Melbourne Theatre Company's Russell Street Theatre, Her Majesty's Theatre and The Comedy Theatre in Exhibition Street, the Athenaeum in Collins Street, and St. Martin's Theatre in St. Martin's Lane, South Yarra. More avant-garde dramatic fare is likely to be on the bill at the Universal Theatre (Victoria Street, Fitzroy), La Mama (Faraday Street, Carlton), the Anthill Theatre (Napier Street, South Melbourne), the Melbourne Writers' Theatre, which has its headquarters in a former magistrate's court and the tiny Theatreworks in Acland Street, St. Kilda. Listings in *The*

Melbourne has a thriving theatre scene of local and imported productions.

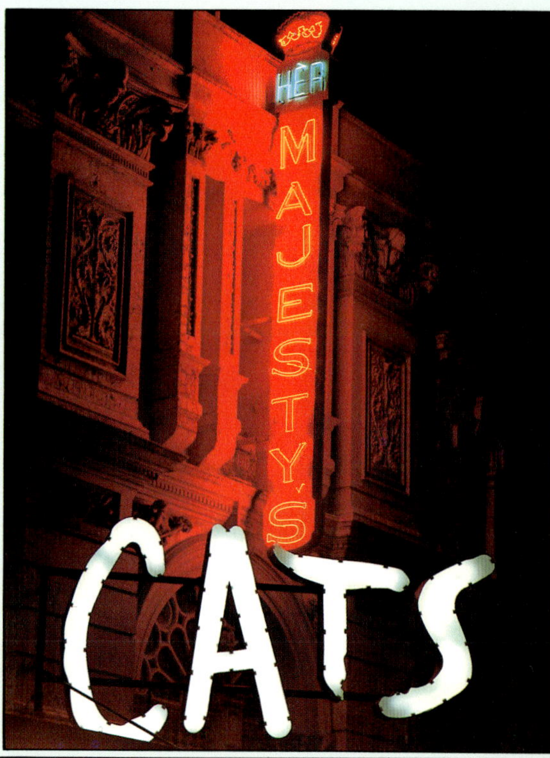

Herald on Thursdays and *The Age* on Fridays give details, along with performances at smaller theatres. The Australian Ballet and the Victorian State Opera both perform at the State Theatre in the Victorian Arts Centre.

Comedy and theatre restaurants: The unique brand of Australian comedy which regularly wows audiences at the Edinburgh Festival was born in Melbourne. The original venue was the now-defunct Flying Trapeze Cafe in Brunswick Street, Fitzroy and the midwife assisting was entrepreneur John Pinder. Pinder's next venture, The Last Laugh (with its upstairs spot Le Joke) is still going strong in Smith Street, Collingwood, although no longer under his management.

At the rest of Melbourne's theatre restaurants, from the long-established Tikki and John's in Exhibition Street to "bawdy" venues like Dirty Dick's (Queen Street, South Melbourne) the danger of being hit by a flying mother-in-law joke is omnipresent.

The city's trams are a special attraction for visitors, and indispensable transport for locals.

Trams

What would Melbourne be without its delightful painted trams (decorated with everything from abstract outback designs to cartoonist Michael Leunig's whimsical little men with teapots on their heads), not to mention its traditional green and yellow ones? For a start, its schoolchildren would have missed out on their tram jokes (Q: What's green and yellow, has wheels on top, and lies in the gutter? A: A dead tram.) and its whole population would have been deprived of a picturesque and relatively pollution-free form of transport.

Look for the special Tourist Tram. This magnificently restored 1920s number departs from the corner of Swanston and Victoria streets, travels through the city on Swanston Street, down leafy St. Kilda Road, then past St. Kilda Beach to the coffee and cake hub of Acland Street. An interesting alternative (but not at peak hour, when it's packed) is to hop on the No. 96 tram in Bourke Street, the light-rail service which will whizz you along the old train line past the Federation and Victorian-style suburbs of Albert Park and South Melbourne, onto Fitzroy Street, past the beach on the Esplanade and Acland Street...all in a mere 15 minutes.

The No. 8 tram to Toorak is recommended, especially for anyone wanting to inspect the tempting Toorak Road shops from the comparative budgetary safety of a tram seat. Those who really get hooked on trams can even dine on one: The Colonial Tramcar Restaurant, the world's first travelling tram restaurant, has special stabilisers giving the smoothest of rides for passengers—and their wine glasses. This 1927 tram has one-way windows, so patrons can enjoy the views of leafy Domain Road and the St. Kilda seascape without non-gourmets gawking at them from tramstops. Call 596 6500 for reservations.

CARLTON

In the late 1960s and early 70s the suburb of Carlton was the intellectual and bohemian centre of Melbourne, with a drug-boosted street culture which was immortalised in Helen Garner's novel *Monkey Grip* and in rock group Skyhooks' song *Lygon Street Limbo*.

The suburb's status as a byword for experimentation owed something to the proximity of Melbourne University. The sex, drugs and rock 'n' roll lifestyle of the Vietnam era students—the last generation of such who could afford to live in the suburb's superb Victorian terraces—permanently altered the flavour of what had previously been a Jewish, then Italian migrant area. But more important than these predecessors in giving Carlton its unique atmosphere was the flowering of a lively experimental local theatre and literary scene.

In 1967, Betty Burstall opened the **La Mama Theatre** in Faraday Street (miraculously, it's still there) with a play by local writer Jack Hibberd. The tiny playhouse quickly became a meeting place for playwrights (such as a young, then unknown, David Williamson), film makers and actors. The La Mama Company metamorphosed into the Australian Performing Group and in 1970 set up headquarters round the corner at the legendary Pram Factory. In that same year the landmark Readings Bookshop opened in Lygon Street. By night, the local literati met at the Albion Hotel on the corner of Lygon and Faraday streets; by day they congregated over coffee across the road in Tamani's (now Tiamo) and went on to Jimmy Watson's Wine Bar (a fixture at 333 Lygon St., since 1935) until it closed at 6 p.m.

Although writers, academics and eccentric lawyers and journalists still meet at Watson's and then move on to the "in" pub of the moment (it went

from the Albion to Stewart's in Elgin Street and is currently The Astor), the universal opinion—and the truth—is that what was akin to the Golden Age ended in the mid-to-late '70s. The final death knell sounded in 1981 when the Pram Factory was demolished.

"Trendyism," it is universally agreed, was to blame, driving up rents in many of the small off-beat Lygon Street shops and in the surrounding streets of Victorian terrace houses—so high that many earlier occupants could no longer afford them. Along the way, some of Carlton's finest iron lace-worked architectural treasures were also damaged by renovators who moved into the houses in Victorian-style squares like Macarthur Place and Murchison Square and sandblasted their walls to get rid of the supposedly "unauthentic" painted surfaces. The effects on the original masonry and joinery were disastrous. The Carlton Conservation Study has subsequently graded all the area's housing, to ensure that historically significant buildings are not further "improved" in this manner.

Lygon Street is now primarily a strip of restaurants and chic clothes shops, with more than 80 eateries of many styles, although Italian predominates. Some of the best coffee shops in Melbourne are still to be found there—including **L'Alba** (280) and **Caffe Notturno** at 177 (both open 24 hours) and the **University Cafe** (257), while the **Grinder Coffee House** (277) sells all the makings for the ultimate cup of home coffee. Lygon Street still has a soul of sorts—not its old alternative soul, but a brash and flashy 1980s personality which is embodied in the European ritual of *La Passeggiata*. Ironically, this evening stroll, in one's best clothes, has taken Lygon Street back to its earlier Italian era and turned it into what local journalist Kevin Childs calls "an Antipodean Via Veneto"—thronged with people whom another less enthusiastic local describes as "all clothes, no person."

Left and right, the refurbished elegance of mid-19th century terrace houses in Carlton.

But, not everything changes. **Readings Bookshop** is still there, albeit in smarter, larger premises, but with its window still functioning as a local bulletin board. The cooks at **Totos** (the first pizza house in Australia, established 1964) are still baking up a storm. And Prime Minister Bob Hawke continues to have his hair cut by the man he considers "the best hairdresser in the world," Tory Marazita, at **Tory's**, 9 Lygon St.

Carlton remains a treat for architecture buffs. Its streets of Victorian terrace housing are a splendid setting for eccentric treasures, like the 1889 **townhouse** at 313-315 Drummond St. on the roof of which perch four chimerical creatures, with dogs' faces, kangaroos' bodies, eagles' claws and lions' tails. Down the road at 48 Drummond St is the floridly Italianate mansion Benvenuta (1892-3), now Medley Hall, a university hall of residence, and one of the most lavish extant examples of "Victorian Baroque." Over on the campus, the Melbourne University's earliest building, The Cloisters (1854-5), which is now the Administration and Law Library, successfully evokes an Oxford/Cambridge mood, while the nearby State College of Victoria at Melbourne (a teachers' college) is a red-brick Edwardian delight, with an elaborate roofline and a highly decorated facade.

There's nothing trendy about death—or is there? While you're in Carlton, take a short, sobering side-trip to the **Melbourne General Cemetery** (on College Crescent, just opposite the University). John Batman is interred here, along with a vast sociological sampling of names from every culture on earth. It's a contemplative necropolis, serene, green and provocative of thoughts on the human trajectory: from fuss to folly. The overwhelming large marble mausolea of many recently departed Italians remind one of Oscar Wilde's quip about "dying beyond one's means."

Lawn lounging on the grounds of Melbourne University.

FITZROY

Where did Carlton's alternative soul go when the suburb gentrified itself into pasta and poseurs? To **Brunswick Street**, Fitzroy, of course, where it slicked back its hair, put on dark glasses and opened a 1950s and '60s fashion shop. Brunswick Street is a spirited, but sometimes uneasy, combination of old and new, and rich and poor, with smart expensive restaurants opening their doors in the shadows of the towering Housing Commission blocks. Young things, chic in 1950s suits, share the sidewalk with drunks from the few bloodhouse pubs yet to succumb to the area's galloping gentrification.

Commercially, the contradiction of Brunswick Street continues, with whimsical ventures like the Fitzroy Nursery (390), and its fantastic Art Nouveau-kitsch gates, sitting palm-by-fender with panel-beating shops and old-style businesses like Max David's Models (401), a dowdily traditional garment factory—"Manufacturers of Costumes, Coats and Ensembles (open to public)" as the original 1950s door sign proclaims. The street still holds its title as the welfare centre of Melbourne (or "Bleeding Heart Row" as cynics have dubbed it) with the Fitzroy Legal Service, the Australian Social Welfare Union (next door to a smart Italian cafe) and a plethora of self-help groups including the Fringe Network, an artists' "resources facility."

The spiritual centre (if that's not too ironic a thing to say) of the "new" Brunswick Street is the quasi-1960s **Black Cat** coffee lounge, where proprietor Henry Maas serves espresso to the local avant-garde.

Brunswick Street, which is open Saturdays and Sundays, is the best place in Melbourne to find unconventional and imaginative clothing and gifts, many of which are made in over-the-shop workrooms. At **Pigtale** (382), pink pottery

Street florist from Fitzroy.

pigs perform improbable athletic feats on top of teapots, or lean seductively over the edge of bowls. They are the stars of a range of exuberantly fanciful kitsch, which includes duck mugs, toucan teapots and, of course, flying ducks. The street is a hat-lover's dream, with headgear from 1930s style cloches to more modern broad-brimmed numbers being well-represented in both new and used clothing shops. **Scally and Trumble** at 331, has new hats in old styles; **Hybrid Hall** at 240 does a fine line in little netted creations, while other retro fashion shops, like **Quarter To Three** (248) and **Grace's Clothing** (313) include old hats among their extensive selections.

Used furniture shops abound, as do browser-friendly bookshops like **Hartwigs** (245), the **Brunswick Street Bookstore** (311) and the **Grub Street Bookshop** (317). **Coyle's Shop** (345)—much-needed proof that there is such a thing as a tasteful souvenir of Melbourne—stocks an eclectic selection of postcards, pottery and jewellery made by local artists. **Hyaza Kites** (441) sells flying extravaganzas, while **Mask of Janus** (334) is the place for endearing hand puppets of sharks and whales, as well as wombats and platypuses. **Fetish** (316-8) screen prints T-shirts and leggings to order. **Misfit Design** (270) has an interesting collection of "special pieces" from a Le Corbusier chair to inventive costume jewellery made by local artists. Proprietor Linn Van Hek also arranges poetry readings in the shop's basement.

Alternative lifestylers can seek refuge from this rampant materialism at the Raja Yoga Centre (256) or compromise by shopping at the **Friends Of The Earth** bookshop and food market (222), located in a resource centre with tenants like the Alternative Technology Association and People For Nuclear Disarmament.

The whole community of yuppies, students and fringe artists, writers and musicians is well-served by coffee shop/meeting places like **Rhumbaralla** (342) with its backroom art gallery, and **Bakers**, now in its new premises at 384, next door to the live music venue **The Troubadour** (386-388). And people flock from all over Melbourne to eat Portugese, Thai, Italian, French, Indian, Afghani, Malaysian, South Indian vegetarian, Japanese and African food in the street's United Nations of eateries.

Beyond Brunswick Street, Fitzroy offers pleasant walks past the fashionable 19th-century terraces on **Victoria Parade** (like Blanche Terrace at 169-179), in and around the Edinburgh Gardens (Brunswick Street, North Fitzroy)—or in the little back streets with their ubiquitous Greek-owned corner stores. Then, for a (summertime) taste of the diversity of the Fitzroy community, try a dip at the 1908-vintage **Fitzroy Baths** (with their misspelt sign "Aqua Profonda") which starred in both the novel and the movie of *Monkey Grip*.

Right, two young Greek participants in an ethnic street festival.

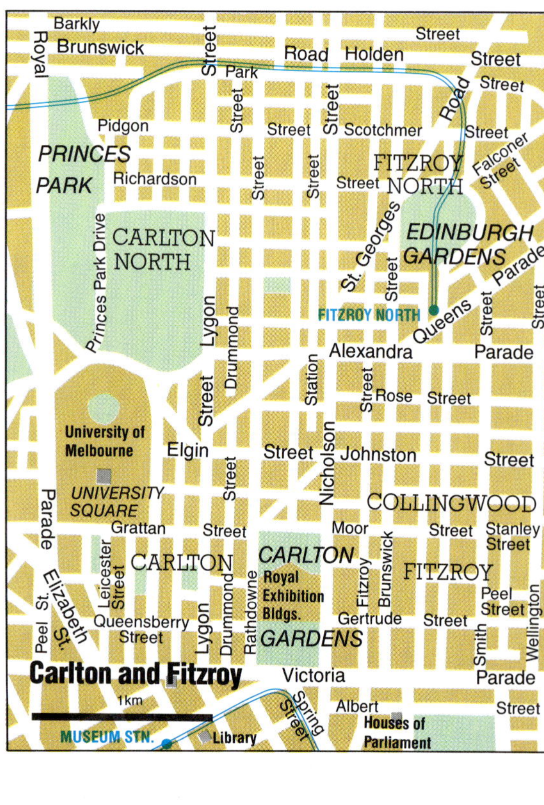

ST. KILDA

The suburb of **St. Kilda**, on the shore of Port Phillip Bay, has been compared to just about everything *except* a summer's day. Visitors have likened its atmosphere to parts of New York, its landscape to Santa Monica, and its general cosmopolitan flavour to that of a European seaside resort. Sydneysiders even claim to have found similarities to their own Bondi Beach—because both beaches feature an esplanade rising to hills which offer magnificent water views.

St. Kilda, however, is no less than its own unique self. Restoration and renovation have recaptured some of the aura of grandeur of the 1890s when the suburb was a seaside resort for the wealthy; when the legendary actress Sarah Bernhardt stayed at The Esplanade Hotel, pronouncing the area to be "just like Europe"; and when the St. Kilda pier was the first port of call for visiting VIPs like the Duke and Duchess of Cornwall, who arrived there in 1901 to open the first Australian Parliament.

The recently restored pier, with its cream and green wooden ceremonial entry pavilion at one end and the beautifully renovated Kerby's Kiosk at the other, now offers a splendid promenade. It's also a popular spot for local fishermen (the foreshore kiosks sell bait and tackle) and an exhilarating place to jog on a crisp, sunny winter's morning, when the sun glints off the masts of the armada of the Royal Melbourne Yacht Squadron, moored in rows across a glassy expanse of bay.

On any sunny Sunday the foreshore is packed with locals and visitors walking, sunbaking, shopping for jewellery or pottery at one of the stalls at the Esplanade market, eating fish and chips from the outdoor section of **Jean Jacques By The Sea** (a fashionable seafood restaurant, formerly the old bathing sheds changing rooms), or heading off for

Moored and stored boats at St. Kilda marina.

afternoon tea with a view at the Stoke House. It's hard to imagine that, little more than a decade ago, St. Kilda Beach was so down-at-heel that only the loyal locals bothered to appreciate her. Outsiders still flocked to Acland Street for coffee and cakes on Sunday, but few wanted more than a quick stroll past a beach that was narrow, dirty and marred by unsightly concrete walls only. The local residents and artists enjoyed the famous pink, purple and orange sunsets over the bay and relished the charm of faded follies like the yawning mouth of Luna Park and the elegantly-domed Palais Theatre. They strolled past the Victorian three-storey terraces in Dalgety Street, admired mansions like Oberwyl in Burnett Street and Linden in Acland Street, and promenaded in the Edwardian landscaping of the Blessington Gardens on Sundays.

Artists and writers have always loved St. Kilda for its air of decaying grandeur, its cosmopolitan atmosphere and its bay views. It wasn't difficult to keep these delights to themselves. The hot sea pools in the dilapidated and domed establishment on the Lower Esplanade, known as "South Pacific," may have been the only ones in Australia—and possibly the last of their kind in the world—but who, except a St. Kilda resident, would suspect there was something pleasant, let alone healthy, behind its neglected exterior? Tourists from other cities—and even other suburbs—were discouraged by St. Kilda's twin local growth industries in the 1960s and 70s, prostitution and drugs, and intentionally avoided the once magnificent boulevard of Fitzroy Street, which had become the centre of these rough trades.

Now all that has changed and, if soaring real estate values are anything to go by, St. Kilda is well on the way to becoming one of the most fashionable suburbs in Melbourne. But this reversal in fortunes has not happened without controversy. No one could argue against the benefits of the beach clean-

One of St. Kilda's best seafood restaurants.

up campaign which saw 90 metres (297 feet) of beach frontage reclaimed and a $97,000 beach cleaner imported to keep the new sand pristine and to even clean the seaweed from the shallows. Most locals applauded the effects of the police campaign to stamp out the criminal activities that had given St. Kilda its "Sin City" image, and are happy that **Fitzroy Street** is now noted for its smart restaurants as well as its sex shops and late night food joints. But many longtime residents are unhappy at the pace of "progress" in the area, fearing that developers are taking "their" St. Kilda and selling it to the highest bidders. Gentrification is rapidly transforming the face of the suburb as well-heeled young couples buy the run-down Art Deco flats and Federation and Victorian houses that were once the preserve of low-income renters.

Yet, for all this, there seems little danger of St. Kilda ever turning into a clone of neighbouring bayside yuppie colonies like Albert Park and South Melbourne. The suburb is simply too entrenchedly and exotically foreign—too Jewish, Polish, Hungarian, Italian, Greek, Lebanese—to degenerate into a slum of bland trattorias and gossip-fountains for designer minds. Census figures confirm the impression gained by a few hours eavesdropping around Acland and Carlisle streets: 40.8 percent of residents were born overseas, while parents of 50 different nationalities send their children to the local primary school.

The first influx of German Jews and other refugees (many of whom abandoned Europe after Hitler came to power in 1933) changed permanently the flavour of St. Kilda. Many opened shops along **Carlisle Street**, which remains a centre for Jewish food (kosher butcher shops abound, serving the local community of Orthodox Jews, while Melburnians of all faiths drive miles on Sunday mornings to buy bagels at **Glicks**, at 330A). Italian shopkeepers followed, although during the war they put up signs, proclaiming they were Greek, in order to avoid anti-Mussolini reactions. And now the street is an international foodie's dream, with Italian, Greek, Middle Eastern and Indian delicatessens, greengrocers and bakeries all vying for custom.

But Carlisle Street serves only the stomach of St. Kilda. Its heart and soul are in **Acland Street**, the coffee and cake mecca of Melbourne, a street whose tourist precinct status allows also butchers, hardware and electrical goods stores to open on Sundays. Then, at the heart of Acland Street itself is **Scheherezade**, opened in 1958 by Polish Jewish emigres Masha and Avram Zeleznikow, in an attempt to recreate the civilised European coffee house (which was only a dream in 1950s Melbourne). Here, Eureopean residents would sit, speaking their native Polish, Yiddish, German or Hungarian, drink coffee brewed on one of Melbourne's first espresso machines, and eat Jewish specialities like blinches or gefilte fish.

Shades of trendiness on land and sea.

PRAHRAN

When the going gets tough, the tough go shopping. In Melbourne, they pack their credit cards and make for Prahran—an area whose City Council has the awesome responsibility of managing seemingly endless bazaars. The "Golden Mile" of Chapel Street, South Yarra (and the "Budget Mile" of Chapel Street, Prahran); the glitzy designer boutiques around the corner in Toorak Road, South Yarra; the retro-chic drag of once-funky Greville Street (by the imposing Town Hall in the heart of Prahran); Melbourne's antique shopping centre in High Street, Armadale; and even the rarefied surrounds of Toorak Village, Toorak fall under its control. Just contemplating the list is enough to exhaust all lines of credit and credibility, but, as long as you pronounce it right they'll never question your credit rating. *Never* say "Prahran." Simply mumble "P'ran."

Chapel Street: Significantly, it was the rebel traders of Chapel Street who by staying open on Saturday afternoons—a radical move which drew shoppers and publicity—forced legislation to make Saturday afternoon shopping legal in Melbourne. The success of the **Jam Factory** shopping complex (the refurbished 125-year-old brick and bluestone factory that now houses a branch of Georges and a host of specialty shops) also encouraged other complexes like the Chapel Plaza and Pran Central to open in the area. The Jam Factory's interior offers architectural as well as shopping interest, with its ancient boilers (themselves housing shops), timber trusses and masses of colourful pipes.

Opposite the stylishly renovated **Prahran Market** (open Tuesdays, Thursdays and Fridays, but a must on Saturday morning for coffee and entertainment in the courtyard) is **Pran Central**, another old building conversion, in which the copper domes, art nouveau stained glass and decorative ironwork of the original Prahran Station have been maintained, while a bright new interior has been created for the centre's shops, offices, professional suites and a fitness club.

The so-called **"Golden Mile"** (the South Yarra stretch of Chapel Street between Commercial Road and Toorak Road) is at its colourful best on Saturday mornings, when little old Greek ladies and harassed suburban mothers with shopping buggies full of Prahran Market produce rub shoulders with sleek youths in search of designer bargains. This part of Chapel Street features boutiques like **Presents** (at No. 467), with its papier mâché zebras and giraffes imported from Thailand; **Moda Moore** (397),which sells high fashion Italian men's labels like Ermengildo Zegna; the **Club Kid** children's boutique (417); and a host of women's fashion shops. The latter include designer boutiques like **Sheldrick** at 555a (with its magnificent hats, in splendid old-fashioned hatboxes, by Melbourne milliners Hatmosphere), **Indigo** (575), and **Big Red Rock** (579) with its idiosyncratic range of hand-painted T-shirts, singlets and leggings. **Mind Games** (593) is the ultimate source for brain teasing games, while the nearby Japanese fish shop does a roaring trade in take-away sushi and sashimi, and **Made In Japan** (with Kazari Japanese Interiors out the back) offers an excellent collection of Japanese treasures, from porcelain and birthday cards to smart black cutlery.

South of Commercial Road, Chapel Street, the **"Budget Mile"** features more discount-oriented clothing and new and used furniture shops, while the original Greek flavour of the area survives in cake shops like the **Special** (at No. 207). Antique hunters are advised to turn left at the Prahran Town Hall into Greville Street, but not before paying a quick visit to the **Chapel Street Bazaar** for a feast of art deco jewellery, furniture and bric-a brac.

Greville Street's days as a hippie hangout are long gone. The street personality that emerged at the end of the 1960s, when members of Monash University's radical Labor Club moved into an old bakery there and declared it a "demilitarised zone" is barely a memory. Today's thriving community of whimsical specialty antique shops, antiquarian bookshops and 1950s clothing boutiques has moved in different directions. The spirit of the street was once epitomised by the Feedwell Food Foundry, a haunt for long-haired, leather-sandalled, herbal tea drinkers. Today, in the bright new **Feedwell Cafe** down the road, women in high heels and men in old suits sip cappuccino and vienna coffees laden sinfully high with cream. Perhaps a more fitting street landmark for today is the *trompe l'oeil* effect of the Victoria Railways train engine which explodes through the facade of the tiny terrace that houses the brewery section of the Station Hotel, as if it had been derailed from the adjacent train-line.

Connoisseurs and collectors of antiques find their spiritual home in the quietly expensive atmosphere of **High Street**, **Armadale**, the site of Australia's leading antique dealers fair, held each year at the Malvern Town Hall. Dealers in fine art and artefacts from both East and West, Persian carpets, genuine Australian colonial furniture and chinoiserie line the street between Kooyong Road and Glenferrie Road, while the splendidly restored Victorian **Kings Arcade** houses a range of special shops, including **The Byerley** and **Chowringhee Indian Art**.

Clothes shops in this street are almost exclusively Australian designer boutiques. More eclectic tastes are also catered for at **Magpie's Nest** (1012) which offers new dresses made from antique lace, and **Boxer Rebellion** (for the quintessential pair of boxer shorts), while "teddyophiles" flock to **Teddy And Friends** (1106).

Left and right, Chapel Street caters for shoppers of all styles and ages.

THE YARRA

Picnickers sprawl on the grassy slopes of the river bank. Before them, the oars of racing shells cleave the water in a rhythm of glistening slashes. An afternoon sun dapples the leaves of the peppercorns, pines, oaks and eucalypts which overhang both the exertions of the rowers and the languid encouragement of the onlookers.

This oasis of calm, only minutes from the city centre, is Melbourne's much maligned Yarra River—the river that's "too thick to drink, too thin to walk on or plough," and—yes, you've probably heard it before—that "flows upside down—with the mud on top."

Melburnians, used to these jibes—especially from smug harbourside-dwelling Sydneysiders—can hold responsible not only founder John Batman but also one Charles Grimes for siting their city upon its banks. Sent by Governor King to make a survey of Port Phillip Bay, Grimes reported in 1803 that the Yarra's banks would be an ideal place for a settlement. The first town plan of Melbourne incorporated the Yarra as a strategic rather than an aesthetic feature, with the town located just below the Yarra Falls at a spot where ships could pull in.

By 1841 a suburb's distance from the Yarra was a measure of its status, with the higher ground of Fitzroy and Richmond hill considered far superior to the lower-lying river flats then known as "East Collingwood." The Yarra, or "Yarra Yarra" (meaning "running water") as local Aborigines called it, was the new city's lifeline—its means of communication, drinking water, supply and drainage. But, despite early descriptions of it as teeming with fish and other wildlife, it is clear that the river was already dangerously polluted as early as 1840, when "colonial fever" (typhoid, cholera and dysentery) claimed many victims.

The Yarra-side cycleway links bowers of serenity with towers of commerce.

While architects were designing elegant buildings to overlook it, the Yarra was receiving the undiluted contents of night carts (emptied straight into it from the Johnston Street Bridge or Penny Bridge), seepage from cesspits dug on poorly-drained ground and waste from the adjacent wool-scouring industry and slaughter yards.

The first permanent bridge over the Yarra was built in 1850 on the site where the Princes Bridge stands today. Before this, punts and ferries had taken people across. By 1888, the Yarra had been deepened and widened and, spanned by the Princes Bridge, looked the sort of river "Marvellous Melbourne" (as it liked to style itself) could be proud of. In 1887 a Royal Commission was appointed to solve a problem which contemporary satirists summed up with the phrase "Marvellous Smelbourne." As a result, in 1891 the Melbourne and Metropolitan Board of Works was founded to manage water works, sewage and drainage, and by 1898, central Melbourne was at last served by a metropolitan sewerage system with an outfall at Werribee and an elegant French Renaissance-style pumping station at Spotswood.

The Yarra's image problem actually stems from its turbidity, which is caused by red soil from the farms on its upper reaches. After a thorough pollution control plan was implemented in recent years, the fish soon came back in schools, closely followed by the fishermen (who need a licence) and hordes of office workers who can have their lunch under the river bank's soaring gum trees—and still make it back to work on time.

On weekdays the permament barbecues which dot the bank are an idyllic spot for a private lunch. On weekends, get there early, or half of Melbourne is likely to beat you to it. To explore the river's further reaches one can hire a Bar-B-Boat from No. 1 South Wharf (corner Yarra Bank Road and Spencer Street) and barbecue your way up river.

A Yarra River rowing regatta.

TOORAK

"Some people would kill to live in Toorak," the Melbourne journalist Keith Dunstan once noted. Certainly people from adjoining suburbs of less status regularly give the impression that they have a Toorak address—thus keeping Toorak Post Office staff busy redirecting mail that belongs elsewhere but has been given the salubrious 3142 Toorak postcode.

In Melbourne, the word Toorak—for those who care about such things—is synonymous with old-fashioned money and class, and is the closest signifier in Australia of the kind of snobbery perfected by the English class system. As Victoria's state historian, Bernard Barrett puts it, "Toorak isn't just a place, it's a way of life and a state of mind." And that state of mind is strictly conservative, with the polling booth at exclusive St. John's Anglican Church (the only place to be married if you're a bride with an eye on the social pages) returning a regular 85 percent conservative vote, while its local Federal seat of Higgins has produced two post-War Liberal (that is, conservative) Party prime ministers, John Gorton and Harold Holt.

Victoria's first Government House, **Toorak House**, was built in this area and the suburb was later named after it. The area's high status stems from its desirable geographic location in the early days of the settlement, when the rich chose the high bank of the Yarra (today's Toorak, Hawthorn and Kew), leaving the swampier lowlands for the poorer settlements. Toorak House attracted other stately homes, built by wealthy squatters after retiring from their sheep stations or by 19th-century merchant princes—the Christian gentry who made up what used to be Victoria's "nobility" of families with "old" money. Nowadays, street names are all that remain of many of the great proper-

The Jam Factory is a most unusually housed shopping centre.

ties of last century. Few of the mansions which survive are now privately-owned. Toorak House is now the headquarters of the Swedish Church in Australia. Illawarra is a National Trust property, and Mandeville Hall is now the Loreto Convent School, in Mandeville Crescent.

In fact, eras have been ending in Toorak, and "old" money has been jostled by the vulgar "new" for nigh on a century. This sociological inevitability may have escaped the notice of some current Toorak inhabitants, whose own parents were probably snubbed half a century ago as "new" money parvenues. "Toorak isn't what it used to be," they lament. "Toorak used to be about school, family, manners. . .and money. Now it's just about money." The old school tie, it seems, has been replaced by the dollar as the local hard currency.

The real end of the "old" Toorak—and indeed, of civilisation as they knew it—came for the die-hard "silvertails" when, in 1987, the West Australian entrepreneur Robert Holmes a'Court paid $5 million to buy Sir Russell Grimwade's grand property "Miegunyah." In the conservative belts of Melbourne (and Sydney), wealth from out of the west is regarded as somewhere between "new" and even "tomorrow's money." Such dyed-in-the-wool attitudes extend to race: "old" Toorak—if it had its way—would have remained WASP, but post-war realities have intruded, resulting in a colourful influx of European Jews, some of whom arrived as penniless migrants, made fortunes in the 1950s and 60s, and celebrated their success by moving into Toorak. Their meeting spot is the indoor coffee courtyard at **The Place** arcade off Toorak Village, a magnificent people-watching spot, but of limited eavesdropping value for non-linguists. For example, many of the bejewelled matrons who are regulars there conduct their afternoon tea conversations in Polish.

Physically, Toorak remains an opu-

High quality Australiana is a growing industry. Following pages: bargain or bust?

lent, hilly expanse of sweeping, tree-lined roads with more private gardens and fewer public parks than any other Melbourne suburb. It's a must on the itinerary for busloads of Japanese tourists who peer in wonder at the superb old houses and ostentatious new ones set in vast gardens of up to one third of a hectare.

The Toorak lifestyle is luxury displayed. Well-heeled shoppers park their Mercedes coupes, BMWs and Rolls Royces in **Toorak Village** and breeze into designer boutiques to buy French frocks and Italian suits and shoes. Taxis draw up outside milk bars, following orders from little old ladies in need of a litre of milk and a packet of cigarettes, who don't mind paying six times as much to have it delivered. Naturally, the suburb boasts Melbourne's highest proportion of millionaires, with the inevitable corollary that 50 percent of Toorak households belong in the highest mortgage repayment category.

In Toorak shopping is raised to a near art form rather than a mere pastime or necessity. And what shops there are, both on the main street and tucked away in arcades like The Place, The Village Way, the Tok H Shopping Centre and the Trak Centre. There are English soaps and perfumes from Crabtree and Evelyn, rich chocolates from Haigh's of Adelaide, wickedly expensive La Perla Italian silk underwear at La Donna, Jasper Conran clothes at Saba and Maud Frizon shoes at Miss Louise.

The prices may be expensive, but for the window-shopper and people-observer, the entertainment is free. A walk along the stretch of shops that begins at Grange Road with a series of mock Tudor buildings, or a cappuccino at one of the pavement tables outside Topo Gigio is an opportunity to take part in what writer and Toorak local John Hepworth describes as "one of the great walking, eating, bargain-hunting, snob window-shopping, perving places in this beloved city of ours."

BOJANGLES

To Do

The range of choices is wide open in and around the city. Will it be exploration of the parks of the "Garden City," idling an afternoon along the Yarra, burying yourself among books or paintings, yelling yourself hoarse in a grandstand, diving into the Bay (preferably in summer), or dancing the night around to day? Melbourne is not short of things to do: where one begins on its menu of distractions is, of course, a matter of each individual's taste and imagination.

The **Melbourne Zoological Gardens** are near the top of the list for both visitors and Melburnians playing tourist at home. One of the city's top attractions, the zoo basks in the reputation of being among the best zoological gardens in the world. Melburnians like to emphasize the "garden" aspect as well as the zoological collection. Just a short tramride north from the city will put you among spacious parks and gardens, a setting far removed from a traditional, closed-in zoo. The zoo was established 125 years ago as a home for exotic animals imported by an "Acclimatisation Society" which wished to add to the diversity of species already found in Australia. (The ravaging of large areas of Australia by millions upon millions of rabbits—whose handful of ancestors were originally introduced for "sport"—was the disastrously logical outcome of this sort of thinking.) From its quaint 19th century beginnings the zoo has become a collection of more than 3,000 animals, which currently includes rare species not on display in other Australian zoos, such as gorillas, the Himalayan snow leopard and the black panther. What makes the Melbourne Zoo so special is the innovative and humane approach to housing its animals. A spacious **lion park**, established in 1966, was the first of this improved accommodation.

At the **arboreal primates display**, a ramp leads visitors up to treetop level where they can watch species of monkeys from all over the world behaving with the same uninhibited panache they do in the wild. In the **platypusary**, the bizarre and endearing platypus is displayed in a large aquarium—that is about the only way these shy, river-dwelling mammals can be seen. **The great flight aviary** is a walk-through area where visitors have close-up views of Australian birds native to the rainforests, the wetlands and the scrubland—including rainbow-hued lorikeets and rosellas, plus the ubiquitous pink and grey galah. The **butterfly house** is another stunning walk-through glasshouse where a cloud of between 600 to 800 butterflies flutters through a hothouse of tropical plants and waterfalls. The **underwater seal viewing area** offers a dramatic new perspective on the Australian Fur Seals cavorting in a habitat as close as possible to nature.

Not far from the zoo you can immerse yourself in one of Melbourne's most

Entrance face to Luna Park, St. Kilda.

tantalising features—the **Queen Victoria Markets** in North Melbourne. Check the day first: it would be a pity to miss them and there are few places as glum as a closed market. They are shut on Mondays and Wednesdays, and open 6 a.m. until 2 p.m. on Tuesdays and Thursdays. Fridays and Sundays, they're exuberantly in business all day. On Saturdays they close at noon. The century-old markets (at the corner of Elizabeth and Victoria streets) cover 6.5 hectares (16 acres) and sell a mind-boggling variety of goods—more than any other market in Australia. There are cheap clothes—new and second hand, antiques, bric-a-brac, flowers, fresh fruit and vegetables. And the cheeses! All of this is housed under one gigantic roof, featuring more of the 19th-century architecture for which Melbourne is so renowned. In contrast to so much lively activity, it is ironic to recall that the site was originally that of Melbourne's first general cemetery. Sunday is a particularly thriving day, both for traders and those who thrill to—or would kill for—a bargain. And don't forget to haggle: it's not compulsory but is perfectly acceptable if the mood takes you.

Completely different, but just as compelling for visitors, is **Captain Cook's Cottage**, in the midst of the Fitzroy Gardens. The stone 18th-century cottage was the home of the parents of the discoverer of the east coast of Australia, that dour and brilliant Yorkshireman, James Cook R.N., who, in three great voyages from 1768 to his death in 1779, did more to clarify the geography of the southern hemisphere than any previous navigator. It is delightfully set in an English cottage garden, such as might have existed in Cook's childhood—many of the trees and shrubs have come from England. Purchased for the centenary of the state of Victoria in 1934, it was dismantled and transported from the village of Great Ayton in North Yorkshire to Melbourne, where it was reassembled. In 1978 it was renovated and upgraded

Left, koalas' affections often wander when they discover that people don't grow edible gum leaves. Right, cheap fresh fruits & vegetables.

and a small museum was created in the stable adjoining the house.

The interior of the mid-18th century cottage is unlikely and fascinating, not only because of its smallness—which is unexpected—but because every detail has been selected with exquisite attention, down to the needlework samplers and the bed-warmers. The simple furniture (all pre-industrial revolution) is handmade. The cottage does not have the stiff, unused feeling of a museum piece, but emanates from its scrubbed stone, a rare warmth and homeliness.

A walking town: Spring and early summer are ideal times to walk through Melbourne, although many Melburnians say that autumn is the best time to see their city. The sleepy beauties of the **Treasury** and **Fitzroy gardens** have long been favourites. Another particularly popular promenade is to follow the walking and bicycle track along the banks of the Yarra River near the city centre. Put on some comfortable shoes and begin your walk at the corner of Batman Avenue and St. Kilda Road. Walk east along the north bank of the river, just before the Swan Street Bridge you will see the **Tennis Centre** (famous for its opening roof, and infamous for the time it takes to open and close); keep going along the river until you come to the very pretty Morell Bridge. Cross here and either go into the Botanical Gardens and walk along Anderson Street into South Yarra, one of Melbourne's most luxurious suburbs; or keep to the river bank, coming up past the picnickers, joggers, cyclists and horseriders, past the boat sheds—there will always be rowers on the river—through the restful Alexandra Gardens before returning to Princes Bridge. This route has become a favourite social promenade, and barbecues, breakfast and evening parties are popular with its cognoscenti.

Before leaving this area south of the Yarra there are several other places of interest to investigate. One looked upon with particular fondness by Melburni-

The cottage of Captain Cook's parents was shipped from Yorkshire and rebuilt in Fitzroy Gardens in 1934.

ans is the **Sidney Myer Music Bowl** in the King's Domain, the gardens next to the Royal Botanical gardens. Completed in 1959, it consists of a soaring aluminium and plywood roof supported by cables attached to steel masts and has an orchestra pit for 100 musicians. The acoustics are excellent and the Music Bowl is used for everything from opera to rock concerts. Every Christmas, thousands of people come out into the summer night to take part in the popular Carols By Candlelight, spilling out onto the grassy slopes surrounding the Bowl. During the winter months the Bowl remains equally popular in its guise as an ice-skating rink.

Also in the King's Domain is **La Trobe's Cottage**, Melbourne's first Government House. When Charles La Trobe arrived in Melbourne in 1839 to take over as Superintendent of the Port Phillip District, he brought with him the timber for this prefabricated house which he called "Jolimont," after his wife's country home in Switzerland. "Jolimont" looks breathtakingly modest compared with the grandly vice-regal **Government House** standing in spacious grounds nearby. (One feels that nothing less than full formal dress would suit that setting.) Government House was built between 1872 and 1876 when Melbourne was at the vulgar height of its "boom." Modelled on Queen Victoria's Osborne House, it has 200 rooms and a ballroom half as big again as that of Buckingham Palace. Government House is Melbourne's stateliest home, but is rarely open to the public. However, its white square tower has become a well-known landmark. When the flag is flying the Governor is at home.

King's Domain also has the **Shrine of Remembrance**, Victoria's tribute to the men and women who gave their lives in war. Surrounded by impeccable gardens it is a solemn building, of a rather too massive 1930s design. The most emotionally moving part of the Shrine is the crypt below the inner sanc-

The Alexandra Gardens still cultivate the original (and best) "greenhouse effect."

tuary, where an inscription reads: "This holy place commemorates Victoria's glorious dead. They gave their all, even life itself, that others may live in freedom and peace. Forget them not."

If walking just isn't your style, another option is to try floating. At **Spencer Street**, near the World Trade Centre one can hire an assortment of boats. There are cruises up and down the Yarra as well as around the docklands. And despite the Yarra being renowned as the muddiest river in the galaxy, it can be a particularly agreeable place to spend time—the views of the city are spectacular.

Just on the outskirts of Melbourne you can enjoy another type of watery pleasure at the **Fairfield Boatsheds** on the Yarra. Here, only five kilometres (three miles) from the city, you descend into real bush then emerge on the river's edge where rowing boats are for hire. You can drift silently along the river, beneath the hanging branches; or just enjoy the quintessentially Australian atmosphere of the old 1920s boatsheds which have been converted into a very relaxed restaurant. It's easy to while away an afternoon, sitting in the sun, having a glass of wine, or a gelato and imagining yourself in 1911.

Even more fashionable than the Fairfield Boatsheds are the Tea Dances that have become a feature of Melburnian weekend life. At the elegant **Burnham Beeches** resort hotel at Sherbrooke Forest, in the Dandenong Ranges, a marvellous Tea Dance is held every quarter, and sometimes more frequently. The dances take place on a Saturday or Sunday—check with the hotel to make sure of the date—and swirl from 2.30 until 5 p.m. Traditional English high-tea is served, along with champagne—naturally. The music of an excellent 1930s big band beautifully matches the decor. You too, may blend beautifully with the decor if you dress for the occasion, as many choose to do.

For those who do not care to drive out to Burnham Beeches, there are several

Symmetrical view of the Shrine of Remembranc

city hotels which also hold regular Tea Dances, including **The Regent**, **Menzies at Rialto** and, naturally, the grand lady of Melbourne hotels, **The Windsor**. The Windsor is worth visiting just for a cup of coffee or a cocktail. To sink into the deep leather in the quiet and cool of this hotel in the high old style of quiet swank is to sink back into time. For those hours when peace or a quiet chat is needed without the terror of enforced Muzak, the best place to go in Melbourne is The Windsor—where they have the good manners to not mind if you sit over one cup of coffee all afternoon. It is one of the few unpretentious, truly civilised places left in Melbourne. It must also be noted that the Ladies Lavatory is said to be the nicest in all of Melbourne.

And then there is shopping. You may notice an unusually high degree of elegance in the garb of Melburnians. Apart from being a major business and retailing centre, Melbourne is the fashion centre of Australia. The department stores are exemplary in their range and sophistication. The exclusive **Georges** of Collins Street, still gives the shopper old-world care and attention in gracious circumstances—but is expensive and can be snooty. Collins Street also has many other exclusive boutiques which are normally very costly, but if you arrive at sale time the bargains are momentous. In the charming arcades (most of which are located between Bourke and Collins streets) you will find more boutiques and speciality shops, as well as restaurants of every dimension. One place of interest is the National Trust classified **Gordon House**, in Little Bourke Street, formerly a hostel for homeless men, but in a dramatic change of fortune now a picturesque complex of exclusive shops. In **Bourke Street**, along both sides of the newly-created mall, Australia's two most venerable department stores, **Myers** and **David Jones** are side by side and you can literally buy anything you want in their vast interiors.

Government House can be seen above the regal green of Kings Domain.

EXIT

ART OF THE CITY

If art is where you find it, a fitting place to start discovering the visual art of Melbourne, the city founded by none other than "Batman," surely ought to be from the air. Its street-plan is a gridded forecast by Empire builders, intent upon plotting a design for prosperity. By day these rectangles may be predictable, but by night from the air they are a sci-fi delight, the angular circuitry of the city's gameplan, a phosphorescent cortex of three million lives.

Back down on earth, the prudent cubes of city blocks soon animate themselves with wonderfully painted trams which roll past dowager-elegant 19th century edifices and lolling parks. "Official" art is well represented where it ought to be, in the galleries, avenues and museums; but also erupting from informal corners, like shop windows and clubs and from a general sense of style, is the vernacular minutiae which tells whether a city has a home-grown or received creativity. Melbourne's muse is the former.

A hanging art: The art of finding art then is in looking around. Here, on the corner of Swanston and Franklin streets are the red walls and cream cupolas of Melbourne's venerable **City Baths**, a beautifully restored vintage billabong of gleaming tiles and heated waters. Nearby, on the corner of Russell and La Trobe are the yellowing gingerbread stones of the **Old Magistrate's Court**—the sort of place in which you could imagine Dracula being sentenced. Next door is the **Old Melbourne Gaol** where they would have hanged him, and indeed where they did hang Australia's best known bushranger, Ned Kelly. Further down Russell, on the corner of Collins, are the sober grey stones and spires of another centenarian, the **Uniting Church**, the sort of chapel in which Drac or Ned ought to have repented.

It's clear that the art of being Melbourne was never vested in one particular notion, place or time of day. Playwrights, planners and poets may hold a few keys to the nocturnal city, but by day it's the art of the domestic architect and the humble gardener which arrests the eye. A few kilometres from the business centre, the suburbs of South Yarra, Toorak and Canterbury epitomise this sort of artistic (and social) history. Cathedral aisles of liquidambar and maple trees overhang meandering streets where modestly baronial Victorian homes represent everything to which Melbourne of late colonial times aspired. The gardens of these havens are thickets of rose and azalea. Australians have so often imitated this type of suburban "art" at the expense of other forms of creativity and imagination, that Melbourne satirist Barry Humphries once derided Australia as "the largest suburb on earth."

To compensate for a blatant land-grab from the local Aborigines by

The National Gallery of Victoria features outstanding art (left) and a magnificent stained glass ceiling by Australian artist Leonard French (right).

founding finagler John Batman, Melbourne worked hard at shoring up its image of colonial respectability, especially by constructing such civic monuments as the Town Hall, Melbourne University, the National Gallery, the State Library, St. Paul's Cathedral, Parliament House and even Flinders Street Railway Station. These were shrines to the edifying effect which European high culture was meant to have on a community of new settlers, old convicts, remittance men, gold rushers and the like.

The rebels: Art, however, is no respecter of such civil and moral engineering, and will out in a form appropriate to the forces of the time. In the shadow of its cultural temples Melbourne has always spawned its own creative freebooters, innovators and fringe visionaries who have worked alone or in groups. During the 1880s a colony of painters in a bush camp at Heidleberg produced fine Impressionist works which dislodged the prevailing Arcadian romanticism and attempted the honest depiction of Australian light, landscape and living conditions. Their 1889 show "The 9 x 5 Impressions Exhibition" was not well received by critics, but its participants, Arthur Streeton, Tom Roberts, Charles Condor and Frederick McCubbin are now regarded as the giants of that era, a reputation which investors in their works continue to assert. Their paintings may be found in all major Australian galleries, including the National Gallery of Victoria.

A later colony of self-consciously bohemian artists and craftsmen was founded in 1935 at Montsalvat near Eltham. The rustic buildings of their hamlet are still open to the public and function as an ongoing work- and market-place for jewellers, musicians and sculptors. Soon after World War II, in the suburb of Bulleen, art patrons John and Sunday Reed gathered to their home (quaintly named "Heide") a group of painters, including Sidney Nolan, Arthur Boyd, John Perceval and Albert Tucker, who were to set the

agenda for Australian Modernism. They too re-defined Australian self-imagery and myths, depicting a view of alienated dwellers in a surreal landscape of bush, desert and city. Their works also are to be found alongside those of Tiepolo, Titian, Gainsborough, Constable, Picasso and Turner in the National Gallery of Victoria, while those of Nolan and Boyd are prominent in the theatre foyers of the Victorian Arts Centre. On the site of "Heide" (7 Templestowe Road, Bulleen) there now stands the **Heide Gallery** and sculpture gardens.

The Victorian Arts Centre on St. Kilda Road is an overwhelming complex of culture and statistics. Twenty four years and $225 million in the making, it houses the National Gallery of Victoria, three major theatres, the Melbourne Concert Hall, an intriguing **Performing Arts Museum** and several restaurants. This government-owned cultural coliseum, which was opened in 1982, is so all-encompassing that it may be described as "state of the art in art of the state." It dominates the Yarra bank, and the skyline, with its 115-metre (380-foot) webbed steel spire—a crocheted cross between Buckminster Fuller and the Eiffel Tower. There are guided tours of the Arts Centre each day, although such a quick look around will not do justice to the complex or its contents.

The Centre's **National Gallery of Victoria** alone can occupy at least half a day if you wish to appreciate its eminent collections of Australian, Aboriginal, Oriental and international art. There is a very strong Chinese collection. Re-housed in 1968 in its permanent home on St. Kilda Road, the Gallery's collection had been accumulating since the rich Felton Bequest early in the century endowed it with the sort of money of which other state galleries only dream. Beside works of the above-mentioned masters, the "Heidleberg School" and "Heide" painters, there are drawings and sculpture by many other

Civic art of different eras: cherubim cooling (left) and hoops and fooling (right).

Australians, plus a sculpture court with a fine Henry Moore bronze. The outstanding architectural feature of the building is the **Great Hall** with its kaleidoscopic stained-glass ceiling (the largest in the world) which Melbourne artist, Leonard French spent five years in creating.

The Centre's Concert Hall and theatres are stunning in the excellence of their layout, decor and acoustics. The 2,600-seat **Concert Hall** has been hand-painted in mineral-like strata, in shades of coral, sand, lavender and grey. The feeling is like that of being within an auditorium quarried from a sandstone hillside. In the foyer of the Playhouse Theatre are 10 superb examples of Aboriginal painting from the Western Desert of the Northern Territory. These "sand story"-based designs depict myths and ceremonies of the primordial Creation or "Dreaming" period, and while the symbols remain inaccessible to the uninitiated, the effect does not. Their imagery is magnetic. By contrast, other foyers in the Centre, with their black mirrors, overloads of Boyd and Nolan, and red and black bordello decor seem too much, too often.

Not all art in Melbourne will sit still on a wall. One of the delights of the city is waiting for a tram which turns out to be a canvas in motion, an electric fresco, a Sistine to go. Since 1978 the ministries of Arts and Transport have employed Melbourne's favourite creative sons and daughters to paint the "old rattlers." Catch one of these off-the-wall creations to the corner of Flinders and Swanston streets for a little pub art. There in the upstairs bar of **Young and Jacksons Hotel** you can admire one of Melbourne's eternal icons, "Chloe." Ms. Forever Fourteen, she modestly turns her gaze away from the rabble of drinkers, who don't necessarily return the gesture. Standing there as naked as the day you'll die, and as beguiling as when Jules Lefebvre painted her in 1875, she is Melbourne's favourite daughter.

Art appreciation in the National Gallery.

The "gallery crawl": An inventory of Melbourne's art and an itinerary of where to view it could take forever. *Art Almanac*, a comprehensive monthly guide to all city and regional art shows is available from most galleries, and should be your operating manual for that time-honoured afternoon ritual, the "gallery crawl." There are scores of galleries (in Toorak, South Yarra, Prahran and many other suburbs) which offer a mixture of traditional and contemporary works in all media—not to mention gems of overheard names-dropping and theory gossip. One craft gallery of special note is **"Makers Mark"** at 85 Collins St. which specialises in high quality contemporary jewellery and small-scale sculpture. Prices range from $50 a piece to several thousand dollars. The **Meat Market** (Courtney Street, North Melbourne) is not a singles bar, but a craft centre where you can watch the best of Victoria's craftspersons at their work and then buy it at bargain prices.

If you're a bibliophile or a bookaholic, the renowned Kay Craddock Antiquarian Booksellers on the corner of Flinders Lane and Russell Street is the place for rare first editions and other gems. A unique place of art and industry is the **Victorian Tapestry Workshop** where they specialise in translating designs by leading Australian artists into giant hand-woven tapestries which, after months or years of preparation, are hung in such locations as the new Parliament House in Canberra. The Workshop is located at 260 Park St., South Melbourne, but telephone first for tour information.

As well as the city's opulent Gold Rush architecture, a very fine **Art Gallery** bears testimony to the great gold rush of the 1850s. Built in 1887, it is the oldest regional gallery in Australia and has a collection which covers the 200 years of European art in Australia, from von Guerard, Gould and T. S. Gill to Fred Williams, Lloyd Rees and John Brack.

Torsos of their time. Left, modern "eggtomorph" and right, undeclared treasure, classical Chloe.

MUSEUMS

Melbourne can lay strong claim to the title of "cultural capital of Australia." Indeed, she may be called "the City of Museums" as truthfully as she is called "the City of Gardens." There are museums galore—some of them formal, others more casual—to illustrate the history of almost every aspect of Melbourne, and Australian, life.

Probably the most formal, and certainly the most comprehensive museum in the state is the **National Museum of Victoria**, which is part of the grand State Library Building on Russell Street. Since its inception in 1853 the Museum has built up a formidable collection of well over four million natural history specimens. There are notable collections of Australian birds, molluscs and minerals as well as significant holdings of Aboriginal artefacts and ethnological displays. The intriguing dioramas of Australian birds and animals in their natural settings are by current standards somewhat old-fashioned, but nevertheless highly informative about their subject matter—and incidentally, also about earlier traditions of museum display.

By far the most popular feature is the mounted hide of the beloved, big-hearted racehorse of the early 1930s, Phar Lap, who, legend has it, was poisoned in California. Preserved, but not quite in the same way, is one of the famous Entombed Warriors of Xian. Regarded as priceless, this is the only one outside China and was a gift to Australia from the People's Republic.

The National Museum also has on exhibition the most complete display of dinosaur specimens in Australia, a fine fossil collection, a children's museum, the Planetarium, the Sunrise School (an experimental school for children in high technologies) and the terrific Experilearn Centre. Gallantly struggling against inadequate financing, the museum is a wholly admirable storehouse of fascinations.

A less conventional museum is the **Old Melbourne Gaol**, a sullen bluestone building on the corner of Russell and Franklin streets. Opened in 1845, it was Melbourne's principal gaol until the end of last century, when the authorities decided to shift the palace of woes to Pentridge Prison at Coburg. During its time as a penal institution, 104 hangings took place in the Gaol, the most notorious being that of bushranger Ned Kelly in 1880. It is now a National Trust Museum where you can see a death mask of Kelly, as well as a suit of bushranger's armour that is probably his, plus many other grim reapings from Victoria's penal past.

Melbourne has a reputation for excellent Chinese food. Before dining in Chinatown, which is right in the centre of the city, drop into the **Chinese Australian History Museum** at 22 Cohen Place, off Little Bourke Street. This is the home of "Dai Loong," the huge

Left, plate metal probably worn by bushranger Ned Kelly. Right, Kelly's death mask.

dragon used during street festivals, celebrations and parades. The exhibitions show the often overlooked but important role of the Chinese in the early years of Australia and attempts to redress the "writing-out" in official histories of their contribution to the nation's development. As miners and merchants they were in the forefront of non-Aboriginal settlement of the continent—in spite of the odious treatment often meted out to them. The museum has a gift shop, as well as audio visual and other displays.

The Performing Arts Museum in the Victorian Arts Centre has the reputation as being one of the best of its kind in the world. This museum of surprises holds costumes, memorabilia, posters and more. There are sight and sound exhibitions exploring the whole spectrum of the performing arts from cinema and musicals to marionettes and circuses.

A treat for those interested in music is the **Percy Grainger Museum** at the University of Melbourne, Royal Parade, Parkville. Grainger (1881—1961), a virtuoso pianist and composer—not to mention eccentric—was among the first classical musicians to value and preserve the folk songs and music of ordinary English people. A great collector, he travelled the world, putting down his field recordings on an old Edison machine. The museum has a vast collection of not only his manuscipts and instruments, but also many personal effects and costumes.

At the Melbourne Cricket Ground in Jolimont, is the **Australian Gallery of Sport**. There is a collection of memorabilia—redolent of the sweat, swearing, tries, overs, ducks, behinds, punts and glories—which covers Australia's famous, and some infamous, achievements in all areas of sport.

At 20 Victoria Dock there is the **Alma Doepel**, a historic sailing ship (built in 1903) which is being restored as a maritime museum and training ship. At the corner of Normamby and

Left, at last a museum that recounts the role the Chinese played in Australia's development. Right, the Old Melbourne Gaol museum.

Phayer streets, South Melbourne, opposite the World Trade Centre, is the dear old **Polly Woodside**, a restored barque, now more than a century old, which is the focal point of a complex which includes a martime museum, an outside activity area with maritime games for children and a licensed restaurant. At Gem Pier, Williamstown, the restored WW II Navy corvette, **HMAS Castlemaine** houses a very comprehensive maritime museum.

Mandatory for philatelists is the **Post Office Museum** at 90 Swan St., Richmond, with its permanent display of historic stamps, as well as postal, telegraph and telephone equipment. Next whistle stop for the museologist is at the **Victorian Railway Museum** at Champion Road, North Williamstown, a fascinating place for railway enthusiasts—and even non-enthusiasts. Situated next to the Newport Railway Workshops, it houses steam locos and passenger rolling stock from every era. In this diesel-electric age when not too many kids say, "I want to be a train driver when I grow up," this one is for both children and their minders, a bygone dream-come-true.

If you fancy an equally nostalgic slide down the fireman's pole, a visit to the **Melbourne Fire Museum** (corner of Gisborne Street and Victoria Parade, East Melbourne) should prove quite exhilarating. Its displays include old fire fighting equipment, uniforms and photographs. Gauge its impact by listening for the sprogs saying "I want to be a fire-man when I grow up." Or, is it "fire-person"?

For former or aspiring *Top Gun* types, 27 kilometres (17 miles) south west of Melbourne at Point Cook is the **Air Museum** at the Royal Australian Air Force Base. On display are a variety of WW II aircraft, including a German V2 rocket, plus a range of uniforms and weapons. Another historic collection of aircraft is located at **Moorabin Airport**, open weekdays and weekends in the afternoon.

Phar Lap galloped straight into national legend, and finally came to rest in the National Museum of Victoria.

FESTIVALS

Whatever the weather, whatever the month, there is a festival being celebrated in Melbourne. For most of these there is a definite theme, but for the largest, and most popular, **Moomba**, there is no theme other than its own Aboriginal meaning—"Let's get together and have fun."

Since 1955 Melbournians have revelled in the pleasures of Moomba during the last days of summer. There are 10 days of festivities in this unpretentious family festival, as well as sporting features such as a water-skiing regatta on the Yarra and important race meetings. There is also the outdoor Art Show, held in the Treasury Gardens; band and musical concerts which are part of the summer festival program of "Fantastic Entertainment in Public Parks"; and wide-ranging theatrical performances. All this culminates on the Monday public holiday of Labour Day, in Australia's largest and best street procession.

This carnival procession is led by the annual monarch of Moomba, and over half a million people pack Swanston Street to watch the marching girls, mixed bands, wildly-decorated floats and clowns parading in a colourful mardi gras. The evening finale is one of those block-buster, take-your-breath-away displays of fireworks over the city.

A newer, and very different type of festival takes place in early September, at the beginning of spring. The **Spoleto Festival** is an arts festival "of three worlds," taking place annually in Italy and America, as well as Australia. Over a period of nearly three weeks it encompasses all the mainstream arts, and brings to Melbourne some of the most exciting and renowned performers in the world. If your taste is opera, drama (traditional or contemporary), music (from chamber to jazz), film, dance or literature then you cannot afford to miss Spoleto. The only thing wrong with all this is having to choose what to miss from such a breathtaking program of offerings. In recent years Spoleto has presented such acts as Ken Russell's *Madam Butterfly*, Nigel Triffitt's *The Fall of Singapore*, the fantastic Royal Ballet of Spain, the Comedie Française, the Aboriginal and Islander Dance Theatre and the Cloudgate Taipei Contemporary Dance Theatre. There have also been writers of the calibre of Nadine Gordimer, Surendra Rendra, Elizabeth Jolly and Kate Jennings speaking at the public forums at the Writer's Festival.

Running concurrently with Spoleto are two smaller and essentially Melbourne festivals: Fringe Spoleto and Piccolo Spoleto. **Fringe Spoleto** presents over 200 events in a variety of venues and is involved mainly with experimental work by local and international artists. The Women's Week has featured performances such as *The*

Left and right, Moomba is Melbourne's great annual party.

Serpent's Fall and *Lilian May*.

Piccolo Spoleto is only very loosely connected with mainstream Spoleto; its aim is to celebrate the particularly Melbourne culture that has arisen from the city's rich cross-cultural mix. It also aims to be geographically and finacially accessible to the average person, something which mainstream Spoleto is not. Piccolo is about Melbourne as a city of things to do—anything from lectures, demonstrations of Indian dancing, mask making or "ghetto gastronomy" and a forum on Trade Unions. It has a distinctly Australian identity and vitality in that it gathers together the threads of cultural diversity in Melbourne.

To commit auto-chiropractic on your funny-bone, book yourself into Melbourne in March for the **Comedy Festival** which presents humour from around the world. It's an exhilarating and exhausting time, but worth a week of aching cheeks. Note that it is not a local comedy festival (although some Australian comedians do participate) but a mainstream international festival. The venues are all over the city, including large theatres and intimate restaurants. For anyone in town at the time, it's not to be missed.

For the younger audience there is, biennially, the **Next Wave Youth Festival**. This one began in order to forge a connection between youth and the arts, and is aimed at a youngish audience, as well as supporting the work of young performers. In its two weeks it presents, astonishingly, over 500 performances and exhibitions. There are lavish productions and small workshop performances and professionals in every field give their time and experience.

There are a host of other smaller festivals in Melbourne, most notably the predominately Italian **Lygon Street Festa** in Carlton for four days during October; the Greek-Australian **Antipodean Festival** in March; the **Spanish Festival** and **Vietnamese Moon Festival** both held in Fitzroy; and again in March, **A Taste of Australia**, a culi-

Spanish frills: ethnic pride on display.

nary festival which spans the entire month, celebrating the delights of Australian food and beverage. In the wintery June there is the **Melbourne Film Festival**. In this "Garden State," there is always a plethora of flower and garden shows—telephone the Royal Horticultural Society for a detailed program.

Melbourne's festivals seem to echo its diversity. As well as being a city of cultural variety and depth, it considers itself one of the world's great sporting cities and has at least three important annual sporting festivals to back up that claim. The **Bells Beach Easter Surfing Classic**, held near the small town of Torquay (about an hour's drive southwest of the city, via Geelong) is one of the world's richest pro surfing contests. International surfers gather for the big autumn swells at Bells and Winkipop—site of the world's first National Surfing Park—to rip and carve their way towards the world title, or perhaps just to personal perfection.

Surfing might be spectacular, but there is nothing quite like the **Australian Rules Football Grand Final**. Sometimes a savage game, and always an intense spectator sport, it stirs the passions of most Victorians. The Grand Final—in September—the last game of this winter sport, is the climax of months of contests. For the weeks preceding this match Melbourne is infected with football fever—stimulating to those who enjoy the game, but infuriating to those who loathe it. Preceding the Grand Final is a noisy and festive week, but only those initiates to the game will really get much out of it.

More accessible is the **Spring Racing Carnival** which culminates in a public holiday for a horse race. But after all, it is *that* horse race for *that* mug—the Melbourne Cup, the holy grail of Australian national consciousness. "Cup Week" is not simply the Melbourne Cup, it is also a dizzy, lively week of fashion and social events that envelop Melbourne in an uncharacteristic levity.

A burst of festival colour.

LICENCED
SPAGHETTATA
Mocopan COFFEE
BISLERI
ACQUA MINERALE
PICCOLO MONDO
Bistro
B.Y.O.

ICCOLO MONDO
Bistro
BISLERI
ACQUA MINERALE
la SPAGHETTATA
RESTAURANT
OPEN FOR LUNCH: 12 NOON - 3 P.M.
FOR DINNER: 5 P.M. - 11 P.M.
Pasta & Seafood: Our Specialties!
BOOKING Ph: 663 6102

THE O
19

FICE Hotel
END
C
CLEARWAY

STAYING

If there was ever any doubt that **Collins Street** is the most desirable address in Melbourne, a glance at the list of top hotels will resolve the matter forever. The Menzies at Rialto at 495 Collins St., The Regent at number 25 and, of course, the Hyatt on Collins at number 123, all sought and found frontages onto Collins Street. In some cases it may be a long walk in from Collins Street and, perversely, other streets seem to be a lot closer to the reception desk, but if there is an entrance from Collins Street, that's the address to have.

It seems that every city has one hotel which is firmly in vogue at any given time. In Melbourne, the **Hyatt on Collins** has pride of place at present. It is the flagship of the Hyatt chain in Australia, a vision in brass, crystal and timber which is almost daunting in its lavishness. A rooftop tennis court, 580 rooms (including 19 suites), four "Regency Club" floors and full Kosher kitchen facilities are just some of the hotel's features. One may question the necessity of the Hyatt's sensory deprivation tank but the spa, swimming pools and steam baths are welcome. Besides the restaurants, bars, ballroom and nightclub within the hotel, the attached Collins Chase Food Court has many more eating and drinking options.

Down the road, the **Regent of Melbourne** is one of a pair of twin towers—a bank occupies the other one. Whenever anyone asks where to go for a good view of the city and the Yarra, the answer is invariably "the bar on the 35th floor of the Regent." Rightly so. The Regent's reputation for service is excellent and the hotel has a high ratio of suites: 52 suites to 311 rooms. Like the Hyatt, the Regent is located at the obsequiously-termed "Paris end of Collins Street" and it too has an attached shopping arcade.

At the western end of Collins Street, the **Menzies at Rialto** is a wonderful combination of old style elegance and modern facilities. The exterior design of the hotel incorporates the elaborate "Gothic Revival" facade of the original Rialto building and the adjoining Rialto Tower is by far the tallest building in Melbourne. The Menzies is definitely located closer to the action-packed end of the city's business district.

Rockman's Regency doesn't fit into the big hotel scene. The convention market and tourists aren't the clients it aims for. Rather, it offers a level of service that ensures it is the favoured haunt of entertainers and business visitors in the know. With only 165 rooms and 20 suites, Rockmans Regency is relatively small, in keeping with its boutique hotel approach. Like the Regent, Rockman's Regency is a member of the prestigious Leading Hotels of the World group.

In Spring Street, opposite Parliament House, is the only five-star property really in tune with the spirit of Mel-

Preceding pages: Lygon Street in Carlton is an Italianate pasta festa; sleeping at The Office is a legitimate excuse in this case. Left, Regent Hotel doorman. Right, Hotel Windsor.

bourne. While the other hotels vie amongst themselves for the grandest in a modern style, **The Windsor**, like so many of Melbourne's historic buildings embodies the grandeur of the Victorian age. It is both classified by the National Trust and a member of Select Hotels and Resorts International. The establishment first opened its doors as "The Grand" in 1883 but changed its name after a visit by the Duke of Windsor in the 1920s. However, by 1980 when the India-based Oberoi group took over the property, much work was needed to restore it to its former glory. Fortunately, the millions required were spent wisely to include all the features essential for a five-star property—including many which aren't immediately apparent, such as a modern fire protection system. Best of all, the renovation included painstaking restoration procedures—even scraping back the walls and consulting the original architects' diaries in order to match the original paint scheme. The Grand Dining Room is spectacular: a symphony in leather, crystal, silver and gold leaf. Following this approach, the furniture in the rooms is a mixture of antique and modern. Outside, throughout the evening comes the clip clop of horse drawn carriages taking tourists past Parliament House opposite. This sound and the feel of the hotel transports the imagination back into last century's era of elegance.

The Hilton International, a well established five-star property, is slightly away from the CBD on Wellington Parade, East Melbourne. This location is countered by a courtesy bus to downtown and the restful ambience of the large park only a few metres away from the front door. On Exhibition Street, the **Southern Cross** is the largest hotel convention venue in Australia. It can handle up to 1,600 delegates and has a total of 419 rooms and suites. Facilities include two restaurants, four bars, tennis court, spa, sauna and heated pool. To the south of the city, the **Parkroyal** on St. Kilda Road is deep in the heart of Melbourne's advertising belt which extends along much of the length of St. Kilda Road.

On the other side of Exhibition Street, the **Noahs Bryson Hotel** (formerly Noahs Melbourne Hotel) has been undergoing a massive $16 million refurbishment program. At the end of the redevelopment, the name will change to the Hotel Bryson.

Another hotel which has been extensively refurbished and upgraded is the **Old Melbourne Hotel** in North Melbourne, on the way in from the airport. In the *Royal Automobile Club of Victoria's (RACV) Guide to Accommodation* (available free to members and members of affiliated clubs) both share four stars, along with six other properties. Both have risen through the ranks from previous faded glory to fill an important niche in the accommodation needs of the city.

Other three-and four-star properties include the **Chateau Melbourne** on Lonsdale Street, the **Rathdowne Inter-**

Left, the foyer cafe of the Hyatt on Collins.

national in Carlton and the **President Melbourne** in Queens Road.

It is only since 1987 that Melbourne has developed the concept of executive apartments. These invariably have much less imposing common areas (such as restaurants and foyers) than equivalent hotels, preferring rather to put the money into the rooms themselves and in keeping tariffs down. **Gordon Place** in Little Bourke Street (which boasts National Trust classification) is one such establishment. At a more modest level is the **Albert Heights** in East Melbourne. However, more executive apartments continue to be built, particularly in the recently gentrified areas of Port Melbourne. As the name implies, the suburbs that make up Port Melbourne are right on Port Phillip Bay and combine the advantages of bayside living and relative proximity to the city. The very stylish **Station Pier Condominiums** well match their pleasant locale. Also, in the very fashionable area of South Yarra there are establishments such as the **South Yarra Hill Suites**, which are luxurious, fully appointed, multi-roomed suites for short stay visitors.

Beyond the CBD, Melbourne has a wide range of accommodation, mainly suburban motels. These have comfortable rooms, provide good parking and always have tea making facilities and a fridge in the rooms. The decor and building design may not be wonderful but they are considerably cheaper than equivalent accommodation in the heart of the city. As a general rule, a four-star suburban property will charge about the same as a three-star in the city. However, it should be borne in mind that the rankings are controlled by the motoring organisations which issue the accommodation guides and do not necessarily correspond with apparently similar rankings overseas.

Melbourne's main airport, Tullamarine, is 22 kilometres (14 miles) north-west of the city. For short stopovers, or where it isn't necessary to head into town, the **Tullamarine Airport Motor Inn** is a four-star property only a few minutes walk from the airport.

There is no central core of backpacker hostels in Melbourne as there are in many cities. However, several hostels in the East Melbourne area attract a lot of young overseas visitors travelling on a budget. There are two **Youth Hostels** in Melbourne, operated by the Youth Hostels of Australia (YHA). Both are in North Melbourne—one on Abbottsford Street and the other on Chapman Street.

New hotels include the four-star **River Bank Hotel**, an integral part of the massive **World Congress Centre**. It will be the flagship of the Interwest group of hotels. Oakford are to open an $88 million all-suite hotel on the corner of Alfred Place and Little Collins Street. This will have 290 suites and will be one of Australia's first all-suite hotels. Four other properties are under construction in the city and are aimed at the three-to four-star market.

Right, Old Shell, new hotel: the Menzies at Rialto.

DINING

Melbourne has always cherished its reputation as a city which takes its eating *very* seriously. The story is still repeated about the former chef at Collingwood's Clichy, Iain Hewitson (now owner of the Last Aussie Fishcaf) absolutely refusing a customer's request for cream on a chocolate dessert. The dessert, he decreed, was to be served just as he, the chef, had created it. And that was that.

Melbourne remains the gastronomic capital of Australia. Here you can eat and drink like a king for a hundred dollars; or feed two people amply in simpler surroundings—and still have change from a $20 bill. In Melbourne, the question to ask before opting for one of the city's 3,000 or so eateries is not "Where is the food good?" (it's good almost everywhere), but "What nationality of food?" and then "For what price?"

Starting at the top of the scale, the restaurant which demands first mention is **Stephanie's**, in Tooronga Road, East Hawthorn. It was singled out by the editors of *The Age Good Food Guide*, as the finest restaurant in Melbourne, for the food, wine, and service in its three handsomely furnished dining rooms. Restaurateur Stephanie Alexander cooks in a style which cannot merely be described as French, because of the many other influences on her cuisine, from Italian, to Chinese, to her own late mother's inspired inventiveness. Stephanie's seasonal menus are a special attraction, although the fact that the owner-chef does not repeat these dishes has led to many an anguished cry from gourmets.

After Stephanie's the next rung on Melbourne's elite gastronomic ladder is occupied by an expensive Gallic gang of four. There is **Mietta's**, upstairs in Alfred Place, for fine French food in a luxurious Victorian dining room with starched linen table cloths, fresh flowers and elegant china and crystalware. **Fanny's**, in Lonsdale Street, famous for its crisped whiting and memorable desserts; and its younger sister, **Glo Glo's**, in Carters Avenue, Toorak—a romantic setting that particularly lends itself to special occasion dinners; and **Rogalsky's**, in Clarendon Street, South Melbourne, an elegant New York-style restaurant.

Other popular licensed French restaurants include **Clichy**, in Peel Street, Collingwood, which has both a cheaper wine bar/bistro and a fixed price restaurant, with a menu that emphasizes French regional cooking; and bright and breezy **France-Soir**, in Toorak Road, Toorak, a noisy brasserie-style restaurant, great for French classics like oysters, boned duckling, pepper steak, steak tartare and pommes frites made in heaven. Meanwhile Jacques Reymond, the chef who helped build Mietta's reputation, has now opened his own restaurant, called—naturally enough—

Left, the balmy, palmy court of Gordon Place. Right, Melbourne boasts a fine daily catch of Bass Strait's freshest.

Jacques Reymond, in Lennox Street, Richmond.

Around 2,500 of Melbourne's restaurants are BYO ("Bring Your Own Liquor") and some of the city's most outstanding French-style ones are among them—like **Tansy's** in Nicholson Street, Carlton, **Maria and Walter's** (Rathdowne Street, Carlton) and **Petit Choux** in High Street, Armadale. Melbourne's stomach is, however, truly international. And there's no more tangible proof of the success of multiculturalism than the proliferation of eateries from a multitude of Asian and European nations. An explosion of grandiose, hi-tech, neo-Italian eateries like **Rosati** (Flinders Lane), which can pack in 500 diners, and its Toorak Road, South Yarra sibling, **Pieroni**, has clearly met a need for seeing and being seen (while munching away on inventive Italian-style food) that had been lying dormant in the Melbourne diner's soul.

Yum Cha, the very sensible Chinese habit of taking your family to a teahouse or restaurant to feast on a tasty procession of small delicacies (known as *dim sum* and served from trollies wheeled past tables of salivating patrons with eyes twice as large as their stomachs) has replaced the Sunday roast ritual for thousands of Melburnians. Many city restaurants now serve *dim sum* during the week as well, from 11 a.m. Chinatown in Little Bourke Street is the obvious place for this, although many suburban Chinese restaurants now also do *Yum Cha*.

The **Flower Drum** (at Market Lane, in the city) is currently regarded as Melbourne's finest licensed Cantonese-style eatery. Its culinary reputation is underlined by regular bookings from visiting Asian delegations. Seafood specialties, like squid stuffed with prawns, abound; they also do an excellent Peking Duck. Chinese chefs from other Chinatown restaurants regularly dine at the late-opening BYO **Supper Inn** (Celestial Avenue), often choosing intriguing dishes like the claypot of

Gordon Place features serviced executive apartments and a quality restaurant.

abalone, sea cucumber and duck's feet. The less adventurous clientele may steer clear of this kind of excitement yet still dine like emperors on tasty crab dishes, the best *won ton* soup in town and excellent garlic spinach (or "garlic Spanish" as one of the waiters always seems to be saying). **Xanghai** (also BYO) in the less prepossessing location of St. Kilda Road, St. Kilda (near the noisy junction) is worth a pilgrimage for its Shanghai provincial specialties—like Shanghai noodles.

Chinatown and the city are home to a few Vietnamese restaurants (like **Golden Bull** in Little Bourke Street and **My Huong** in La Trobe Street), but the best place to get the flavour of the large Vietnamese community who have made Melbourne their home is in Bridge Road, Richmond. Its grocery stores are full of the aromatic lemon grass, coriander and fishy *nuoc man* sauce which are key ingredients in Vietnamese cooking. Among its simply furnished, family-run restaurants (many of which are owned by former "boat people"), **Que Hong**, at 176, is a favourite of those who know their *cha gio*, as is **Hue**, down the road at 282 Victoria St., Richmond, is home to the popular **Van Mai** (372) and **Vao Doi** (120).

Japanese food has taken Melbourne by storm over the past few years. Once concentrated in the city, Japanese restaurants (most of them BYO) have now spread to the suburbs, even penetrating the pizza/pasta push of Carlton (e.g. **Toki**, in Grattan Street) and the continental citadel of Acland Street, St. Kilda (**Osaka**, in Belford Street). **Akari** in Brunswick Street, Fitzroy, offers stylish snacking at its aluminium sushi bar, while **Edoya** in Russell Street reproduces the Tokyo habit of displaying plastic moulded models of the house specialties in the window. **Akita**, at the corner of Courtney and Blackwood streets, North Melbourne and tiny **Kuni's** in Crossley Lane, city, remain favourites after many years.

Pellegini's on upper Collins Street is a legendary part of Melbourne's caffeine culture.

Those who like sushi with rock music on the side can try the sushi bar at the restaurant/nightclub **Zanies**, on the corner of Russell and Lonsdale streets.

For the ultimate Japanese meal, the place is **Kenzan**, at the plush Regent Hotel. Famed for the quality of its sashimi, Kenzan is also noted for introducing the art of the *Kaiseki* to Australia. In this ritual, based on the traditions of the Japanese teahouse ceremony, the diner receives one exquisitely arranged taste treat after another, each selected and prepared according to the seasons, and served on stoneware chosen to harmonise with each dish.

Melbourne's thinner-walletted Japanese foodies have also discovered the delights of take-away sushi and sashimi, to be eaten at home, or at picnics in a nearby park or down by the sea. Some visit the place many Japanese restaurateurs patronise: **Oceania**, in Chapel Street, South Yarra, where fish can be bought already cut for sushi or sashimi. Others favour **Michael Canal's Seafoods** (Glenhuntly Road, Elsternwick or Nicholson Street, North Carlton) where you can order platters, or **Bottom Of The Harbour** (Malvern Road, Toorak) where take-away sushi is available Thursdays, Fridays and Saturdays. Sushi day at **Fishmongers** (Edsall Street, Malvern) is Friday.

Other sushi lovers go to the **Myer Food Hall**, the gastronomic temple for a city that worships food. This recently-upgraded monument to the glories of gluttony sells 2,000 sandwiches a day, made on any of six kinds of bread, five sorts of rolls and three varieties of pocket breads.

When the debate about what and where to eat grows tiresome, when one partner wants to eat African at **African Tukul**, in Chapel Street, South Yarra, and the other wants Argentinian at **Enri's** in Bridge Road, Richmond, and the kids are squabbling over the merits of Egyptian at **Al Pharaoh's** in Glenhuntly Road, Caulfield or Arme-

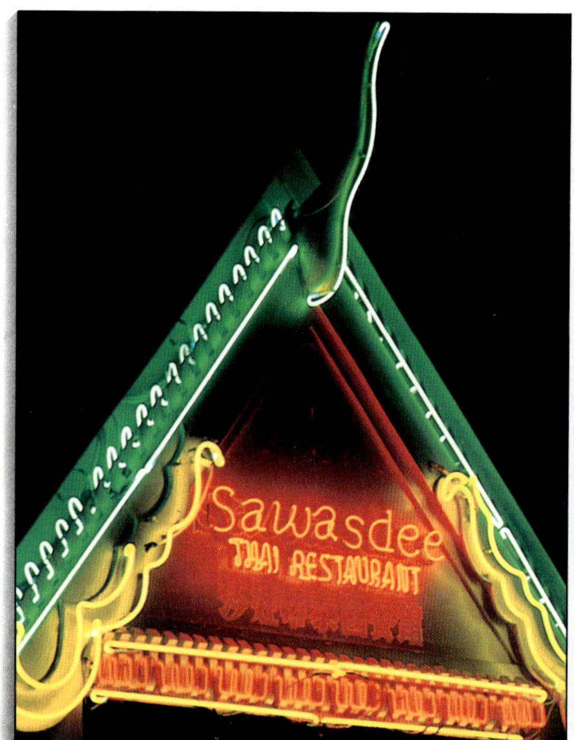

nian and Ethiopian at **Armenia** in Ross Street, Toorak, an easy solution is to head for one of the two great eating strips of Lygon Street, Carlton and Brunswick Street, Fitzroy. Here you can read the menus in the windows, smell the cooking aromas, and let your noses fight it out.

Lygon Street, home of 1,001 Italian treats, has its share of overpriced tourist traps, but there are also plenty of cheapie treasures like **Casa di Iorio** (139) which looks like any other pizza joint, but serves a fine selection of daily special pasta dishes and provides cheap and highly drinkable wine. You don't have to eat Italian just because you're in Carlton. **Nyonya**, at 191, serves the Malay dishes cooked by Straits Chinese: coconut milk and tamarind-based curries, and the spicy noodle dishes that are the staple fare of Penang street hawkers' stalls. Or there's **Chenny's** (320), a welcome break from the red lanterns and Oriental calendars school of Chinese restaurant decor. The freshness of approach reflected in the cappuccino machine, *dim sum* bar and elegant white crockery is also in evidence in the restaurant's crisply appetising cuisine. Meanwhile, down the road, **Shakahari's** vegetarian restaurant (329) is still packing in the herbivores with food that shows a piquant Asian influence that has banished all thoughts of the boring old brown rice days of the early 1970s.

The city offers dining options which range from formal Japanese (far left) to fiery Thai (left) to traditional Chinese (below).

Over in **Brunswick Street**, the menus span the globe, from Afghanistan at the **Afghan Gallery** (327) to Malaysia at **Sri Malacca** (262), to Thailand at **Thai Thani** (293), India at **Shahnai** (359) and Portugal at **Cafe Lisboa** (413). The latter occupies an old furniture factory owned by the Portuguese Community Trust and is hung with maps, photographs and paintings of Portugal—the perfect setting for traditional favourites like grilled sardines.

Good fish restaurants are also on the increase in Melbourne, with **Max's** at the Hyatt (123 Collins) enjoying the title of the city's finest and most glamorous seafood establishment. Across town at Iain Hewitson's **Last Aussie Fishcaf**, in Park Street, South Melbourne, the emphasis on style evident in the cafe's sea blue walls and dark green tables carries through to the inventive food, which ranges from fish and chips done the way they should be (but almost never are) to Creole blackened fish fillets and tempura prawns. Famous for the 1950s jiving at night—and for the fact that you have to book weeks ahead to get in for dinner—the Fishcaf usually manages to have some space left at lunchtime.

For seafood with a view, **Jean Jacques By The Sea**, in the renovated St. Kilda Road bathing pavilion offers oysters and charcoal grilled fish in its indoor licensed restaurant, or fish and chips to take away and eat at its outdoor tables. A few hundred metres south, **La Marina**, by the boat harbour at St. Kilda Marina, serves excellent seafood straight out of Bass Strait.

DRINKING

The most "Melbourne" place to drink at present must be the downstairs lounge of **Mietta's** restaurant in Alfred Place. Here you can choose a cocktail from a formidable selection, or a bottle from one of the most interesting (but not cheapest) wine lists in the city—and drink until 3 a.m. in a room whose lovingly restored Victoriana evokes the spirit of 1880s Melbourne.

For a tipple in an atmosphere redolent of more raunchy Melbourne history, try **Young and Jacksons**, opposite Flinders Street Station, an 1861-vintage watering hole famed for its portrait of Chloe, a haughty nude who has won an enduring place in the soul of Melbourne men. Chloe has since been spirited upstairs to the more elevated atmosphere of the bistro, where her much admired charms, classified, like the pub, by the National Trust, are now displayed behind glass.

All the older Melbourne suburbs have their corner pubs, but the ones with the most character tend to go up-market and put in a bistro as soon as the old clientele turn their backs. The old white **Esplanade Hotel** (where Sarah Bernhardt once stayed) remains the best place to watch the magnificent St. Kilda sunset. These days, a roughish rock 'n' roll pub, The Esplanade is currently under threat of redevelopment. Nearby, the **Village Belle Hotel** in Acland Street has an old section, where the pre-trendy customers still drink.

At the other end of the social scale, the watering holes for designer dressers are the legal eagles' haunt, the **Red Eagle** in Albert Park and the advertising crowd's local, the **Botanical Hotel** in Domain Road, South Yarra. The long red bar at the black and white tiled **Caffe Maximus** in Acland Street, St. Kilda is also a favourite cocktail spot. A must for night owls is **Le Monde**, at the top of Bourke Street, once a 24-hour coffee

Exercising arms at the Sportsman's Bar in Fitzroy.

lounge, now a round-the-clock New York Italian-style bar. Patrons sit on black bar stools at a corrugated iron bar, described by its designer as "a homage to Australian building surfaces."

Melbourne's five-star hotels offer a choice of opulent drinking settings. The Hyatt on Collins (123 Collins) has its elegant 1930s-style **Deco Bar**, or for noisier ambience there's **The Chase Bar** in the hotel's Collins Chase Food Court. A cocktail with a view of Melbourne that stretches right to the bay is the obvious choice at the 35th floor bar in the Regent Hotel at the top of Collins Street. Or the alternative, at the other end of Collins, is a view of the passing parade from the plushly intimate atmosphere of the **Edinburgh Bar** in the Menzies at Rialto. Or, for some traditional Grand Hotel style imbibing, there's the lounge at the historic Windsor Hotel in Spring Street.

For Melbourne beer drinkers, the latest trend is the pub brewery, where you can choose from a range of beers made on the premises, and watch its replacement being made while you're drinking. At the **Station Tavern and Brewery** in Greville Street, Prahran (the one with a train engine bursting out of the brewing house) patrons can view the beer being made through signal box windows; while at the new **Tiger's Head Brewery**, in Flemington Road, North Melbourne, drinkers in both upstairs and downstairs bars can watch the labyrinth of copper brewing vats and shiny pipes through the glass walls that separate the pub and the brewery.

And when the sun is shining, where better to be than a beer garden? Try the **Fawkner Club** (in Toorak Road, South Yarra)—enormous but so popular that it can still be difficult to get a table on a fine day; the **Lemon Tree Hotel** in Grattan Street Carlton; the ferny surrounds of the **New Argo Inn** in Argo Street, South Yarra; or **The Cricketer's Arms Hotel** in Cruickshank Street, Port Melbourne—which also serves great food.

Below and right, liquid choices adorn these well-known pubs.

ROCKING

Melbourne is synonymous with Australian rock 'n' roll. In other cities, one can never be sure of the commitment: over the years they have flirted with exotic sub-strains, but grittier Melbourne has held fast to the basic beat. Less flash, more thunder. Australia's earliest rock 'n' roll groundswell occurred in Melbourne and seeped out through the extensive Town Hall and Ballroom Circuit. While Sydneysiders were stomping by the beach in board shorts, the Yarra-ites were leather-clad and impeccably greased, checking out such heroes as The Thunderbirds and The Chessmen. It is not uncommon to find scores of perfectly preserved rockers cruising the streets in their equally authentic Ford Customlines.

In the '60s, the city housed dozens of stylish discotheques which would offer up to eight "scream sensation" bands in a single night to exceptionally aware and demanding audiences. Young ensembles from all over the country made a bee-line for Melbourne in search of fame. Many found it. By the early '70s, a fascinating experimental, acid-culture rock underground had taken root around the bohemian inner suburb of Carlton. The uncompromising, cult-politico bands nurtured by this extreme creative environment, such as Spectrum and Skyhooks, provided Australia with some of its finest musical moments of the era.

Melbourne's standing as the rock capital of Australia has not been allowed to lapse. Every night, scores of young hopefuls join established bands in eking out a living in the vast network of small pubs and clubs throughout the city. As with most cities in Australia, live music revolves around places where people congregate to drink and socialise. This basic factor has shaped the nature of Melbourne rock. Small-time bands who went on to find international success—Split Enz, Men At Work, Crowded House, Big Pig, Hunters & Collectors, Australian Crawl/James Reyne—were forced to create a music that could instantly grab the attention of drinkers and ragers. This meant either being very brash and exhibiting fine showmanship, or playing songs that were brief and powerfully melodic. When these bands hit the world market they were quickly lapped up, either for their dynamic live shows or their AM radio orientated records. To wit: Men At Work, who crawled out of the Cricketers Arms Hotel in the inner suburb of Richmond and right to the top of the American and British single and album charts.

The desires of any Melbourne visitor with a taste for rock music are remarkably well catered for. Bands range from smooth jazzy combos playing to up-market yuppie audiences, to alternative, grubby, psychedelic, punk or gothic efforts barely out of the rehearsal room. The core of the live rock scene is the city-area pubs and clubs (often with a capacity of only 300 or so) which give over a corner of the bar or lounge to enthusiastic young promoters who promise to keep the bar cash registers ringing. This is where the staunch fans are found; cheering on young outfits with such exotic names as Swinging Sidewalks, Vacation In Harlem and Spot the Aussie, or taking in a showcase set by "Off-Broadway" recording bands the likes of Black Sorrows, Sacred Cowboys or Triffids.

Admission to these venues runs at about $6 -$12, depending on the calibre of the act. There's rarely a dress code, the atmosphere is dank but spirited, the audiences enthusiastic and knowledgeable. Most of them are within 10-15 minutes drive from the city central and include the **Esplanade Hotel** (St. Kilda), **Corner Hotel** (Richmond), **Music Station** (Richmond), **Loaded Dog** (Fitzroy), **Evelyn Hotel** (Fitzroy), **Cricketer's Arms** (Richmond), **Duke of Edinburgh** (St. Kilda), **Smith Street**

Left, guitar guru Carlos Santana doing his thing at a Melbourne concert.

(Collingwood) and **The Club** (Collingwood). They tend to disappear and reappear like field mushrooms, according to the financial state of the "scene" at a given time.

Therefore, it's always best to check out the scene first from the latest sources, to avoid disturbing a group of wharfies at their favourite watering hole. This is best done through rock papers like *Juke*, which has a national Gig Guide section, or Melbourne entertainment papers such as *Beat* and *Im-Press* which are distributed to nightclubs, hair salons, colleges, etc., and have comprehensive run-downs on the week's theatre, fashion and rock shows. Daily newspapers, *The Age* and *The Herald* also have quite comprehensive listings.

Moving out into the suburbs, you find the larger pubs where the bands with hit singles come to play. These sprawling edifices can hold 2,000 and regularly serve up names like Chantoozies, Boom Crash Opera, Party Boys, Angels, Eurogliders, Hoodoo Gurus and Noiseworks. Some of the more prominent venues are: **The Village Green** (Glen Waverly), **Sentimental Bloke** (Bulleen), **Mentone Hotel** and **The Palace** (St. Kilda) and **Edwards Tavern** (Prahran). Entrance will generally set you back about $10 and there is a "neat casual" dress code. Usually a lengthy taxi ride from the city, they tend to be strictly policed, particularly on Saturday nights.

Melbourne takes rock music more seriously than any other Australian city. It is a catalyst for new trends and directions and the breeding ground for imaginative, barrier-stretching bands. Even the obvious affectations of transient style have an earnestness that can't be ignored.

This musical magic extends to other music genres. Lovers of classical music, for example, will appreciate the world-class Melbourne Symphony Orchestra. Elton John, after his highly successful Australian tour with the

The Troubadour is home to Melbourne Folk.

MSO in 1986 (he wore black tails and a green Mohawk wig over a pink pony-tail; they wore glasses) swore he'd finished with ordinary rock 'n' roll backing groups for ever. Even so, the MSO, like so many of Melbourne's attractions, remains a well-kept secret. "I am very proud of this orchestra," says its conductor since 1974, Hiroyuki Iwaki, recently honoured by the Suntory Foundation for his contribution to contemporary music.

Since the opening in 1982 of the **Victorian Arts Centre Concert Hall**, the orchestra has had the opportunity to play in a venue worthy of its talents. The Concert Hall itself is Melbourne's pride and joy. Barry Humphries, Kiri Te Kanawa, the London Philharmonic, the Berlin State Orchestra, Yehudi Menuhin, Elvis Costello and Joe Jackson have all graced its stage. The Concert Hall is also the key venue for the annual summer Melbourne Music Festival, a program which regularly attracts great musical talents of both the classical and pop world, from violinist Pinchas Zukerman to guitar virtuoso Leo Kottke. Other Melbourne venues for major concerts by local and overseas artists include the **Dallas Brooks Hall**, and the **Sports and Entertainment Centre.**

Outdoor concerts always attract a crowd.

The city is full of live jazz and folk music pubs. The Bridge Hotel, Bridge Road, Richmond; the Emerald Hotel, Clarendon Street, South Melbourne; and Bell's, corner Moray and Coventry, South Melbourne—to name just a few—all offer jazz at various times of the week. Check the *Thursday Herald's* "After Hours" magazine or *The Age's* "Entertainment Guide" for detailed information. **The Troubadour** in Brunswick Street, Fitzroy and **The Green Man** in High Street, Malvern are both legendary Melbourne folk music venues.

The **Sidney Myer Music Bowl**, site of many memorable open air rock concerts over the last two decades, is now a key summer venue for an organisation that has managed to become one of the world's biggest free entertainment programs, while, simultaneously, keeping a low profile. FEIPP, or Fantastic Entertainment In Public Places, is a later incarnation of the old Free Entertainment In The Parks, which started with a production of the opera *Cosi Fan Tutte* in the Fitzroy Gardens in 1973, and grew into a huge program which has brought free opera, jazz, pop and puppets to millions of Melburnians over the years. Funded by private sponsors, the Melbourne City Council and the Ministry Of Arts, FEIPP uses indoor venues like the Melbourne Town Hall in winter. In summer the organisers' imagination is the only limit, with settings for musical entertainment including The Royal Botanic Gardens, the Victoria Market and Little Bourke Street, where the finals of the FEIPP Busking Championships have been held.

Contact the **Melbourne Visitors Bureau** for a copy of the latest FEIPP program.

NIGHTCLUBBING

All kinds of pernicious libel is spread about Melbourne's nightclub scene, like the T-shirt in Sydney souvenir shops, which features a big black square... and the caption: "Melbourne's night life." Uncharitable jibes like this may have had some foundation 10 years ago, before the arrival of **Inflation** or **The Underground** (both still going strong in King Street). Since then, literally scores of clubs have sprung up all over Melbourne, so that there are now some 30 dance spots in the central city and inner suburban area alone. Guides like the Thursday *Herald's* "After Hours" magazine or *The Age's* "Entertainment Guide" provide full listings of the different clubs' "theme" nights, their opening hours, and their entry charges. Many clubs are closed Monday nights, although **Billboard** (Russell Street), **The Grainstore**, Inflation, **The Hippodrome** and Underground (all on the "disco drive" of King Street in the city) are there for clubbers who don't believe in resting on the eighth day.

The city's hottest new club is **Checkpoint Charlie** (South Yarra), a grey-toned dance temple of cement and steel girders. This designer bomb shelter (which reportedly cost $5 million to build) only holds 800, which means it has a door policy that is selective. The club, open Wednesday-Saturday, also serves dinner and supper, and waives its cover charge for diners.

The Metro, a hi-tech disco in Bourke Street, is the place where football glamour boys like Warwick Capper tend to be seen. It is said to be Australia's biggest nightclub, and alternates between its "Shooters Club" (students and young professionals) on Thursday nights, jazz on Fridays, mainstream dance music Saturdays and soulful dance music Sundays. The Grainstore in King Street and **Zuzu's** in Exhibition Street also offer a line up of theme "clubs" which changes nightly, such as Zuzu's "Seventh Heaven" gay night on Sundays.

Left, stepping out at the Metro.

Across the Yarra, cosy and stylish **IDs** in Greville Street, Prahran, presents hip local groups like The Bachelors From Prague and Miss Dorothy And His Fools In Love, while **The Linden Tree** in Fitzroy Street also draws a more off-beat crowd. Dancers who are allergic to disco music can bop every night of the week in Melbourne, totally safe from Donna Summer records. Funk, reggae and African music nights are a regular fixture at several clubs, like Thursday night's "The Boat" at the **Bridge Road Nightclub**, while "Rubber Soul" (Friday night at the **Carron Tavern**, Spencer Street, North Melbourne) and Thursday night's "Limbo Club" (**Central Club**, Swan Street, Richmond) play '60s music. Musical monomaniacs should check the listings for clubs like "The Beehive" (Saturday night at the Carron Tavern) which devotes whole nights to the sounds of a particular group, such as INXS.

There is another dance club scene which plays mostly imported dance discs from Britain, Europe, Japan and the States. This is where the ultra-fashionable hip things gather. Often these clubs—such as **Club for Heroes** (City), **Thrash Dance Club** (Richmond) and **Chasers** (South Yarra)—maintain their hipness and one-upmanship by staging fashion shows to highlight the latest designs from abroad.

More conservative clubbers congregate at **Lazar International** (King Street, city), a dress-up place for over 25's; at **Warehouse** (Claremont Street, South Yarra); at **Juliana's** at the Hilton, (Wellington Parade, East Melbourne), or at ritzy **Monsoons** at the Hyatt (123 Collins St.).

Finally, for those who love to dance, the **Club Dancing Bar** (Smith Street, Collingwood) has a Latin night on Wednesdays, with cha cha, samba, rhumba, tango and jive.

Marong
Bendigo
Axedale
Waanyarra
Lockwood South
Stuart Mill
Goldsborough
Laanecoorie
Lockwood
Mosquito Creek
Heathc
Dunolly
Leddington
Navarre
Lake Eppalock
Natte Yallock
Red Bank
Harcourth North
Maldon
Moonambel
Landsborough
Maryborough
Carisbook
Castlemaine
Redesdale
Craigie
Newstead
Avoca
Rodborough
Elphinstone
Guildford
Elmhurst
Talbot
Malmsbury
Dunneworthy
Campbelltown
Kyneton
Lexton
Clunes
Ararat
Daylesford
Woodend
North Learmonth
Newlyn
Trentham
Mt. Macedon
Eurambeen
Beaufort
Creswick
Burrumbeet
Rossbridge
Lake Burrumbeet
Pootilla
Gisborne
Lake Goldsmith
Ballarat
Carngham
Ballan
Myrniong
Sunb
Snake Valley
Egerton
Bacchus Marsh
WERRIBEE GORGE NATIONAL PARK
Me
Skipton
Streatham
Scarsdale
Scotsburn
Lake Bolac
Linton
BRISBANE RANGES NATIONAL PARK
Lake Bolac
Cape Clear
Durdidwarrah
Ripley
Pura Pura
Meredith
Werribe
Woorndoo
STEIGLITZ HISTORICAL PARK
Anakie
The You Yangs
Flinders Peak
Rokewood
Lismore
Lethbridge
Derrinallum
Darlington
Cressy
Shelford
Bannockburn
Lake Gnarpurt
Point Wilson
Lake Martin
Inverleigh
Portarlington
Mortlake
Corangamite
Lake Corangamite (salt)
Geelong
Drysd
Beeac
Mt. Moriac
Gnotuk
Camperdown
Queens
Terang
Lake Purdiguluc (salt)
Lake Colac
Winchelsea
Ocean Grove
Barwon Heads
Pt. Lonsda
Jans Junction
Por
Stoneyford
Colac
Birregurra
Torquay
Cobden
Dean Marsh
Anglesea
Aireys Inlet
Timboon
Simpson
Gellibrand
Lorne
Peterborough
Port Campbell
Carlisle River
Haines Junction
Wye River
PORT CAMPBELL NATIONAL PARK
Ferguson
Kennett River
Tasman
Princetown
Lavers Hill
Cape Horn
Skenes Creek
Lower Gellibrand
Glenaire
Apollo Bay
OTWAY NATIONAL PARK
Cape Otway

South Victoria
30km
Euroa
Nagambie
Graytown
Longwood
East
Lima South
Strathbogie
MOUNT
SAMAIA
STATE PARK
Toombullup
Avenel
Barjarg
Merton
Bonnie
Doon
Maindample
Mansfield
Seymour
Tallarook
Trawool
Lake
Eildon
Pyalong
Kerrisdale
Yarck
FRASER
NATIONAL
PARK
Goughs
Bay
Merrijig
Cathkin
Molesworth
Alexandra
Broadford
Yea
Eildon
Thornton
Howqua
Strath
Creek
Acheron
Upper
Thornton
ELIDON
STATE
PARK
Kilmore
Jamieson
Flowerdale
Taggerty
Wallan
CATHEDRAL
RANGE
STATE
PARK
Kinglake
West
KINGLAKE
Glenburn
Buxton
NATIONAL
Kinglake
Toolangi
Marysville
Whittlesea
St.
Fillan
PARK
Merrie
Junction
Hurstbridge
Craigieburn
Matlock
Licola
Yarra Glen
Healesville
Tullamarine
Bundoora
Yerinberg
Aberfeldy
Warrandyte
Yarra
Junction
Cheynes
Bridge
WARRANDYTE
STATE PARK
Lilydale
Warburton
Toorongo
Mount Baw Baw
1562
FERN TREE
GULLY
NATIONAL
PARK
Woori
Yallock
Beardmores
Camberwell
Powelltown
BAW BAW
NATIONAL
PARK
Hobsons
Bay
CHURCHILL
NATIONAL
PARK
Emerald
Cockatoo
Noojee
Gembrook
Walhalla
Cardinia
Res.
Mordialloc
Dandenong
Neerim
Sth.
Cowwarr
Beaconsfield
Pakenham
Robin
Hood
Rokeby
Willow
Grove
Frankston
Drouin
Glengarry
Cranbourne
Drouin
Sth.
Warragul
Traralgon
Tooradin
Yarragon
Moe
Koo Wee Rup
Trafalgar
Mornington
MOUNT WORTH
STATE PARK
Morwell
Western
Port
Lang Lang
Hastings
North Arm
Allambee
Dromana
Poowong
Mirboo
Nth.
Rosebud
Nyora
Loch
Hallston
Boolarra
MORWELL
NATIONAL
PARK
BULGA
NATIONAL
PARK
NEPEAN
STATE PARK
Balnarring
Grantville
Bena
Balook
Cowes
Korumburra
Limonite
English
Corner
Tarra
Valley
TARRA
VALLEY
NATIONAL
PARK
Flinders
Leongatha
Pulpit
Rock
Anderson
Kongwak
Madalya
Ryton
Cat Bay
San Remo
Yarram
Meeniyan
Alberton
Wonthaggi
Foster
Inverloch
Port
Albert
Sea
Welshpool
Cape
Paterson
Tarwin
Lower
Fish
Creek
Barry
Point
Entrance
Point
Yanakie
Walkerville
Sandy
Point
WILSONS PROMONTORY
NATIONAL PARK
Cape
Liptrap
Monkey
Point

SOUTH AROUND THE BAY

The Bellarine Peninsula: The two peninsula arms which seem to draw Port Phillip Bay upwards into the heart of Victoria have always drawn their share of visitors as well. Either arm makes an ideal day trip from Melbourne. The Bellarine Peninsula, beyond Geelong, is less well known than its eastern counterpart, the Mornington Peninsula, but just as attractive. Wild and exposed on the Bass Strait side, but gently undulating towards the calmer waters of the bay, the Bellarine offers a balance of quiet pleasure and vigorous excitement. The surging waves of Point Lonsdale and Ocean Grove and the quiet charm of Queenscliff, with its dark cypresses and Victorian hotels, provide both active and passive delight in an historically important location.

When John Batman landed at **Indented Head** in 1835, he could survey the entire Port Phillip Bay from this vantage point: the You Yang ridges to the west, Arthur's Seat and the Mornington Peninsula to the east and, to the north, the coastline where he was to found Melbourne. Today, from the same location, you can just make out the shapes of the towers of Batman's city and trace the course of your road journey from it around the western edge of the bay.

The first leg of such a trip from Melbourne is across the West Gate Bridge, then along a dead straight freeway across a basalt plain. It's not an auspicious beginning but the monotony can be broken at **Werribee** where **Chirnside Park** is a National Trust showpiece, an example of the opulent mansions of the graziers who thrived in Batman's wake, turning the volcanic plains into the rich profits of the wool trade and the basalt into bluestone masonry. The Italianate design and the elegant furnishing of the period are balanced by the bizarre decor of the trophy room where the firebox has been fashioned out of the preserved foot of an elephant. Perhaps it's not so strange that the estate is now used to provide a broadacre range for the larger herbivores of the Melbourne Zoo.

Geelong is a provincial city with many of its older bluestone buildings still intact. Once a direct rival of Melbourne, it's still known as "The Pivot" by some of its ardently loyal denizens. (Others call it "Sleepy Hollow.") During the gold rush, it offered newcomers easier access to the diggings and it remains the outlet for the enormous agricultural production of Victoria's west. But Melbourne really was more central, so it rose naturally to ascendancy. **Dights Falls**, where the lava flow from Mount Macedon reached the Yarra, is probably the place where Batman conned the Aboriginals whose land it was into letting him run his sheep on their pastures. At **Buckley's Falls** in Geelong, where the lava meet the Barwon River, an old water

Preceding pages: skiing, the Victorian Alps; old-fashioned bathing boxes, Port Phillip Bay; map of South Victoria. Left, characterless face but nice hat. Right, aged lighthouse, Williamstown.

mill, from the days of first settlement, still exists. It's not a tourist attraction and hasn't been restored. It's simply there, a bluestone marvel of towers, arches, mill races—everything apart from a working wheel. The mill and Buckleys Falls are best seen from **Queens Park** in Highton.

A diversion around Eastern Beach and central Geelong is well worth while on the southward journey. Upon reaching the peninsula itself, the use of bluestone for industrial purposes is evident in the Old Mill at **Port Arlington**. Dating from 1857, and unlike the mill at Geelong, this one was steam powered and has been restored by the National Trust and is open to the public. At **Fort Queenscliff**, the battery that was set up to guard the Heads is also built of the characteristic Port Phillip bluestone.

The **Bellarine Peninsula Tourist Railway** runs a steam service on weekends and holidays from Drysdale to Queenscliff, using locomotives and rolling stock collected from throughout Australia. The line was originally constructed to service the fort, but it became popular with the Victorian holiday makers who came to enjoy the seaside pleasure and the elegant hospitality of Queenscliff's hotels and guest houses. The **Ozone Hotel** in Gellibrand Street dates from this period. Its tower and iron balustrades give it prominence on the foreshore among the smaller buildings. The name catches the Victorian faith in the health-promoting virtues of sea air, but the chief attraction to the modern visitor is the seafood, which is superb.

Queenscliff sits right at the Heads to the bay, the point of greatest strategic importance. The **South Channel Fort** was built during the 1880s when the Crimean War sparked fears of Russian or French invasion. Yet another bluestone construction, it can be visited from Queenscliff or from Sorrento on a number of pleasure cruisers. Neither the guns of Fort Queenscliff, nor the

Lush Victorian greenery.

heavier ones of South Channel were ever fired in anger. The real danger at the Heads has always been the violent rip, a ferocious undertow. **The Maritime Centre** at Queenscliff has a display which demonstrates the vital importance of the lifeboats stationed there. The restoration of the "Queenscliffe" marks the homage of the people of Victoria to a boat which saw half a century of service. Many Victorians have ancestors who passed through The Rip before the protecting arms of the two peninsulas gave shelter to their ships.

Next door to Queenscliff is **Point Lonsdale** and along the coast, with an ocean beach, is **Ocean Grove**, a mixture of country town and holiday resort which has space for thousands of caravans and tents along its shores. **Barwon Heads** (near Ocean Grove) is the nearest town to some of the best surf on the coast, at **Thirteenth Beach** (part of it is next to the thirteenth hole at Barwon Golf Club). North of Queenscliff, across Swan Bay is **St. Leonards**, a small seaside community with a camping area, good fishing spots and a boat ramp. Port Arlington is at the northern most point of the Bellarine Peninsula, and the shoreline heads west from here, back to Geelong. In between lies an unspectacular, beachless coastline which is really best suited for fishing or just sitting above and watching.

The Peninsula also has diverse attractions such as nurseries, an **old steam railway** (Queenscliff to Drysdale; tel. [052] 522069), a donkey stud, yacht clubs, Sunday markets, arts and craft galleries, a **"U-pick blueberries"** farm at Drysdale (Tel. [052] 513468), museums and a **nature reserve** (at Grubb Road, Ocean Grove [052] 264667).

Mornington Peninsula: The first permanent settler to brave The Rip was John Batman, but three decades earlier, in 1802, David Collins had led a party of convicts, marines and free settlers to establish a settlement on the Mornington Peninsula at Sorrento. The move to

The venerable Queenscliff Hotel.

occupy territory on the shores of newly discovered Bass Strait was prompted by fears of French intentions. Governor King in Sydney knew that the French explorer Baudin had sailed through the Strait, and sought to secure the vital passage.

The settlement failed, but the remarkable story of the convict William Buckley links the Sorrento landing with Batman's later camp across the water at Indented Head. Buckley fled from Collins' party at Sorrento on Nov. 9, 1803 and in three days had travelled right around the bay, joining up with Aborigines who adopted him. Thirty one years later, John Batman was astonished by the appearance of a "wild white man" at his camp at Indented Head. Buckley virtually had to re-learn his mother tongue before he could give a coherent account of how he had sat on the beach and watched Collins' ships leave the bay.

Today it is possible to cross from Queenscliff in the west to Sorrento in the east on the Queenscliff-Portsea-Sorrento ferry, the **"Peninsula Princess,"** which can carry 35 vehicles and 200 passengers, and operates daily between Sorrento and Queenscliff (Information: [052]523171). There is always something satisfying about a round trip, but to take in both peninsulas, one needs to give them a day each. So, one must stay overnight in Queenscliff before taking the morning ferry, or find accommodation on the Sorrento side after a late afternoon crossing.

You can easily reach the Mornington Peninsula directly from Melbourne by road, train or bus. Trains travel frequently to **Frankston**, the major peninsular town and a bus service connects with the rail to take visitors throughout the southern peninsula. For those who want to get straight off the plane and into the water (well, almost), an "airport to peninsula" shuttle bus operates many times every day from Tullamarine to Frankston and Rosebud.

Melbourne's suburbs reach east and

The "Great Australia" plied the England-Australia route in the 1800s (*The Illustrated London*, December 1660).

THE GIGANTIC CLIPPER-SHIP "GREAT AUSTRALIA," RECENTLY BUILT FOR MESSRS. BAINES AND CO., OF LIVERPOOL.

south around the bay. From St. Kilda Road, the bayside suburbs sprawl along the Nepean Highway to Frankston. The Nepean Highway then continues to curl around the shoreline all the way to Portsea, while the Frankston Freeway now links Frankston with the Princes Highway to the north. From Frankston, it's best to head further south to the Western Port side of the peninsula, to make it possible to take in the whole peninsula in one loop. Take the Franston to Flinders road but diverge to the right just beyond Baxter. Coolart Road leads to the shore of Western Port Bay and the **Coolart Reserve** where the homestead and its splendid gardens date back to the squatting era. In the 1840s settlers began to take up "runs" in the area. Initially they had no title to the land, and although they became active in asserting their claims, some of them weren't too concerned about the rule of law.

Georgiana McCrae who, with her husband Andrew, established the run at Arthur's Seat, records a duel between two of her neighbours. Edward Barker held runs in the Cape Schanck area and Maurice Meyrick was established at Boneo. The duel took place in one of the sand swales or "cups," near the point where the Cape Schanck Road leaves Boneo Road. "Out of the wind, and lighted by the rays of a hidden sun, the men stood, pistols in hand, ten paces apart. Meyrick fired first, and the bullet flipped his enemy's ear; whereupon Barber, taking aim, not at Meyrick, but a gull on the wing, killed it."

From **Cape Schanck**, a narrow coastal park runs out to the newly opened **Point Nepean National Park**. There is access to the park from several points which are clearly signposted. Erosion of the delicate dune systems had become a major problem by the 1970s, so it is essential to keep to the defined tracks. Recommended are the walks along the cliff wall and surrounds, such as **Coppins Track**, starting from Sorrento Ocean Beach, and

Hang gliding is popular among those who prefer to sail above the waves.

Bushrangers Bay Track near Cape Schanck.

The thundering surf of this coastal strip has attracted eager visitors (and drowned its share of them) since the last century when many travelled down the bay by steamer to Sorrento. George Coppin, who had the Victorian spirit of enterprise and the romantic passion for Nature in her wilder moods, built a steam powered tramway to carry tourists to **Sorrento Back Beach**. His name survives in the lookout and the track to **Jubilee Point**. The most dramatic event in the history of this beach occurred in 1967 when Australian Prime Minister Harold Holt disappeared while swimming alone in these rip-prone seas.

The old **Quarantine Station** at the very end of the Nepean Highway is an interesting building and reaching it provides a sense of completing a journey. Returning along the quiet front beach foreshore, you pass the **Early Settlers Graves** and the monument to Collins' brief settlement. At **McCrae**, the homestead where Georgiana painted and compiled her diary can be visited. **Arthur's Seat**, which she loved so much, is the most commanding vantage point in Victoria: "We go to the summit. There the view was beautiful: on one side of us, the sea as far as one might look, on the other Port Phillip Bay." The view up and down the peninsula, from the 300-metre high lookout, today is not much different than in her time, but the ascent by car or chairlift is considerably easier. By the way, Arthur's Seat was named after neither Arthur nor his seat but a mountain which early explorer Matthew Flinders remembered back in England.

From Portsea back to Frankston, along the Bay's shore, safe beaches provide plenty of swimming, boating and picnic spots. There are boat ramps and recreation areas, most of which are out of bounds for your dog during summer. Peninsula **information centres** have the latest word on picnic and barbecue facilities, including news

Historic Williamstown is a classic sea-port settlement and great tourist attraction.

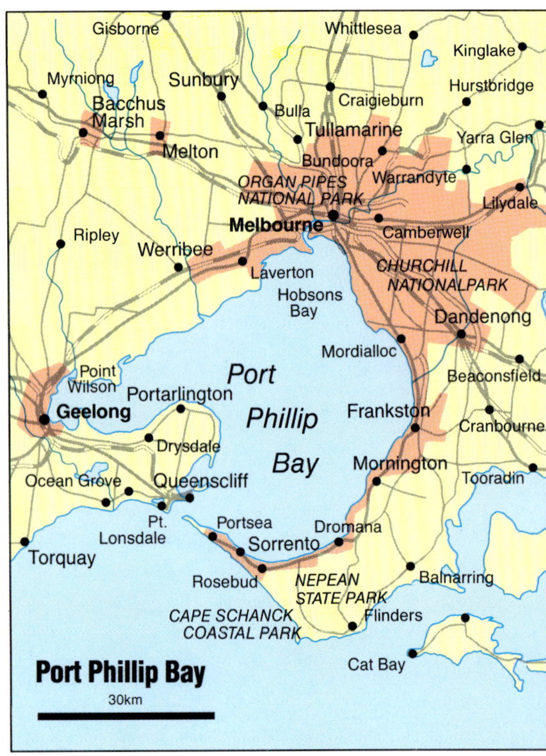

of the all important "fire ban" days, and can be dialled on (03) 7815244—Frankston, (059) 751644—Mornington and (059) 873078—Dromana. Much of the southern coast is spectacular and crisscrossed with walking tracks and there are good walks near bush at Arthur's Seat and **Main Creek** and in the **Nepean State Park**.

There are so many activities available for the visitor to the Mornington Peninsula that a detailed rundown is impossible here but here are a few of the peninula's "greatest hits." The **Red Hill Market** (second Saturday of the month, September to May; Rosebud Primary School, Nepean Highway, Rosebud). For something "different," the **train to Stony Point**—not old enough to be antique and not modern enough to be with it, but enjoyable for many. The **Manyung Art Gallery** at **Mount Eliza** ([03] 7872953). **Sages Cottage** (orchids, herbs, plants—Sages Road, Baxter [059] 711337). **Native plant nurseries** in the Red Hill area. A barbecue or picnic at **"Seawinds"** gardens near Arthur's Seat. Finally, check out **Coolart Farm and bird sanctuary** at Lord Somers Road, Somers.

Phillip Island: The chief attraction of Phillip Island is the famous **penguin parade**, the regular nightly return of the fairy penguins to nest among the grasses in the dunes. Undeterred by spotlights and tourists, they totter up the beach like miniature revellers coming home late from a ball in dinner suits. For many visitors to Melbourne and, indeed, Australia, this is one of the highlights of their trip and the evening parade is perennially popular.

Koalas are plentiful and tame on Phillip Island. During the decades when their numbers were dangerously low, the island was a sanctuary where they were able to continue to breed. At the **Nobbies** is a thriving colony of seals. The Cowes Ferry Service runs a two-and-a-half-hour cruise which includes a close approach to the seals and provides the best means of viewing them.

A molten summer sun burnishes the waters of Port Phillip Bay.

To The East

"The Blue Dandenongs": Seen from the distant city they are little more than a hint on the horizon, something solid behind a hazy blue mist. Yet, an hour's drive east of Melbourne there they are, the lovely ranges which the Aborigines called "Corhanwarrabul" and later settlers named "the Dandenong Ranges." Being so accessible—only 35 kilometres (22 miles)—from Melbourne they are a great tourist feature; so, if possible, visit them on a weekday rather than the weekend when the winding, and at times, narrow roads can become irritatingly busy.

The first white settlers came to the area in 1870, to log and to mine for gold, activities which in turn opened the way for immense subdivision of the area. In 1900 the railway came as far as **Ferntree Gully** in the foothills, which saw the establishment of the Dandenongs as a tourist weekend-holiday retreat. The village of **Kallista** became a haven for creative workers including impressionist painter Tom Roberts and poet C. J. Dennis, author of *A Sentimental Bloke*.

Much harm was caused by the original settlers and their felling of native trees for subdivision (which continued late into the 1930s) and for their own aesthetic purposes. The "Arcadian" vision of that era preferred the landscape to be occupied by deciduous northern hemisphere trees, rather than by the anarchic grace of Australian eucalypts. Today, many of those cleared areas have regrown but there is now concern that, as the Dandenongs have become increasingly "commuter belt" territory, there is a real danger of them becoming over-populated.

Despite their Eurocentric notions of sylvan beauty, much of credit for the charm of Dandenong buildings is due to those early settlers. They constructed beautiful weatherboard guest houses

Puffing Billy makes the climb through the Dandenongs from Belgrave up to Menzies Creek.

with enormous verandas, charming churches of stone or timber, and village shops which these days cannot escape the tag of "quaint." Even the names of the villages have a ring of delight: Kallista, Clematis, Olinda, Sassafras, Ferny Creek. At the aptly-named **Silvan** there are spectacular bulb farms which should be visited in September and October to see acres of tulips. (Contact 737 9305 for information.)

Evidence of the earlier settlers and holidayers is abundant, despite the ravages of frequent bushfires. They planted many of their "exotics" (including rhododendrons and azaleas) in spectacular gardens which, when their colours rust or burst in spring and autumn—the best times to visit—give the Dandenongs the reputation for being one of the prettiest places in Australia. The destruction of the original environment by the loggers and settlers, and the subdivision (since the 1890s) of the ranges into small blocks, has meant that very few of the splendid mountain ash that once covered the ranges are left. Much of the lower storey of the natural bush, a haven for many bush creatures and noted for its rare wildflowers and orchids, has also been decimated. A more recent problem is the feral cats which threaten the native birds, particularly the tiny finches, and the smaller marsupials. On an even more sombre note, the Dandenongs are designated one of the three most fire prone areas in the world.

Kangaroos and wallabies keep their joeys in the pouch to an advanced stage.

A village atmosphere is maintained in most of the 23 small townships scattered through the ranges. Nurseries, antique shops and markets all flourish, as do restaurants, picnic areas and walking tracks. Scenic view points are strategically located; from some you can gaze back at the dreaming spires of Melbourne's CBD—and probably prefer to dream a little longer here in the hills.

One delightful way to see the Dandenongs is to travel on "Puffing Billy," a narrow gauge tourist steam-train which twists and whistles through 10 kilometres (six miles) of lush bushland between Belgrave and Emerald. (Emerald is an idyllic township on the edge of a lake and the site of the Dandenongs' first settlement in 1858.) The little steam engines of "Puffing Billy" carried passengers and freight until 1953 when a landslide blocked the line. For many years the service was out of action, but The Puffing Billy Society has now completely restored the line. A ride on "Billy" is for kids aged from four to 104, a real hoot. "Puffing Billy" carries more than 180,000 passengers a year, running every weekend from Belgrave: on Saturday at 11 a.m. and 2 p.m., and on Sunday at 10:45 a.m., noon, 1:35 p.m., and 3:10 p.m. It also runs daily during the week, leaving Belgrave at 10:30 a.m., 11:45 a.m. and 1:15 p.m. (For timetable information ring (03) 870 8411.) The Steam Museum at Menzies Creek, behind the "Puffing Billy" Station, houses a unique collection of locomotives and machinery. It opens Sunday only from 11 a.m. to 5 p.m.

The Dandenongs are world-renowned for specialist nurseries and many fine gardens. Along Sherbrooke Road is one of Australia's finest private gardens, belonging to the mansion, **Burnham Beeches** which is itself a wonderful monument to headaches. Alfred Nicholas, the inventor of the aspirin, had this magnificent retreat built between 1872 and 1930, in high art deco style. He and his family lived there until World War II, and later the mansion became a laboratory for the Nicholas company, during which time many aspects of the interior structure were ruined. In 1981, John Guy bought the mansion, along with the staff residence and the 22 hectares (56 acres) of garden for $3.5 million dollars. With extraordinary attention to detail, he set about recreating the mansion as Nicholas had intended it to be, beginning with the five impressive upstairs bedrooms.

Burnham Beeches now operates as a country house hotel (it's a member of Select Hotels and Resorts International). Here relaxation is the ultimate aim. From the vast sunny windows of any bedroom, all of which overlook Sherbrooke Forest, you can watch the native rosellas, galahs, kookaburras and tiny finches feed from the huge seed bells hung along the verandahs. Peacocks strut across the lawns, and the most pleasurable bushwalks lie just across the road. If walking is too energetic, you can enjoy the fine food and wine in the restaurant. (Ricard Lovatt, the chef, was Australia's Chef of the Year in 1988.) Prices range from $145 to $475 per night. Burnham Beeches is situated in one of the best forest settings in Victoria.

Across the road from Burnham Beeches is **Sherbrooke Forest Park**, famous for its falls, scenic walking tracks, and wildlife—and especially for the elusive, and endangered, lyrebirds. These exquisite birds with the lacey, lyre-shaped tails of the male are mimics of all forest sounds and can be found by the early and patient watcher not far into the forest. Here there are great stands of mountain ash and gullies of giant tree ferns. However, unless you are accompanied by someone familiar with the area, it is best to stay on the well sign-posted walking tracks, because one can all too easily become lost in the bush.

Among the many tourist attractions of the Dandenongs, a great favourite is the **William Ricketts Sanctuary**, near the town of Mount Dandenong, where the sculptor Ricketts has paid homage with an enchanting complex of works depicting the area's strong Aboriginal heritage.

Another day trip, this time 60 kilometres (37 miles) north-east from Melbourne (an easy drive along the scenic Maroondah Highway), is to the **Colin McKenzie Wildlife Sanctuary** on the outskirts of the rural township of Healesville. (**Healesville** itself is worth a visit, especially for a cup of tea in its picturesque park with its bandstand and

Left, koalas aren't bears at all—in fact, they are marsupials.

creek.) The Wildlife Sanctuary is one of the most comprehensive fauna parks in Australia, covering 32 hectares (79 acres) and surrounded by 142 hectares (350 acres) of bushland reserve. It was opened in 1929 as a picnic ground, and originally used by Sir Colin McKenzie, a noted Australian surgeon and director of the National Museum, to further his studies in the comparative anatomy of marsupials.

There are 200 species of native birds, reptiles and mammals on display in large, natural enclosures planted with indigenous flora. Here you can surround yourself with a colony of 800 ibis or enter walk-through aviaries that bring birds of the wild, including the lyrebird, close at hand. The glassed-sided platypus house is a special feature, where these unique and surprisingly small creatures can be easily observed playing in their pool. In 1943 platypuses were first bred in captivity in this sanctuary. The Nocturnal House is wonderful in providing a chance to see tiny marsupial rats and possums that are rarely seen in their natural habitat. Stroll through the paddocks of kangaroos and wallabies, watch the emus and wood ducks cross your path—and steal your food—and see the koalas and various reptiles (the latter safely isolated from visitors). It is quite pleasant to sit on the grass with a picnic lunch, but there is also a licensed bistro, a snack bar and a gift shop.

Back in the surburbs in the bushy Shire of Eltham, 15 kilometres (nine miles) north-east of Melbourne, is the intriguing community of **Montsalvat**. It is unique in Victoria, and probably in Australia, because it was founded purely as an artistic colony—for painters, potters, silver and goldsmiths, craftspeople, writers and musicians—and it still functions in much the same way. The charismatic painter and architect Justus Jorgensen bought land near the **Eltham** township in 1935, and, with the help of his followers and students began to build Montsalvat, a grand scheme that was to house a community.

Jorgensen—who died before his project was completed—was profoundly impressed by the Europoean buildings of the Middle Ages and designed his own after this style. The result, Montsalvat, is a marvellous, albeit quirky, creation which remains partially unfinished today because the members of the community do not want his work—the final expression of his artistic vision—disturbed in any way. The buildings are of varied design and construction techniques, but of particular note is the Great Hall, which was handmade in 1938 of local mudstone. This revival of *pise* construction was highly influential in the work of Alistair Knox, a renowned architect whose work is most visible in the Eltham district. In its early years life at Montsalvat was culturally and artistically vivid and the Eltham area is still a centre for arts and crafts. Montsalvat today is a complex set in 9.4 hectares (23.2 acres) and used for concerts and receptions.

Right, sulphur-crested cockatoos make a raucous screech that can be heard right through the bush.

GREAT OCEAN ROAD

The Great Ocean Road is a driver's road: not dangerous, but demanding total concentration at the wheel, for which it offers wonderful rewards. The driver's pleasure is an active one, pursuing this sinuous shoulder of the coast; but the passenger can relax and take in the constantly changing views of ocean and spray, cliff face and tea-tree, eucalypt forests and fern gullies.

This is perhaps Australia's most breathtaking drive, and at almost every curve or crest another spectacular fan of land and seascape spreads before you. It isn't easy to fight the urge to push on. But the regular stopping points and lookouts are there for the driver's pleasure as well as convenience. In fact, the only satisfactory way to appreciate the Great Ocean Road is to take these opportunities to swap roles. Let your passenger drive a while.

Like the Yarra Boulevard in Melbourne, the Ocean Road was one of the relief works of the Great Depression. An army of the unemployed swung picks and pushed barrows on these precipitous slopes and struggled through mud slides when the icy squalls from the Southern Ocean soaked skins and hillsides. The road is officially dedicated to the fallen of the Great War, and many of those who worked on it knew both the mud of Flanders and the mud of these roadworks.

The commemorative arch between Fairhaven and Devil's Corner recognises the role of Major McCormack, the honorary engineer to the Great Ocean Road Trust, and of his men. The arch has a little history in its own right. The original structure was built in 1937, but was replaced in the 1970s. In 1983 when the devastating "Ash Wednesday" bushfires tore along the coastline, it too was destroyed. The new arch incorporates all the plaques of its predecessors. The memory of the fires of 1983 haunts this area and blackened tree trunks mark the progress of the holocaust that razed hundreds of houses in Anglesea, Aireys Inlet, and Lorne. But regeneration and rebuilding are as remarkable as destruction. This is a coastline which can see the fiery northerly winds of summer scorch the earth and the howling gales of July drench the hills with Antarctic sleet. From extremes comes resurgence.

The journey west along the Great Ocean Road begins at **Torquay**, at the end of the Bellarine Peninsula, and heads towards Anglesea. This leads close to **Bells Beach**, a legend among professionals and serious surfers as *the* great beach of the southern coastline. When the full moon of Easter brings the tides to their peak and the cold Southern Ocean swell surges, conditions are ideal for the lunatic masters of the waves. **Anglesea** is a popular tourist resort where the surf is rather more benign than at Bells. In the summer it is ideal for swimming and has a well patrolled beach. The golf course is well known for its kangaroos which placidly munch the fairways as players attempt to negotiate these unorthodox hazards. There is no record of anyone scoring a pouch in one.

From Anglesea the road becomes slower and more winding. There are many sheer drops to the water, and **Angahook Forest Park** still displays the aftermath of "Ash Wednesday." The red ironbarks have begun to regenerate but much of the melaleuca scrub seems to have suffered badly. The park offers an interesting contrast to the wetter forests further on to the southwest. At **Cinema Point** (an intriguingly obscure name), on the flank of Big Hill (considerably less so), the view towards Lorne and back towards the Aireys Inlet lighthouse is superb. This is the point of highest elevation on the road and is an ideal place to change drivers for the downhill stretch.

Lorne is an older seaside town than many of the others along this coast because it pre-dates the Ocean Road. Access down through the Otway

Preceding pages: the Twelve Apostles as seen from the Great Ocean Road. Below, the perfect point waves of Bells Beach attract surfers even in winter.

Ranges from Deans March made it one of the summer retreats in the early 20th century of the Western District "squattocracy," and the older houses between the town centre and the Pacific Hotel reflect these beginnings. With their wide verandas and green lattice work gone shabby in the salt air, these comfortable old houses rest a little warily among the tea-trees, waiting for the developers. At Lorne the surf is even gentler than at Anglesea, and the original name of the town, Loutit Bay, bore witness to the shelter it offered Captain Loutit after a battering from the Bass Strait gales. In the hills behind the town, **Teddy's Lookout** gives a fine view of the coastline ahead, and **Erskine Falls**, eight kilometres (five miles) inland offer the first taste of the rain forest to come. This hinterland is densely wooded and much of it is included in the **Lorne Forest Park**. Here the moist gullies are thick with tree-ferns and you can still pick out the relics of the timber tramways which brought lumber down to the coast in the first decades of the century.

Beyond Lorne, the forest of the **Otway Ranges** closes in and the road crosses a series of fast flowing streams. The **Cumberland River** offers a short walk through luxuriant fern gullies to the falls. Just two kilometres (1.2 miles) on and up, the road reaches the **Mount Defiance Lookout** before continuing between forest and ocean to **Wye** and **Kennett rivers**. These are pleasant holiday towns with comfortable accommodation. The **Cape Paton Lookout** and **Carisbrook Creek** are both recommended stopping points.

Towards **Apollo Bay** the forest gives way to cleared hillsides of intense green. Bracken fern in the gullies tends to accentuate the moulded shape of the hills as they slope towards the sea and the openness of the scenery comes as relief after the confining forest. This is a farming landscape around an old established fishing port. The serenity of the pasture land tends to

Geelong still retains some character from its early days as a Gold Rush port.

mask the threat of the sea. Apollo Bay was settled in 1850, and no fewer than three jetties were built there before 1881, all of which were washed away in storms. Today, the town still has a fishing fleet which braves the Strait, but the current pier where the catch is landed has stood the test of time. Apollo Bay is a suitable place to break your journey and ample tourist accommodation is available.

The stretch of the Great Ocean Road from Apollo Bay to Cape Otway leads through the deepest and wettest section of the Otway Ranges. The sloping pastures are left behind and the **Otway National Park**, with its high rainfall species (mountain ash, manna gum, myrtle beech and a vast range of ferns and mosses), engulfs you with its characteristic dank aroma. The fauna here include the tiny marsupial phascogales and dunnarts as well as the larger bandicoots and possums. Larger still is the poteroo. But the egg-laying mammals, the platypus and echidna, here and elsewhere in Australia, are the most bizarre examples of an ancient line which still survives in this island continent.

There is also a rich bird life in the forest, with satin bower birds, white goshawks, yellow tailed cockatoos and jet black gang-gangs some of the most notable species. The Ocean Road passes inland at this stage but access to the coast, 21 kilometres (13 miles) from Apollo Bay, takes you into the **Commonwealth Lighthouse Reserve**. Along the waterline you can see herons, egrets and ibis, while terns and albatrosses patrol the open sea.

The Cape was first noted by James Grant in the *Lady Nelson* as she made the first west to east passage of Bass Strait in 1800. Once this route to New South Wales (considerably shorter than going around Tasmania) was discovered, **Cape Otway** became the point of landfall for the thousands of ships which sailed the "great circle" from the Cape of Good Hope. Taking advantage of great circle navigation

principles and the westerly gales ('The Roaring Forties") of sub-Antarctic latitudes, virtually all the settlers of 19th century Australia were swept for weeks through mountainous seas before coming abruptly to this rocky coast.

The need for a lighthouse was obvious, but it was not until August 1848 that one was successfully established. Many ships had foundered before then. Even after the lighthouse was built, the *Marie Gabriell*, the *Fiji*, and *Eric the Red* were wrecked near Cape Otway. Beside the lighthouse you can see the graves of drowned sailors who washed ashore from the *Lady Loch* in 1896. It is possible to be shown over the lighthouse on Tuesdays and Thursdays between 10 a.m. and midday or 2 and 4 p.m., but it is wise to phone beforehand (052) 37 9240.

The alternative inland route from Apollo Bay takes you through the timber country of **Beech Forest** and **Weeaporinah**, some of the wettest places in mainland Australia, and rejoins the Ocean Road at the tiny timber and potato growing town of **Lavers Hill**. From here you make a descent along cleared ridges towards Princetown, at the mouth of the Gellibrand River where the **Port Campbell National Park** begins. This final section of the Great Ocean Road is quite different: wide, open and windswept with stunted heath and occasional banks of tea-tree. A flat plateau drops to the sea. The limestone cliffs have been subject to the sculpting of wind and water into ledges, caverns, tunnels and bridges.

The first of these dramatic features is the line of isolated columns which stand amid the turbulent surf as the **Twelve Apostles**. Beyond them is the bulk of **Mutton Bird Island**, the nesting ground of these remarkable migratory birds which travel 24,000 kilometres (14,880 miles) to the Bering Strait in their annual pursuit of a second summer. Hatchlings have to reach maturity in a season to be ready to make the astonishing journey when the flocks are ready to leave in April. There is a spectacular blowhole between the island and Broken Head. Thunder Cave and the Island Archway lead to **Loch Ard Gorge** where two survivors from the wreck in 1878 of the *Loch Ard* were miraculously washed ashore. The headstones of four less fortunate passengers stand just to the west of the gorge.

Such grimness is left behind in the sheltered haven of **Port Campbell**. The quiet water of the Campbell Creek inlet and the Norfolk Island pines provide a pleasant respite from the rugged coast. But the limestone cliffs and stacks continue almost to Peterborough and the most dramatic of all is probably **London Bridge**, a huge archway which seems likely to collapse under the weight of a single visitor. Beyond Peterborough one can continue on towards the provincial city of Warnambool and the classic bluestone maritime village of Port Fairy or head back to Geelong through Colac and the rich grazing country of the Western District.

Left and right, tree ferns and vast tracts of bush in places like Sherbrooke Forest are ideal for bushwalks.

GREAT OUTDOORS

It is no coincidence that much of the advertising which accompanies Australia's tourism push features natural assets: rainforests, rivers, beaches and eucalyptus bushland. These are the most distinctively "Australian" things about Australia, and there is an accelerating awareness of the continent's natural heritage from both an environmental (protect them) and a tourism (see them) perspective.

There are several great outdoor areas in Victoria, a state which, because of its relatively small area, provides the visitor with an accessibility and easy choice not available in some other parts of Australia. There are the hauntingly spectacular stretches of coastline along the Great Ocean Road, the alpine beauty of north-east Victoria, the "wide brown land" of north-west Victoria and the aquatic attractions of Port Phillip Bay.

Left, a famous rock with an equally famous view of the Grampian Ranges. Below, autumn at Lake Guy.

One of the regions making a start in promoting "natural tourism" is **East Gippsland**—a dazzlingly lush area stretching from the ocean to the snowfields and up to the NSW border.

Under reasonably visionary policies, many parts of Victoria have been protected, and this is particularly the case in East Gippsland, where a conservation strategy in place means an expansion of the national parks system. Rivers, inlets, freshwater lakes and ocean beaches provide numerous camping and fishing spots, and for the more energetic there is an abundance of bushwalking trails, as well as rafting thrills, such as going down such hefty streams as the Snowy River. The area also features **Croajingolong National Park**, one of Victoria's finest, and the unique **Errinundra Plateau** with its sub-alpine rainforests and gnarled trees thousands of years old.

Car Touring and Bushwalking by Grant DeCosta is a reference book, history lesson and touring atlas to East Gippsland, all in one, which will serve well any visitor to the region. For a first journey you need look no further than a tour of the forests of the **Rodger River** (one of Victoria's most enchanting spots) detailed in DeCosta's book (Tour 6). The Rodger River's eucalypts in a virgin setting make it a majestic and inspiring destination. The upper Rodger River, one of the State's last great wilderness areas, has a high rainfall and sometimes freezing conditions but sensible precautions (food, water, wet weather gear and warm clothing) can easily outweigh these hardships and allow visitors to enjoy the area to its fullest. There are several superb camping areas for those making this great trip, which can be coupled with some of the best bushwalks in Victoria. The **Waratah Flat**, **Black Snake Creek** (recommended for its waratah flowers, not its black snakes) and **Monkey Top Big Tree** walks are particularly worthwhile.

The Gippsland region also features

some of Australia's great rafting and canoeing rivers and these can easily be enjoyed in conjunction with car touring. The **Mitchell River** from Stratford, takes paddlers (and those just hanging on!) through great mountain and cliff country in **Glenaladale National Park**. The **Snowy River**, joined from Buchan, is pure Australia, and carries you through a superb variety of landscapes. The **Mitta Mitta**, (reached from Omeo) is a thrilling river, combining gorges, rapids, white water and more white water, and the Blue Duck Lodge for a meal or two around an open fire. The **Goulburn River**, nearer Melbourne, is a good introduction to river rafting as it is an easier grade and there are plenty of serene reaches to provide respites from rapids.

The relatively high population density of most of Victoria means there is ample opportunity for car touring and staying in country pubs, where hotel-style accommodation includes classic Aussie "bed and breakfast" arrangements which make your money go as far as you want. There is now an **"Aussie Pub Bed and Breakfast Holiday Pass"** which gives you special access to this style of accommodation. At last count, there were 34 pubs as members of this system. The accommodation in these hotels does not include a private bathroom but, on the plus side, most of them serve a full Australian hot breakfast—tea or coffee, toast, sausages, eggs, cereal. You can buy a "Aussie Bed and Breakfast Pass" from any Victour office, RACV office or direct from "Aussie B&B Holidays" on (03) 5924375.

The historical Victorian gold centres, around Bendigo, Ballarat and places south, are also of great appeal for car tourers, and the accommodation matches the history with lovely old hotels available in such towns as **Daylesford** (Central Springs Inn) and **Bendigo** (The Shamrock). There is also plenty of accommodation other than hotels. For instance, up to eight people can stay in regal splendour at Halcombe Homestead Country Retreat (Halcombe Road, Glenyon) in the Central Highlands, or at Pond Cottage at Piper's Creek, only one hour's drive north of Melbourne.

All the major rental car companies operate in Melbourne, and there are also some specialist firms, dealing in campervans and 4-wheel drive vehicles, which are found in the columns of the Yellow Pages business phone directory. Brits Rentals (112 Bell St., Preston. 03-4800291) has "one way" rentals for interstate trips and for Victorian trips. Toyota long wheel-base 4-wheel drives adapted to camper style are readily available and will go almost anywhere there is a track. For less off-road touring "poptop" campervans are spacious, even though not as rugged as a 4-wheel drive. Other 4-wheel drives which seat 11 and sleep three (the other eight might like to take a tent) are ideal for the more rugged parts of Victoria's varied terrain.

Water, water, everywhere: views of Archron Creek (left) and McKenzie Falls (right).

BALLARAT

These days, it's a comfortable hour and a half of freeway driving from Melbourne to the sedate and elegant Victorian city of Ballarat. However, it was a difficult climb for the original 1850s gold diggers who trudged up from the coast through the Pentland Hills to reach the elevated area known to the Aborigines as "Balla-arat," or "resting place." But resting on arrival was the last thought of these men from Europe, China and the Americas who believed they were within a pick's swing of a golden future on the swarming diggings.

Not everyone struck it rich, but the gold here was more than enough to build this classic Victorian town and a community. The need to form syndicates to drag the pay-dirt 20, 30 or more metres to the surface united the freebooter diggers into a coherent political group. So it was that the miners of Ballarat struck the veins of wealth and democracy, that strangely mixed ore from which much of the modern world has been smelted.

Walking along **Lydiard Street** (from the School of Mines and the Anglican Church, past Craig's Hotel, the Royal Memorial Theatre and the Post Office on Sturt Street corner), one comes to the **Mining Exchange**. The Exchange became the real economic focus of Ballarat as the quartz mines drove ever deeper into the earth and the early syndicates gave way to companies. The contrast of the heavy stone arches and airy iron lacework along Lydiard Street captures that Victorian fusion of rectitude and confidence which extends into the private houses beyond.

Back in **Sturt Street** on the Dawson Street corner, the **statue of Peter Lalor**, the leader of the rebel miners at the Eureka Stockade (see Box), stands between St. Patrick's Cathedral and St. Andrew's Kirk. In front of him and to his right, is the flamboyant iron of the Golden City Hotel. Lalor wears his parliamentary speaker's wig: the Irish radical became the sober patriarch. Again, the disparate elements that made Australian society seem to be drawn symbolically together.

Sturt Street is one of the great streets of Australia. Its generous central plantation is embellished with monuments, sculptures and rotundas. In front of City Hall is a fine equestrian bronze commemorating the Boer War. The civic pride generated in the gold rush days continued to flourish. A city which hosts Australia's most famous eisteddfod, Ballarat has always been a centre for music, and the **Titanic Rotunda** is one of the more curious expressions of this. It was built by the bandsmen of Ballarat to honour the courage of those musicians who continued to play *Abide With Me* as the great ship sank below the icy waves of the Atlantic.

Nearby is a **statue of Robbie Burns**, much loved by the descendants of the many Scottish miners. Even the most dour of Scots in the bleak Ballarat winters had their lighter side: their Highland bard was located so close to Craig's Hotel that it looks as though he might just slip in for a dram. The town's **statue of Queen Victoria** even shows her in a less severe mood than usual. She looks just a touch smug, as if to say that she heartily approves of the endeavour and steadiness of the people who built this town and the colony's contribution to the British coffers. And no doubt she did approve, even though she may have been less amused by some of the goings on in the hotel.

Craig's Hotel is one of those pubs with long horse racing affiliations and an extraordinary story of a dream come grimly true. Walter Craig owned a horse called Nimblefoot. One night in 1870, he told the drinkers in the billiard room that he'd had a dream in which Nimblefoot carried his colours across the line in the Melbourne Cup. Craig could remember every detail—even that the jockey was wearing a black arm band. Out of the banter in the bar came a bet with the bookmaker, Joe Stack, that Nimblefoot would win the Cup and a horse called Croydon would win the Sydney Metropolitan, a long-shot double for which Stack would pay a thousand pounds, or Craig a round of drinks. Croydon duly won the Metropolitan, and Nimblefoot completed the double—but before his dream came true, Craig himself was dead—so Nimblefoot's jockey wore a black arm band in mourning.

Despite its boomtime mix of Florentine, French and Scots turrets, Craig's Hotel is too substantial to be mistaken for a dream. Like so much of Ballarat West, it has the imposing aura of solidity. It's hard to find so much unspoiled Victoriana in such a compact area anywhere else in the world as there is in this town in Victoria which has so many links with the Victorian age. Further west you come to the old **Ballarat West Fire Station**, now an antique shop, with its octagonal bell tower and bulky crenellations, and the **City Oval** which still has its splendid Victorian grandstand. Beyond is **Mary's Mount**, a relic of 19th century Catholic architecture at its most lavish.

A classic Ballarat street vista.

At the western end of Sturt Street the parklands of **Wendouree** begin. Just as 19th century as the buildings, the grand sweep of lawns, gardens and lake evoke images of Sunday afternoon promenades. The Ballarat Tramway Preservation Society maintains a **museum** and you can take a ride around the lake in one of their proud little trams. The ornate kiosk and the boatsheds add a further touch of old world leisure, and the oarsmen ploughing their way through flotillas of black swans remind you that Lake Wendouree was an Olympic Games rowing venue in 1956. Along the western shore are the Botanical Gardens with their varied plantings of exotic trees and spectacular flower beds. The begonia conservatories are perhaps the most splendid feature of the gardens, and in celebration of them Ballarat has a famous annual Begonia Festival in mid-March. Then, there is **The Avenue of Prime Ministers**, a series of stone busts in an intriguingly solemn homage, which might well cause derision in other Australian cities, but the Right Honourables sit very comfortably upon the West End of Ballarat.

Ballarat East is another story, although its modern face belies the cramped chaos of the early years. The canvas city which sprang up overnight in 1851, soon became a rabbit warren of bark shacks and shanties. Prone to both flood and fire, the houses of the miners were wiped out last century. But **Montrose Cottage** in Eureka Street is an authentic relic of the 1850s. Built of bluestone and handmade bricks by the Scottish miner, John Alexander, it dates from 1856 and has been fully restored and furnished appropriately for the period.

SOVEREIGN HILL

Total reconstruction is the only way to achieve the complete effect of gold rush life. This is what the Ballarat Historical Park Association set out to do when they embarked on the Sovereign Hill Settlement. Since it opened in 1970, the settlement has steadily developed into an elaborate and scrupulously accurate reconstruction of the gold town in the 1850s. The enthusiasm of the initial vision still survives, if just a little dulled. Ironically the weathering of the buildings has enhanced the sense of authenticity. The knowledge and flair displayed by the guides, shopkeepers (who sell traditionally-made wares and food) and various historical characters who drift around the settlement is remarkable given the daily repetition they must face. Chickens and ducks, cats and even a rather shabby dog wander about, adding a little more realism.

There is certainly no historical park in Australia that even approaches Sovereign Hill in terms of comprehensiveness and accuracy.

A visit to the **Gold Museum** with its array of nuggets, bullion and coins, can whet the appetite for Sovereign Hill by playing on the universal lust for gold, but the experience in the alluvial gully, with your feet sodden and your pan still empty puts one very close to the reality of the 1850s. "This Ballarat—a nuggety Eldorado for the few, a ruinous field of hard labour for many" were the grumblings of an Italian miner that still ring true in this setting. But then there are the pleasures of the time to be enjoyed in the hotels and the bakery, theatre and the various craft shops. The trades of the period, the wood turning, printing works and the all-important smithy are there to be taken in at first hand.

Certainly Sovereign Hill is all a good deal cleaner than the historical reality would have been, but it's a realistic attempt to bring one age to life in another. The school house is used by thousands of Victorian children each year. They live out the past in period clothes and even delight in their struggles with copperplate writing. The **Chinese Joss House** brings home the unrecognised contribution of the Chinese to the growth of the nation.

At the top of the hill is the poppet head of the deep mine, the massive battery equipment and the steam engines that drove the cables and worked the pumps. Here you begin to see the significance of the deep mining of Ballarat which forced men to co-operate in syndicates, and ultimately to use the engines of capitalism—the mining company and new technology—in their quest for gold. The latter response produced the visible wealth of Victorian Ballarat. But the first was crucial to setting the stage for Eureka and notions of political independence. Ballarat and Sovereign Hill tell the cultural, political and technological story of Victorian Australia in vivid style.

Left, panning for gold. Right, dressing the part, a 19th-century citizen of Sovereign Hill.

EUREKA

In a room of its own in the **Ballarat Fine Art Gallery** are the carefully preserved remnants of a tattered flag bearing the starry grid of the Southern Cross. On the morning of Dec. 3, 1854, this flag flew above the stockade at Eureka on the Ballarat gold-fields as 300 troops charged down upon 130 rebel miners.

For months before the attack miners had been smarting under the imposition of a one pound per month licence fee, payable whether they struck gold or not. Thuggish police enforced the law and collected for themselves half of each fine levied against defaulting miners. Mass gatherings of protesting miners culminated in a meeting on November 29, during which 12,000 men demanded universal franchise and then made a bonfire of their mining licences.

Led by an Irishman, Peter Lalor, and opposed by the Governor of Victoria, Sir Charles Hotham, 500 miners of many nationalities built a stockade and swore "to defend our rights and liberties." Above it they hauled, in place of the Union Jack, the emblem of the Southern Cross. By the early hours of December 3, the miners' numbers had dwindled to around 130. It was then that the 300 troops charged, leaving six soldiers and 24 miners dead.

Lalor managed to escape, but 13 other miners were charged with high treason. After much public furore all charges were dropped and an amnesty for Lalor and the other leaders proclaimed; the licence fee was abolished. While the incident was replete with tragedy and even farce, it was a symbolic point in Australian political evolution. Australian politician Dr. H. V. Evatt considered that "Australian democracy was born at Eureka." Since then the starry Eureka flag has continued to symbolise the movement for political independence and an Australian republic.

BEECHWORTH

Did Daniel Cameron, a flamboyant Gold Rush politician, really ride through Beechworth on a horse shod with golden shoes at the head of a procession of fabulously attired miners? They say that he wore off one ounce of gold during his celebrated ride.

Sceptics like to claim that the gold was merely gilt, but the tale, fanciful or true, gives some indication of what Beechworth was like in its 19th century heyday. The town had, incredibly, 61 hotels and a theatre where international celebrities performed. Nellie Melba sang at the **Regency House** theatre, and here, it is said, ill-fated explorer Robert 0'Hara Bourke broke his heart over an opera star.

Beechworth is situated 267 kilometres (166 miles) north-east of Melbourne on the edge of the Victorian Alps, between Wangaratta and Myrtleford, and in the centre of the historic Ovens goldmining region. The National Trust has only classified two entire towns in Victoria as worthy of preservation. One is Maldon, the other Beechworth. Locals claim that even a week in Beechworth will not do justice to it and its beautiful surrounding areas. Certainly, given the fact that it is a considerable distance from Melbourne it would be advisable to plan to spend some time there. It's heavenly in autumn, dazzling with red and gold; and merely gorgeous in spring when the wild violets and orchids are out—not to mention glittering in winter. Facilities for tourists are comfortable and varied, ranging upwards from a clean Youth Hostel located in the historically-classified **Star Hotel**.

As well as being at the centre of a gold strike area, Beechworth has a more notorious claim to fame—it is at the very heart of **"Kelly Country."** During the late 1870s, Ned Kelly, Australia's most famous, or infamous bushranger (opinions vary, and seem to depend largely upon one's Irish ancestry) stood trial twice in the present courthouse and was held in custody in the gaol. Standing in the grim room where Kelly was imprisoned can still have an extraordinary effect on the visitor.

Because of its close associations with the Kelly Gang the area around Beechworth became known as Kelly Country, the boy-os being familiar with every detail of this landscape. The tourist industry has fanned poor Ned's posthumous fame very hard in this region. One particular scenic route from Wangaratta to Albury is even known as the Kelly Way. Only about three kilometres (two miles) further than the Hume Highway route, it is recommended for those interested in a uniquely Australian and historic landscape. Looking at the rugged countryside, it is not difficult to imagine how Kelly's little Irish crew managed to ambush the gold coaches then disappear into the scrub for weeks.

Beechworth was first settled by white men in 1839, and gold was discovered in 1852 and mined until 1920. It was one of Australia's richest gold-fields until early this century and was also the administrative centre for north-east Victoria—thus the relatively sustained prosperity of the township. What is so pleasing about Beechworth is that everything is genuine. There is none of that obvious "touristified" aspect of many other historic settlements. With very little effort, and almost no "tarting-up," Beechworth seems to have survived in an agreeable timewarp.

Throughout the township are many historic buildings, but perhaps the most sensible place to begin is at the **Rock Cavern**, in the centre of the town, opposite the Post Office. This is a former Bank of Victoria, built in 1867, with a restored cottage at the side and the original gold vault still intact. It is now a Visitors' Information Centre and a mineral museum. There is also a stunning chandelier of over 4,000 crystals. Just down the street is the **Carriage**

Museum, a National Trust project. It is situated behind the gracious **Tanswell's Commercial Hotel** and within a coach house and stables which date to 1859. Inside there is a fascinating and eye-opening collection of horsedrawn vehicles and saddlery from a bygone era. Just how tough these pioneers were is obvious with one look at the unsprung open omnibus.

Stroll further down the street and find **Ned Kelly's cell**. This oppressive room is tucked just beneath the rear of the Town Hall and was where Kelly was kept immediately after his conviction in 1880. The atmosphere is chilling and a quick visit only is recommended. Continue straight across the gardens at the rear to the Burke Museum. Also worth noting are the five impressive granite structures opposite the Town Hall, the old Government Buildings.

The **Robert 0'Hare Burke Museum**, named after the explorer who died tragically in the central Australian desert, and who had earlier been a police constable in this area, is recognised as one of the finest country museums in Victoria. Established in 1856, it houses a huge collection of documents, pictures and relics of Beechworth's past, including those of the Chinese miners and predictably, Ned Kelly.

Further across the town there is the old **M. B. Brewery and Cellars**. Built on a local granite base, of handmade bricks and oregon beams, the building remains virtually the same today as when constructed in 1872. It was still brewing stout until 1956 but now concentrates on aerated water, cordial and the famous herbal beer, Ecks. In the cellars there is a priceless collection of old bottles and utensils, as well as machinery and tools used by brewers over the past century.

While in town, the **Gardens**, dating from 1875, should not be overlooked. The designer of Melbourne's Botanical Gardens, Baron Von Mueller, had some influence in selecting the trees: the sequoias in particular are remarkable. If you can drag yourself from the enticement of Beechworth's galleries, museums and tourist shops (which are somewhat superior to the usual ticky-tacky trinket emporia) there are many worthwhile features just outside town. One essential visit is to the **Chinese Burning Towers and Prayer Desk**, within the cemetery. It's a reminder that over 5,000 Chinese worked these goldfields.

A visit to the **Powder Museum** is also worthwhile. This was the storage keg for the powder used during the gold rush days, and the National Trust has restored it to its 1859 solidity. If you feel inclined to venture down one of the many old mine shafts in the area, this can be arranged through the Visitors' Information Centre. You'll need to be adventurous, because it can be a difficult climb—and old mines have a horrible stench. You'll emerge full of admiration for those who worked these cramped, dank and dismal shafts for hours and days at a time.

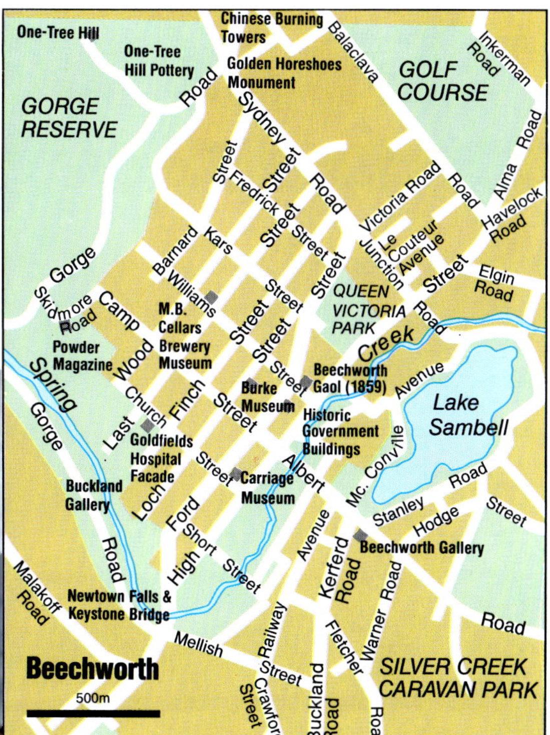

SNOWFIELDS

Skiing in Australia tends to have two apparently contradictory trajectories: physically, it is a (predictably) downwardly mobile activity, but socially, it is definitely upward. Victoria has some very pleasant and accessible skiing areas, which suffer less from the high fashion compulsions of the New South Wales meccas, Thredbo and Perisher Valley, but which, nevertheless, have a class of their own. The proximity and relatively easy access of skiing at Victoria's five resorts has meant that skiing here is a fairly democratic activity. Victoria's mountain resorts stretch in an arc from north-east of Melbourne to almost directly east of the capital. They dot the finest alpine country in the state, the high plains of which slope gracefully along to the Snowy Mountains of the Australian Alps.

Mount Buller, labelled "Big, Bold and Beautiful" by its promoters, is a comfortable and pretty three-hour drive from Melbourne, 237 kilometres (146 miles) away. Before arriving, you pass through Mansfield, a mountain town 50 kilometres (31 miles) off the Hume Highway. It takes well under an hour to travel from Mansfield to Mount Buller (47 kilometres away/29 miles), but the journey is through archetypal *Man from Snowy River* country. Here there are more Akubra hats, Drizabone coats and elastic sided boots than anywhere in the world—with the possible exception of London.

If you're not interested in driving, there is the Melbourne to Mount Buller coach service, via Mansfield, which operates daily. The fare ($55 for adults) includes "oversnow" transport to the lodge door. Buller is certainly "big," being by far the largest of the five main ski centres in Victoria. The car parking space is generous, the sleeping accommodation (7,000 beds) copious, and even the verticle drop in the snowruns is the biggest—400 metres (1,320 feet). With a claimed skiable area of 400 hectares (988 acres), Mount Buller is almost four times as big as the next largest resort, Falls Creek. It has a fairly even spread of grades on its slopes. Twenty-four lifts, including eight T-bars and six quad chairs are said to be able to handle 36,000 people per hour.

Buller's peak, at 1,804 metres (5,953 feet) is the high point on a spur which shoots out from the Great Dividing Range, the spine of mountains which runs up Australia's eastern flank. That spur separates the sensationally beautiful Howqua River and Delatite Valleys. Around the village (1,600 metres/5,280 feet above sea level), there are also some good cross-country ski trails, although the 11-kilometre (six-mile) total distance of these trails is relatively small, and Buller tends not to be at the top of the list of priorities for many keen cross-country skiers. However, it does provide access to Mount Stirling, to the north, where there are generous doses of

Left, frozen fronds in the High Country. Right, snow gums give Australian snowfields a unique appearance.

all grades of cross-country skiing.

The snow resort most distant from Melbourne is **Falls Creek**, which is 30 kilometres (19 miles) from Mount Beauty and 377 kilometres (234 miles) from the city. The five-hour drive is definitely worthwhile, for Falls Creek is in one of the most spectacular parts of Victoria.

There are some particularly "hairy" and exciting runs at Falls Creek, and only 17 percent of the slopes are for beginners. But for many, it is in cross-country skiing and ski touring that "Falls" and its surrounds really excel. In the **Nordic Bowl** on **Sun Valley**, there are 20 kilometres (12 miles) of groomed cross-country trails, all for beginners or intermediate skiers. Further afield lies the real jewels: the **Bogong High Plains**. There is good skiing around **Rocky Valley** (on the edge of the Plains) and from Falls, there is access to **Healthy Spur, Pretty Valley** and **Mount Bogong**, all worthy challenges for experienced alpine skiers.

The alpine expanse of high plains is one of extreme and rugged beauty, which seems to satisfy the most ardent adventurer and skier. If you are a typically individualistic cross-country skier you may prefer a solo experience; but for some, the safest and most enjoyable way is to have it organised for you, in the company of others who, presumably, feel the same way. Several adventure travel operators run trips throughout this area. Apart from introductions to cross-country skiing and snowcraft, there are five-day ski safaris through superb wilderness from Falls Creek to Mount Hotham. Such a trip costs around $400. This traverse of the Bogong High Plains cannot be surpassed as a wilderness skiing route. In the summer, spring and autumn, the same high plain and its beauty provide numerous opportunities for bushwalking, camping and trout fishing.

Another superb little sub-alpine town in Victoria is **Bright**. Bright and beautiful indeed. Two ski resorts, Mount Hotham and Mount Buffalo, are nearby, and the five-hour drive from Melbourne to Bright provides you thereafter with plenty of choice. **Mount Hotham** is 367 kilometres (278 miles) from Melbourne, via Bright (55 kilometres/34 miles away). Hotham has the highest "lifted point" in Victoria, at 1,868 metres (6,164 feet), and a relatively high village at 1,750 metres (5,775 feet). (Well, it's high for Australia: you've got to remember that Australia's loftiest point, Mount Kosciusko, is one-quarter the height of Mount Everest. Australia's snowfields are extensive but they certainly aren't on towering peaks.) Hotham also boasts great cross-country skiing, on Wire Plain and Whisky Flat, as well as acess to Mount Loch. Mount Hotham also has some superb wildlife, including rare mountain pigmy possums which cross the Alpine Road safely (we hope) by going under it along a tunnel built expressly for that purpose by the Victorian Road Construction Authority.

All geared up to hit the slopes.

Mount Buffalo, 32 kilometres (635 miles) from Bright, or 320 kilometres (198 miles) and five hours driving from Melbourne, is a fairly small resort. There are only 230 beds there. It's also the cheapest (by far) with more than 15 kilometres (nine miles) of cross country ski trails, mainly for beginners, with more demanding areas in the **Cresta Valley** accessible from Buffalo. Mount Buffalo has some fine accommodation, in any season, including the splendid anachronistic **Mount Buffalo Chalet**.

The last of the big five ski areas in Victoria is in Gippsland, at **Mount Baw Baw**. Less than three hours' drive from Melbourne, Baw Baw boasts numerous attractions, not the least of which are its panoramic views across the La Trobe Valley to Bass Strait. In recent years, Baw Baw has been transformed, with new car parks only minutes from slopes and cross-country areas. Visitors can take advantage of almost as much skiable area as at Mount Buffalo. The cross-country trails also present excellent intermediate skiing, and all grades of ski touring are accessible at **St. Gwinear**, "the secret mountain" (until now).

The mountain areas of Victoria are winter playgrounds or hideaways, and summer retreats or fields of adventure. There is now a greatly improved supply of information available for the skiing community of Victoria, mostly provided by the **Victorian Ski Association booking service** (03) 693655 or (03) 6994413 or its **"Snow-Line"** (03)11545. The **Alpine Resorts Commission** can provide information and booking facilities for on-mountain accommodation. Its phone numbers are: Falls Creek (057) 58335, Mount Buller (057) 776280, Mount Hotham (057) 593636. **Snow Report** phone numbers are: Buller (057) 776067, Hotham (057) 593531, Falls Creek (057) 583366, Baw Baw (051) 651126, Buffalo (057) 551216. For road conditions, telephone the Road Construction Authority on (03) 8602290.

A snowman, by gum.

THE GRAPE ESCAPE

Winemaking in Victoria began as early as 1834 when Edward Henty settled in Portland and planted, among other things, a vineyard. Encouraged by the first Governor of Victoria, Charles La Trobe—who established a vineyard in the gardens of the first Government House—several respected winemakers from Europe migrated to Victoria where they continued their craft.

From the 1840s there were thousands of hectares of vineyards in Melbourne suburban areas, as well as in the country areas—often established by gold-diggers who had not struck it rich and began planting vines as a source of income. In the last four decades of the 19th century winemaking became a considerable industry and with its light dry wines winning gold medals in Europe, Victoria was considered to have a brilliant future in winemaking.

Then, late in the century, the *phylloxera* mite ravaged the vineyards, and vignerons were forced to burn all the old stock and to plant *phylloxera*-resistant stock. This setback was followed by the economic depression of the 1930s. Throughout all these trials, Australians continued to show a distinct preference for beer to wine.

The end result was that, by the middle of the 20th century, many of the more famous vineyards had closed. Fortunately, some vineyards managed to hang on, but it was not until the 1960s that Victoria once again began producing excellent wines. Since then, enthusiastic new winemakers in small family wineries have joined the more established businesses. With a month to spare you might find time to explore all of Victoria's wineries. However, a realistic excursion within a comfortable day's drive from Melbourne is to the Yarra Valley area, which specialises in delicate light wines.

The prettiest way to the **Yarra Valley** (you will need a map) is to drive north-east from Melbourne to the charming township of Warrandyte, a bushy outer-suburb that is home to many artists and potters. Continue on to rural Wonga Park and to the **Kellybrook Winery** and restaurant. Established in 1970 and originally making a name for a wide range of apple champagne ciders, it has 10 hectares (25 acres) under vine, producing (as do all the wineries in the area) pinot noir, cabernet sauvignon, Rhine reisling, chardonnay, shiraz, traminer and merlot. The shiraz is the star—a delightfully peppery "Victorian" taste.

Keeping your map open, drive across Victoria Road, Lilydale, to the **Bianchet Winery**. Founded in 1977 by Lou and Therese Bianchet, this winery is a tiny, but very worthwhile concern, producing a remarkably wide range of wines from such a small estate. Its chardonnay recently won a gold medal at Ballarat against many more famous and well-established wineries, and the recently released derduzzo—a generous, fragrant white burgundy style—is said to be the best in Australia

It is a short drive, through the busy township of Lilydale then north-east along the Maroonda Highway, to Coldstream, where you will see, just as the Yarra Glen Road leaves the Highway, the huge yew hedge that surrounds Coombe Cottage, Dame Nellie Melba's favourite home. A little way further on is **St. Hubert's Wines**. Re-established in 1966, it has 20 hectares (50 acres) under vine and has recently been taken over by the West Australian based firm of Regional Vineyards. The new wine maker, Brian Fletcher, has impressed by producing a brilliant pinot noir. St. Hubert's may also boast about having won the highest point ranking ever in an international show with a near perfect score. The wine, which won a double gold medal in Canada, is the 1985 beerenauslese Rhine Reisling, an elegant dessert wine.

From St. Hubert's, continue through

Left, the lushness of an up-country Victorian vineyard.

strawberry fields and rich pasture land to the idyllic township of Yarra Glen. Seven kilometres (four miles) past Yarra Glen, at Dixon's Creek is **Fergusson's Winery**. Its very stylish cabernet sauvignon has won many awards and the estate also has a rustic restaurant, run by the winemaker's wife, herself a professional chef. Reservations are essential. Also at Dixon's Creek is the **Chateau Yarrinya** winery, recently taken-over by the DeBortoli family, the biggest Australian company in the Yarra Valley. Their chardonnay and pinot are highly recommended, and they specialise in dry table wines made from the "noble" varieties.

If you're a fast mover and haven't overdone the tasting so far, there are other excellent wineries in the immediate area. These include the **Lillydale Vineyards**, which produce a particularly classy chardonnay, is situated in the gorgeous little mountain town of Seville (rather better known for its orange growing than its grapevines). At Yarra Junction, the **Yarra Burn Vineyard** should be visited. It is run by the dynamic Christine and David Fyffe, who produced the valley's first *methode champenoise* in a delicate rosé style, using pinot noir. Their unusually spicy chardonnay, which has been aged in German oak, is certainly worth a try.

As you turn again for Melbourne, think about returning via Monbulk and calling in at the **Monbulk Winery**. Paul and Ruth Jabornik grow a variety of grapes on the red volcanic soil of the mountains, but their particular speciality is their kiwi-fruit wine that they have been making since 1970.

The significance of the Yarra Valley to Victorian winemaking may be gauged by the fact that the French company, Moet et Chandon, have recently bought hundreds of hectares in the area. They plan to produce their famous champagne in a few years time.

A longer excursion, and one which will include an overnight stay—especially if you are a dedicated taster—is 270 kilometres (167 miles) north-east of Melbourne to the state's oldest and most significant winegrowing area. Most of the vineyards are still managed by the descendants of their founders and are much larger concerns than those in the Yarra Valley. The **Rutherglen** area is noted especially for its dark reds and ports, flor sherries and muscats, while the nearby **Millawa-Glenrowan** district is renowned for individual table wines with good body and style. **Buller's Winery** near Rutherglen was established in 1921 and has 32 hectares (79 acres) under vine. Three generations of Bullers in Rutherglen have preserved the estate's traditional style. There are robust reds and a fine range of fortifieds, including vintage ports, but the muscat is the jewel in the crown.

At Glenrowan is **Bailey's of Glenrowan**, widely known for its fortified wines, particularly an excellent muscat. There is also a pleasant picnic area, as well as an old-style cellar. A short distance away is **Taminck Cellars**, estab-

Heavily laden grape vines coming into harvest time.

lished in 1900 and renowned for its sophisticated reds. Beautifully situated, it also offers superb views of the surrounding countryside.

At Milawa, 16 kilometres (10 miles) south of Wangaratta is the renowned **Brown Brothers Milawa Vineyard**. Brown's were the leaders in the renaissance of Australian wines and the first to capture the market with individual varietal table wines—where they are still leaders in the field. Their 1986 chardonnay is particularly well recommended. The estate welcomes guests and there is a tasting room as well as picnic and barbecue facilities—but, with characteristic modesty, they recommend the food at the Old **Emu Gallery** in Milawa. In 1989, Brown Brothers celebrated its centennary.

Not far from Brown Brothers at Oxley is **John Gerhig Wines**, the first of the new "boutique" wineries to be established in the north-east region, although its proprietor is a fourth generation winemaker. His pinot noir and merlot are remarkable, and his champagne, the first commercial one to be grown in the district for 100 years, is very pleasant—and not overpriced. Located on the banks of the King River it is an attractive place for a barbecue.

Sampling the finished product.

The rich river flats of the **Goulburn Valley** are also ideal for table wines and this area, just 122 kilometres (76 miles) north-east of Melbourne, is one of the most picturesque winegrowing areas. Features include the century-old cellars of **Chateau Tahblik** and also **Michelton Winery**, which comprises a winery, vineyard and restaurant on the banks of the Goulburn River. There is also a swimming pool for the overheated but non-inebriated. They make excellent oak-matured marsanne, semillon and chardonnay, all of which show great depth, integration and varietal flavours. Osocka's Vineyard, Walkershire Wines and Longleat Wines are some of the other specialist wineries in the Goulburn region. Longleat in particular is low profile, but most interesting, producing rich, fuller-bodied red table wines in the traditional style, and generous whites.

Two hundred kilometres (124 miles) west of Melbourne is the little town of **Great Western**, famous for its champagnes. If you can only visit one winery here, try the delightful **Best's** run by Viv Thompson. This ancient property is part of the state's winemaking heritage, with its 100-year-old cellars and vineyards, in which some varieties remain from last century. Their hermitage is soft and rich, and the pinot meunier is a classic light-bodied wine. It's imperative to try any sparkling wine that you might see—the chardonnay is fantastic.

And then . . . well, the tippler's tour goes on. And remember: if wine is the mirror of the heart (as Aeschylus thought), keep an eye on the rear-view one too. The most likely view for the unfortunate driver who picked the short straw to drive, not drink, will be of his or her passengers catching a well-deserved nap after a hard day's tasting.

MELBOURNE
FOUNDED
-1864-
BOWLING CLUB

TRAVEL TIPS

GETTING THERE

BY AIR

Melbourne's Tullamarine Airport is 22 kilometres (14 miles) from central Melbourne. All international flights and the vast majority of domestic flights use Tullamarine. Some short haul domestic flights use Essendon Airport which is 11 kilometres (seven miles) from the city centre.

As Australia's second largest city, Melbourne has a large number of domestic flights to the country's major population centres.

Domestic Airlines with flights to and from Melbourne:

Ansett Airlines
489 Swanston St.
Tel: 668 1211
Australian Airlines
294 Collins St.
Tel: 665 3333
East-West Airlines
489 Swanston St.
Tel: 668 1211
Kendell Airlines
489 Swanston St.
Tel: 668 2222

International direct flights from Melbourne:
Melbourne has direct flights to and from the following list of cities; many of those not listed can be reached with a connection through Sydney.

Flights which depart Melbourne:

Air Caledonie International
543 King St.
West Melbourne
Reservations and flight information: 329 8066
to Noumea: Sunday only

Air Nauru
80 Collins St.
Reservations: 653 5209
Flight information: 339 4700
to Nauru Island: Tuesday, Friday

Air New Zealand
154 Swanston St.
Reservations: 654 3311
Flight information: 654 1166
to Auckland: Wednesday, Thursday, Friday, Sunday
to Christchurch: Daily except Thursday

Air Pacific
440 Collins St.
Reservations: 602 6751
Flight information: 602 6122
to Nadi: Tuesday, Thursday, Saturday

Alitalia
143 Queen St.
Reservations: 670 0171
Flight information: 338 2022
to Bombay: Tuesday, Thursday, Saturday
to Rome: Tuesday, Thursday, Saturday
to Singapore: Tuesday, Thursday, Saturday

British Airways
330 Collins St.
Reservations: 602 3000
Flight information: 602 3000
to Bangkok: Friday, Saturday
to Dubai: Tuesday
to London: Tuesday, Friday, Saturday, Sunday

Continental Airlines
13th Floor, 575 Bourke St.
Reservations: 602 4899
Flight information: 602 4899
to Auckland: Monday, Thursday, Saturday
to Honolulu: Daily
to Los Angeles: Daily
to New York: Wednesday, Sunday

Garuda Indonesia
45 Bourke St.
Reservations: 654 4311
Flight information: 602 6122

to Denpasar (Bali): Tuesday, Friday, Saturday, Sunday
to Jakarta: Daily except Monday, Thursday

JAT Yugoslav Airlines
124 Exhibition St.
Reservations: 654 6524
Flight information: 654 6524
to Belgrade: Wednesday, Sunday
to Dubai: Wednesday, Sunday
to Singapore: Wednesday, Sunday

KLM Royal Dutch Airlines
80 Collins St.
Reservations: 654 5111
Flight information: 338 4881
to Abu Dhabi: Friday
to Amsterdam: Friday
to Colombo: Friday

Lufthansa German Airlines
454 Collins St.
Reservations: 602 1155
Flight information: 338 4733
to Bangkok: Monday
to Dubai: Wednesday, Saturday
to Frankfurt: Monday, Wednesday, Saturday
to Kuala Lumpur: Monday, Wednesday, Saturday

Malaysia Airlines
1 Collins St.
Reservations: 654 3255
Flight information: 338 8197
to Kuala Lumpur: Wednesday, Saturday, Sunday

Olympic Airways
84 William St.
Reservations: 602 5699
Flight information: 339 5755
to Athens: Wednesday, Saturday
to Singapore: Wednesday, Saturday

Philippine Airlines
121 William St.
Reservations: 629 1321
Flight information: 602 6122
to Manila: Monday, Wednesday, Friday

Qantas Airways
114 William St.
Reservations: 602 6111
Flight information: 602 6122
to: Amsterdam Thursday
to Athens: Wednesday, Sunday
to Auckland: Daily except Thursday, Friday
to Bahrain: Daily except Thursday, Sunday
to Bangkok: Daily except Monday
to Bombay: Wednesday, Friday, Sunday
to Christchurch: Tuesday, Wednesday, Saturday
to Denpasar (Bali): Friday, Sunday
to Frankfurt: Tuesday, Thursday, Saturday
to Honolulu: Daily
to Jakarta: Thursday
to Kuala Lumpur: Thursday, Saturday
to London: Daily; Twice daily on Wednesday, Friday, Sunday
to Los Angeles: Twice daily except Monday
to Manchester: Tuesday, Thursday, Saturday
to Manila: Tuesday
to Nadi: Tuesday, Thursday, Saturday
to Noumea: Sunday
to Papeete (Tahiti): Wednesday, Friday, Sunday
to Rome: Wednesday, Sunday
to San Francisco: Daily except Tuesday, Saturday
to Singapore: Twice daily except Monday, Friday
to Tokyo: Daily except Thursday, Sunday
to Vancouver: Thursday

Singapore Airlines
1st Floor, 416-420 Collins St.
Reservations: 605 2555
Flight information: 339 5088
to Singapore: Daily

Thai International
60 Market St.
Reservations: 629 6132
Flight information: 602 6122
to Bangkok: Monday, Thursday, Friday, Saturday

BY SEA

The only sea connection with Melbourne is to and from Devonport in Tasmania.

TT-Line's good ship *MV Abel Tasman* is a very comfortable vehicle and passenger ferry with two-, three- and four-berth cabins, some with private facilities. Fares are split

into three seasons with one-way fares starting in the winter at $147 per person (Aug 1988).
Departs Devonport 6 p.m. on Tuesday, Thursday, Sunday.
Arrives Melbourne 8.30 a.m. on Wednesday, Friday, Monday.
Departs Melbourne 6 p.m. Monday, Wednesday, Friday.
Arrives Devonport 8.30 a.m. Tuesday, Thursday, Saturday.
Reservations: Melbourne Tel. (03) 645 2766 Fax. (03) 646 3867
Elsewhere in Australia Tel. (008) 030344 Toll Free.

OVERLAND

Buses: There are a large number of express coach services between Melbourne and other state capitals. The following is a list of the major companies:-

Deluxe Coaches, 58 Franklin St., City (03) 663 6144
Firefly Express, 177 Flinders St., City (03) 654 8788
Greyhound, corner of Franklin & Swanston streets, City (03) 668 2666
Inter-Capital Express, 260 Latrobe St., City (03) 6634900
Pioneer Coachline, corner of Franklin & Swanston streets, City (03) 668 2422
Sunliner Express, 260 Latrobe St., City (03) 663 4900
Trans City Express, 181 Flinders St., City (03) 650 4044

To save time in getting reservations and the cheapest fares, it is possible to contact a travel agency that specialises in Express Coach Travel:-

Interstate Bus Services
Shop 4 Princes Plaza,
Corner of Swanston & Flinders streets.
Melbourne.
Tel: (03) 654 8477
Tollfree from anywhere in Australia: 008 088112

TRAINS

Advanced reservations for seats and sleeping berths are recommended. Long distance train services offer first class and economy class seating and sleeping berths (supplement payable).

Dining cars or buffet cars are provided on all interstate trains. Lounge cars sell liquor and other refreshments.

There are daily train services between Melbourne and:-

Adelaide, Canberra, Mildura and Sydney. Detailed fares and schedules can be obtained by contacting: V/LINE, at Spencer Street Station Tel: 619 1500, or any other railway station in Australia.

The Victorian countryside is easily accessible by train. For example, the traveller can take a train to Glenrowan in the heart of Ned Kelly country.

CARS

The drive to Melbourne is interesting no matter from which direction you approach. The route through the Australian Alps is rugged but spectacular whilst the direct route from Sydney down the Hume Highway goes past some fine wineries in the historic north of Victoria. The renowned drive along The Great Ocean Road from Adelaide passes through some superb coastal scenery, and the long route along the Princes Highway following the coast from Sydney is most rewarding.

ROAD DISTANCES

Melbourne to/from
Sydney via Hume Highway: 869 km
Sydney via Canberra: 931 km
Sydney via Princes Highway: 1045 km
Adelaide via Dukes and
Western Highways: 728 km
Adelaide via
Princes Highway: 918 km
Canberra via Albury: 647 km

Travel Essentials

VISAS & PASSPORTS

Visitors require a passport and visa to enter Australia. Exception is made only for New Zealanders, who require a passport but no visa. Visas are free and valid for up to six months. Applications should be made to the nearest Australian or British Government representative. Visitors must also produce an onward or return ticket and must have sufficient funds for their time in Australia.

MONEY MATTERS

Australia's currency is dollars and cents. Coins come in 1, 2, 5, 10, 20 and 50 cent pieces, as well as $1 and $2 denominations. Notes are $5, $10, $50 and $100. There is no limit to the amount of foreign or Australian currency that you may bring into the country, but you may only take out a maximum of $5,000 in cash.

EXCHANGE RATES

Most foreign currencies can be exchanged at the airport when you arrive. City banks will exchange currencies between 9.30 a.m. and 4 p.m., Monday to Friday. International class hotels will exchange major currencies for guests. It is recommended that you change money at the airport or major city banks as it can be difficult elsewhere. The bank will advise you on current exchange rates. New Zealand dollars are not legal tender.

At the time of writing A$1 buys approx.: $US 0.80; C$ 0.98; $NZ 1.31; UK pounds 0.47; German marks 1.48; French francs 5.04; Japanese yen 107; Swedish kroner 5.12.

CREDIT CARDS

The most widely accepted and recognised are American Express, Diners Club, Mastercard (and its affiliates) and Visa Card (and its affiliates). You may encounter difficulties with lesser known overseas cards.

CHEQUES

All well-known international traveller's cheques are widely used in Australia and can be readily cashed at international airports, banks, hotels, motels and other similar establishments. Offices of Thomas Cook and American Express are in the city centre.

HEALTH

Standards of hygiene in Australia are high, particularly in food preparation. Doctors and dentists are highly trained and hospitals well equipped. Most doctors will make house calls, and a list of doctors and their telephone numbers can be found in the Yellow Pages Telephone Directory under "Medical Practitioners."

DRINKING WATER

It is safe to drink tap water in any Australian town.

INSECTS & PESTS

Melbourne enjoys a cool Mediterranean climate in which mosquitoes have difficulty surviving. Flies are common in Melbourne and Victoria, but otherwise the state is relatively bug free.

SUNBURN

The summer sun is strong in Melbourne, and it is easy to believe that you are not burning on a day with cool air temperatures. A sunscreen or a broad brimmed hat should be worn if you are going to spend more than an hour outdoors.

PRESCRIBED DRUGS

Visitors to Australia may bring up to four weeks' supply of prescribed medications. For large quantities it is necessary to produce a doctor's certificate.

WHAT TO BRING/WEAR

Check the temperature chart (later in this section) before selecting clothes to pack. For Spring and Summer in Melbourne bring light to medium weight clothes and for Autumn and Winter medium weight clothes with some heavier pullovers or jackets. Melbourne can experience all four seasons in one day, so it is prudent to carry a raincoat always...regardless of what the weather forecast says.

Australians are informal dressers, but for special occasions, business meetings, concert halls or dining at better class restaurants, men may need a jacket and tie or suit; women a cocktail dress or smarter designer clothes.

ANIMAL QUARANTINE

Australia is rabies-free and all incoming animals are placed in quarantine. Dogs and cats travelling from England and Europe must spend one month quarantine in England and five months in Australian quarantine. Those from the USA are placed in one month quarantine in Hawaii and four months in Australian quarantine. From the Pacific countries, dogs and cats are placed in Australian quarantine for nine months. For any other type of pet, check with customs in your home country well in advance. In short, forget it.

CUSTOMS

Visitors may bring personal effects into Australia duty free and those over 18 years of age may include 250 cigarettes or 250 grams of cigars or tobacco and 1 litre of alcohol, provided this is carried with them. Other dutiable goods to the value of $400 for adults and $200 for children under 18 years in personal baggage are duty free. Australia has strict regulations on the importation of narcotics, food, plants, animals and their by-products. Heavy penalties apply to drug offences.

BAGGAGE/PORTER SERVICES

There are Left Luggage offices at the airport and at Spencer Street Railway Station. Luggage lockers are available at bus terminals and at the railway stations. The Travellers Aid Society,169 Swanston St., City Tel: 654 2600, also provides a left luggage service.

Porters are thin on the ground at the airport, but if you find one the tip is optional. Railway porters have a fixed charge for carrying bags. The more expensive hotels have porters who won't say no to a tip.

RESERVATIONS

Transit/Transfer: It is important to reconfirm onward reservations within 72 hours of travel. Failure to do so could result in the cancellation of the reservation. The telephone numbers listed at the beginning of this section will connect you with the airline reservations.

EXTENSION OF STAY

To extend your stay, contact the Department of Immigration one month before your visa is due to expire. In order to be granted an extension, you will have to show evidence of sufficient funds and a return air ticket. The maximum time allowed to visitors, including extensions, is one year. Check in the front of the phone book under Immigration Department in the Commonwealth Government listings to find the nearest office. Head office is 190 George St., Sydney, Tel: (02) 258 4555.

ON DEPARTURE

Melbourne Airport is at Tullamarine, 22 kilometres (14 miles) northwest of the city, and is served by Skybus Airport Coach Service (Tel: 663 1400). The bus service leaves 58 Franklin St. in the city at regular intervals for both Domestic and International terminals. The transfer time is 35-40 minutes and the one-way fare is $6 at time of writing. This compares with 30 minutes travel time and a fare of approximately $16 by taxi.

DEPARTURE TAX

There is a Departure Tax of $10 imposed on all international travellers except those under 12 years of age. The tax stamp can be purchased at the airport or a post office.

GETTING ACQUAINTED

GOVERNMENT & THE ECONOMY

Victoria is a State in the Commonwealth of Australia. Melbourne as Victoria's capital is the seat of the State Parliament. Victoria has a bicameral Parliamentary System. A Legislative Assembly of 81 members is elected every three years and a Legislative Council of 40 members every six years. Responsible Parliamentary Government in the State began in 1856, and functions in every legislative sphere, except Defence, Customs, Post and Telegraphs, External Affairs and several minor matters which since Federation (1901) are responsibilities of the Federal Government. The Crown is represented in Victoria by a State Governor appointed by the Sovereign.

Melbourne's economy is based on light and heavy manufacturing industry which is concentrated in the western portion of the city. There is a great deal of wealth (as is evidenced by the mansions of Toorak and Malvern), a legacy from the gold boom of last century.

GEOGRAPHY & POPULATION

Victoria is the smallest mainland State of Australia being 223,712 square kilometres (89,485 square miles), just a little smaller than the United Kingdom's 244,102 square kilometres (97,641 square miles). Melbourne's area is 6,129 square kilometres (2,452 square miles).

Melbourne is home to 2.9 million people (out of Victoria's total of 4.2 million). It is a truly cosmopolitan city, reputed to be the world's third largest Greek city (after Athens and Thessaloniki). It was chosen as the destination within Australia by thousands of Italian, British, Irish, Vietnamese, Lebanese, Polish, Chilean migrants of other nationalities.

TIME ZONES

Melbourne is 10 hours ahead of Greenwich Mean Time, except when Daylight Saving is in place for the summer months (between October and March) when Melbourne is 11 hours ahead of G.M.T. There are three time zones within Australia, and Victoria together with the other eastern States works to Eastern Standard Time which is half an hour ahead of South Australia and Northern Territory, and two hours ahead of Western Australia.

CLIMATE

Melbourne's seasons are the opposite to the Northern Hemisphere's.

Spring
September-November
Summer
December-February
Autumn
March-May
Winter
June-August

Melbourne has a mild temperate climate with the attraction of four distinct seasons.

Generally summer is warm to hot with an average maximum temperature of 26 degrees Celsius and higher for short periods.

Winter is cool with an average maximum of 13 degrees Celsius in the coldest month of July when night temperatures can be cold. Frosts in Melbourne are rare.

Snow falls on the alps only and there is good skiing within three to four hours' drive of Melbourne.

Spring and Autumn are delightful in the Garden City.

Average Temperature and Rainfall

	Average Maximum (Celsius)	Average Minimum (Celsius)	Average Rainfall (mm)
January	26	14	48
February	26	14	50
March	24	13	54
April	20	11	59
May	17	8	57
June	14	7	50
July	13	6	48
August	15	6	49
September	17	8	58
October	20	9	67
November	22	11	59
December	24	13	58

CULTURE & CUSTOMS

Multicultural Melbourne is a treasure trove of different cultures: China Town in Little Bourke Street, Little Vietnam in Victoria Street, Richmond, and an Italian enclave in Lygon Street, Carlton. Almost every religion in the world is represented in Melbourne. One of the largest Jewish communities in the world can be found in and around Caulfield. All of this makes for a rich cultural mix that manifests itself in festivals, dress, food, language and temperament and is evident wherever you go in Melbourne.

WEIGHTS & MEASURES

Australia uses the metric system of weights and measures. For those not familiar with the metric system, the following conversions are offered as a guide:

*25 millimetres (mm) is approximately one inch.
*1 metre (m) is a little more than a yard
*1 kilometre (km) is approximately 5/8 of a mile.
*1 kilogram (kg) equals 2.2 lbs.
*1 litre (l) equals 1.75 pints (UK) and 2.10 pints (US).

*60 kilometres per hour (km/h) is just over 35 mph.
*25 degrees Celsius (C) is a warm 77 Farenheit degrees.

CLOTHING SIZES

Women's dresses and suits

Australian	10	12	14	16	18	20	22
American	8	10	12	14	16	18	20
British	32	34	36	38	40	42	44
Italian	40	42	44	46	48	50	52
French	38	40	42	44	46	48	50
German	36	38	40	42	44	46	48

Men's suits, overcoats and sweaters

Australian	87	92	97	102	107	112	117
American	34	36	38	40	42	44	46
British	34	36	38	40	42	44	46
European	44	46	49	51	54	56	59

Shirts and collars

Australian	36	37	38	39	40	41	42
American	14	14.5	15	15.5	16	16.5	17
British	14	14.5	15	15.5	16	16.5	17
European	36	37	38	39	40	41	42

ELECTRICITY

The domestic electrical supply in Australia is 240 volts, 50 cycles alternating current. Universal outlets for AC 110 volts (Electric razors and small appliances) are available in most hotels. You may need to buy a voltage converter and a special flat three pin adaptor, if your hotel cannot supply one.

BUSINESS & BANKING HOURS

Melbourne shops open from 9 a.m. to 5.30 p.m. from Monday to Thursday, with some of the major stores in the city and the suburbs staying open till 9 p.m. on Thursdays. Most shops stay open late on Friday night (til 9).

On Saturdays most shops stay open from 9 a.m. till 5 p.m., while some close at lunchtime. Very few shops open Sunday.

Banks open from 9.30 a.m. to 4 p.m. Monday to Thursday and until 5 p.m. on Friday. All banks close on Saturdays, Sundays and Public Holidays.

Restaurants, snack bars, bookshops, and corner stores are open till later in the evening and often all weekend. Seven Eleven stores sell a wide range of convenience goods and are open from very early to very late.

Post offices open from 9 a.m. to 5 p.m. Monday to Friday, and close on Saturdays, Sundays and Public Holidays.

PUBLIC HOLIDAYS/FESTIVALS

All banks, post offices, government and private offices, and most shops close on public holidays. Many hotels and restaurants surcharge their tariffs.

January
New Year's Day
the Monday closest to 26 January
Australia Day
first or second Monday in March
Labour Day
April
Good Friday (varies)
Easter Monday (varies)
Easter Tuesday (varies)
25 April
Anzac day
second Monday in June
Queen's Birthday
last Thursday in September
Melbourne Show Day
first Tuesday in November
Melbourne Cup Day
25 December
Christmas Day
26 December
Boxing Day

RELIGIOUS SERVICES

Multicultural Melbourne has every conceivable religious service available. Details of worship times may be found by telephoning numbers in the telephone directory under the name of that religion. The Catholic and Protestant service times are published in *The Age* on a Saturday.

COMMUNICATIONS

POSTAL SERVICES

Australia post offices are open 9 a.m. to 5 p.m. Monday to Friday. The GPO in Bourke Street Mall is open 8 a.m. to 6 p.m. Post Offices will hold mail for visitors (address it to Post Restante at the Post Office nearest to where you will be). Thomas Cook Travel and American Express will also hold mail for clients.

Postal Charges (at time of writing)

	Letter	Postcard
Standard	39¢	37¢
Priority Paid (guaranteed next day delivery)	plus$1.20	
Airmail:		
UK & Europe	$1.00	63¢
Hong Kong and India	70¢	58¢
Singapore, India and Malaysia	65¢	47¢
New Zealand	55¢	42¢

Post Offices also offer electronic mail services:

LETTERGRAM, Lodge up to two pages by telephone or at any Post Office for guaranteed delivery across Australia in two hours or the next working day. Service/information phone: 1291. For more information call 609 4562.

TELEPHONE & TELEX

Public telephones are situated in a wide variety of public places including: hotels, restaurants, shops, stations, and Post Offices. Local calls from a public phone booth cost 30¢ for an unlimited time. STD (Subscriber Trunk Dialling) long distance calls may be made from red or yellow phones. Time charges apply to long distance calls and are cheapest between 10 p.m. and 8 a.m.

International calls can be made through Gold phones. Instructions on how to make international calls and the charge rates may be found in the front of the telephone directory. Most hotel rooms have telephones that can be used for making international calls. The overseas access code is 0011.

Telephone Interpreter Service: 662 3000.

Telegrams and cables can be made through the operator (dial 015) or at the Post Office. Cables can be sent at urgent, ordinary, or letter rate.

Faxpost: Facsimile and delivery service is available from many Post Offices which are listed in the front of the telephone directory under Australia Post. Information about this service can be obtained on (03) 329 5111.

MEDIA

Radio: There are 20 radio stations to choose from, 13 on AM and 7 on FM. Programs are published in daily newspapers with detailed weekly information in Thursday's *Age* and Monday's *Herald*. Radio Australia, the overseas service of the Australian Broadcasting Commission, beams programs worldwide. For details write to Radio Australia, GPO Box 428G, Melbourne, Victoria 3001 .

AM Radio

3AR 621 kHz
In-depth talk with cerebral music. ABC.
3LO 774 kHz
Journalistically based talk with middle-of-the-road music. ABC.
3CR 855 kHz
Community radio.
3UZ 927 kHz
Racing, talk and music.
3TT 1026 kHz
Classic hits of yesterday and today.
3KZ 1179 kHz
Contemporary hits.
3EA 1224 kHz
Ethnic radio.
3AW 1278 kHz
Populist talk. Information based.
3GL 1341 kHz
Local Geelong station, sport, news and music.
3MP 1377 kHz
Easy listening music.
3XY 1422 kHz
Contemporary hits.
3AK 1503 kHz
Contemporary middle-of-the-road music.
3RPH 1629 kHz
Radio for the print handicapped.

FM Radio

RPP 98.7 MHz
Mornington Peninsula local station.
FOX 101.9 MHz
Rock 'n' roll.
RRR 102.7 MHz
Contemporary music.
MBS 103.5 MHz
Classical music.
MMM 105 MHz
Contemporary rock 'n' roll.
ABC 105.9 MHz
Fine classical music.
PBS 106.7 MHz
Wide variety of music.

TELEVISION

There are five television channels (PAL system) available to viewers in Melbourne. Most hotels and motels have colour televisions available in rooms. Programmes are published in daily newspapers, *Australian Visitors News* and *Discover Melbourne* (see Newspapers and other Publications).

Channel 2 ABC (Australian Broadcasting Corporation). A government funded station that offers "quality" television and caters to minority interests with no commercial breaks.

Channel 28 (UHF) SBS. A government

sponsored multicultural TV station, with many subtitled movies, excellent international news, and programs to interest a wide cross section of the migrant population. No commercial breaks.

Channels 7, 9 and 10. These three commercial channels show movies, soap operas, current affairs programs, news, weather and sport with frequent advertising segments. Much of the content is American.

PERIODICALS

Newspapers and magazines can be bought at newsagents, hotels, and kiosks, at railway stations and city street corners.

The Australian is Australia's national daily, but more Melburnians read:-

The Age: Melbourne's quality morning paper.

The Herald is the afternoon paper (if you're ever late to a morning appointment you may be asked why you didn't bring *The Herald*).

The Sun News-Pictorial is a morning daily tabloid.

The Truth is also published in Melbourne, and is known for its photographs of bare-breasted women and its racing form guide. It is printed twice a week.

There are many suburban weekly newspapers, usually delivered free to every home in the area.

Publications of interest to the visitor to Melbourne are:-

Australian Visitors News, a weekly tabloid with a TV guide, map and other useful information about places of interest.

Discover Melbourne, a weekly pocket-size visitor information guide with maps, TV and entertainment guide, as well as information on tours, restaurants, and accommodation.

This week in Melbourne, a general weekly tourist information magazine.

These three publications are free of charge, and available at hotels, tourist attractions, and tourist information centres.

Pedestrian Guide to Melbourne is available from Melbourne Town Hall, on the corner of Swanston and Collins streets.

LIBRARY

The State Library of Victoria is a magnificent Victorian building in Swanston Street (03) 669 9888. It has a comprehensive collection of books and historic documents. Open: 1 p.m. to 9 p.m. on Monday, 10 a.m. to 9 p.m. Tuesday to Thursday, 10 a.m. to 6 p.m. Friday, Saturday, Sunday and public holidays.

Closed on Christmas Day (December 25), ANZAC Day (April 25).

Good Friday (date varies from year to year).

There are many suburban libraries, and university libraries which can be used for reference by the public. Borrowing books, magazines, videos, audio tapes, toys and equipment is possible on production of proof of residence or in the case of an educational institution, proof of being a student.

EMERGENCIES

Melbourne is a relatively "safe" city to visit. There are no "no-go" areas, but as with all large cities, women, in particular, should excercise caution walking alone after dark.

If you face an emergency, find a telephone and dial 000 for connection to Police, Fire or Ambulance.

SECURITY & CRIME

General Police: Telephone Russell Street, City Tel: 667 1911.
General Fire: Brigade enquiries Tel: 662 2311.
Missing Children: 762 1592.
Rape Emergency: Queen Victoria Medical Centre Tel: 665 5111.

COUNSELLING

Life Line Centre: For anyone who can't cope, who needs someone to help Tel: 662 1000.
Gay Line: Homosexual Telephone Counselling Service Tel: 329 5555.
Interpreter Service: Tourist help, 24-hour free service, 102 languages. Call 662 3000.

MEDICAL SERVICES

Poisons Information: call 345 5678.
Dental Emergency Service: 41 0222
Emergency Road Service R.A.C.V: 540 2211
Alcohol and Drug Problems: 614 19
Chiropractic Emergency Service: 1000
Pharmacy Day and Night:
Ian Herbert, 449 Swanston St., City 6704; Leonard Long, corner of Wil Road & High Street, Prahran 51 397.

GETTING AROUND

ORIENTATION

ON MELBOURNE:
Victour, 230 Collins St.,
City. Tel: (03) 619 9444.

The Melbourne Tourism Authority
20th Floor, Nauru House, 80 Collins St.
City. (03) 654 2288

The Travellers Aid Society
2nd Floor,169 Swanston St., City. (03) 654 2600. And at Spencer Street Station.

This organisation offers showers, lockers, snack bar, lounge, pusher hire, baby changing and feeding facilities, and gold phones in its Swanston Street branch at modest fees. They can also arrange for elderly or disabled travellers to be met. Open Monday to Friday 8 a.m. to 6 p.m., and Saturday and Sunday 10 a.m. to 4 p.m. for information and advice.

The Melbourne Telephone Directory contains much information of interest in the Information Services pages, including Leisureline (11671) to keep the visitor informed of current happenings.

ON AUSTRALIA
Australian Tourist Commission
Level 3, 80 William St.
Woolloomooloo, Sydney 2011
Tel: (02) 360 1111
Fax: (02) 331 6469
Telex: 22322

ON CANBERRA:
Canberra Tourist Bureau
247 Collins St.
Melbourne 3000
Tel: (03) 654 5088
Telex: 22785

ON N.S.W.
The Travel Centre of NSW
353 Little Collins St., Melbourne 3000
Tel: (03) 670 7461
Fax: (03) 642 1260
Telex: 32240 GOVTOUR

ON NORTHERN TERRITORY
Northern Territory Government Tourist Bureau
415 Bourke St., Melbourne 3000
Tel: (03) 670 6948
Telex: 31450

ON QUEENSLAND
Queensland Tourist and Travel Corporation
257 Collins St.
Melbourne 3000
Tel: (03) 654 3866
Fax: (03) 650 1847
Telex: 30200

ON SOUTH AUSTRALIA
South Australia Government Travel Centre
25 Elizabeth St., Melbourne 3000
Tel: (03) 614 6522.
Fax: (03) 614 6967
Telex: Satour 82487

ON TASMANIA
Tasbureau, 256 Collins St., Melbourne
Tel: (03) 653 7999
Fax: (03) 650 4421
Telex: 30165

ON WESTERN AUSTRALIA
WA Tourist Centre Melbourne
33 Elizabeth St., Melbourne 3000
Tel: (03) 614 6833
Fax: (03) 614 1346
Telex: (03) AA32147

FROM THE AIRPORT

Major **car rental** companies have desks at the airport. Advanced reservations should be made to ensure that there will be a car available. **Taxi cabs** ranks are outside both international and domestic terminals. The ride to the city takes about 30 minutes at a cost of about $16. Skybus **Airport Coach Service** takes only a little longer to drive to the city at a cost of $6. The city terminal is at 58 Franklin St., Melbourne. Tel: 663 1400.

DOMESTIC TRAVEL

As the smallest mainland state, Victoria has few intra state flights. Kendell Airlines has flights to such places as Mildura in the far north west corner of Victoria, but otherwise most of the flights out of Melbourne are to major cities in other states.

THE METROPOLITAN TRANSIT AUTHORITY (THE MET)

The Met is Australia's largest public transport system. It is an efficient, integrated system that brings buses, trains and trams together in a way that allows one ticket to be used on all three modes of transport. The Met ticket gives the right to travel for a period of time in a particular area and enables the passenger to transfer from train to tram to bus without the need for separate tickets. It is possible to take unlimited rides around Melbourne and its inner suburbs for a whole day using trams, buses and trains for just $2.40 (at the time of publication). Other tickets will give the passenger two-hour unlimited travel within an area and others like the Anywhere Card give a wider geographic range. Weekly cards are also available. Information is available from the Met Kiosk in Royal Arcade, or any rail station, bus or tram depot. Alternatively, telephone: 617 0900.

WATER TRANSPORT

There are many opportunities to travel by water in Melbourne.

There are sightseeing cruises up the Yarra River that depart from Princes Bridge (Tel: 32 2054). Boats that cruise the lower Yarra River and Williamstown Bay depart from the World Trade Centre. Station Pier in Port Melbourne is the departure point for Port Phillip Bay cruises, and for steam enthusiasts there are Steam-Tug Cruises from North Wharf, Port of Melbourne.

PUBLIC TRANSPORT

Bus: The red and white Explorer Bus runs at hourly intervals from Flinders Street Station on a 50-minute journey around Melbourne's landmarks. It runs every hour from 10 a.m. to 4 p.m. every day except Mondays at a cost of $8 for adults and $4 for children. Passengers may get off and rejoin along the route.

TAXIS

Taxis operate all hours. The three ways of securing the services of a taxi are:-

i) Hail a cab in the street.

ii) Go to a taxi rank (at most major intersections in the city, at hotels, and at transport terminals).

iii) Telephone a cab (30¢ surcharge) by ringing:-

Arrow Taxis: 417 1111
Astoria Taxis: 347 5511
Embassy Taxis: 320 0320
Regal Combined Taxis: 810 0222
Silver Top Taxis: 345 3455
Yellow Cabs: 810 0222

If the taxi dome light is illuminated, the taxi is for hire. Two tariffs apply, a daytime tariff (Flagfall $1.90 plus 10¢ each 177 metres), and a higher tariff ($2.90 flagfall plus 10¢ each 148 metres) which applies between 8 p.m. and 6 a.m. during the working week and from 1 p.m. on Saturday afternoon till 6 a.m. on Monday morning.

PEDICABS

Pedicabs Australia operate colourful three-wheel pedicabs in and around the city. They can be hired at the main rank in Bourke Street Mall or telephoned on 663 2746 ($2 booking charge).

Pedicabs can be hired by the hour or for a complete tour.

PRIVATE TRANSPORT

Car: Because of a draughtsman's error Melbourne streets are twice as wide as was planned which makes Melbourne a joy to drive in.

There is, however, a unique driving rule that has visitors to Melbourne baffled when they first encounter it: at the major intersections in the heart of the city if a motorist wishes to turn right he must pull over to the **left** hand lane and wait for the lights to turn amber before making the turn. These intersections are marked by overhead signs. The rule has a sound logic in a city with trams, but it is hard for new-comers to see this at first.

Motorists may not overtake a stationary tram unless directed to do so by police or a uniformed employee of the Met, and then only on the left hand side of the tram at no more than 10 km per hour (6 mph).

When turning left off a major road, motorists must give way to oncoming traffic wishing to turn right.

If possible the city should be avoided between 8 a.m. and 9.30 a.m. and again between 4 p.m. and 6 p.m. when police control every major intersection and will not allow any left or right turns.

60 km per hour (37 mph) is the maximum speed permitted within the city limits. In the country the limit is 100 km per hour (62 mph) except where indicated otherwise, such as on freeways where the limit may rise to 110 km per hour (68 mph). Further details on the Rules of the Road can be found in the *Victorian Road Traffic Handbook* which can be bought ($2.10) from bookshops and Road Traffic Authority offices.

The Royal Automobile Club (Tel: 700 2211) will come, at no cost, to the aid of motorists who belong to a motoring organisation with reciprocal agreements.

There are plenty of parking metres in the city (thev eat 10¢ and 20¢ coins), but there are also plenty of cars, so that people have to resort to the more expensive and less convenient multi-storeyed car parks.

LIMOUSINE SERVICES

The following companies offer large, chauffeur-driven luxury cars at rates that are established by arrangement (higher than taxis):-

Astra Hire Cars: 489 7777
Budget Chauffeur Drive: 320 6161
Hughes Chauffeured Limousines: 646 1550

BICYCLES

Melbourne has more than 110 kilometres (68 miles) of cycle track, including the Bayside Track and The Yarra River Track, both highly recommended.

Bikes can be hired at:-
Yarra Bank at Princes Bridge (near the Arts Centre). Tel: 288 5177
Como Park at the corner of Williams Road and Alexandra Avenue. Tel: 527 6340
St. Kilda Pier at St. Kilda. Tel: 818 2871

20 Tours are outlined in The Bicycle Institute of Victoria's Melbourne Bike Tours.

ON FOOT

The fact that Melbourne is reasonably flat and has a temperate climate makes it a suitable city for walking. What makes it ideal is the River Yarra, the bay and the many parks, gardens and cycle tracks (that double as walking tracks). There are 90-minute guided Heritage Walks (Tel: 241 1085) or the National Trust at Tasma Terrace have pamphlets outlining walks.

HITCHIKING

Hitching is not permitted in Victoria and police will move offenders on in a friendly way, but have never been known to press charges.

COMPLAINTS

Complaints regarding transport should first of all be taken up with the operator and if satisfaction is not given there, reported to:-

Consumer Affairs
500 Bourke St.
Melbourne
Tel: 602 8123

WHERE TO STAY

Australia has no official classification system for accommodation. This guide has graded the various types of accommodation into the following standards:

Superior: Quality, first class and deluxe establishments with international standard amenities. These are the finest hotels and motels in Melbourne.

Moderate: Covers a range of properties with comfortable, clean rooms and suites. Levels of services will vary with price and location.

Budget: Clean and simply furnished, these properties have modest facilities. Suitable for the younger or more economy-minded traveller.

In Australia a hotel must provide a public bar, and pubs are often referred to as hotels; hence our category Tourist Hotels. Motels on the other hand are not obliged to have bar areas, although some do, but only for guests and invited guests and friends.

Advance reservations are recommended in Melbourne, especially during the week when business bookings are heavy. If you are going to arrive after 6 p.m., telephone ahead to prevent the room from being released. Check-in is from 11 a.m. on, and check-out at 10 a.m.

HOTELS

Superior

Chateau Melbourne
131 Lonsdale St., Melbourne 3000
Tel: 03-663 3161
Central
Room only 1-2 persons $A140

Hilton International
192 Wellington Parade, East Melbourne 3000
Tel: 03-419 3311
1 km from downtown
Room only 1 person $A185
2 persons A$205

Hotel Windsor
103-115 Spring St., Melbourne 3000
Tel: 03-630 0261
Central
Room only 1 person A$185, 2 person A$215

Hyatt on Collins
123 Collins St., Melbourne 3000
Tel: 03-657 1234
Central
Room only 1-2 person A$240-A$300

Menzies at Rialto
495 Collins St., Melbourne 3000
Tel: 03-620111
Central
Room only 1-2 persons A$190

Noah's Melbourne
Corner of Little Bourke & Exhibition streets, Melbourne 3000
Tel: 03-662 0511
Central
Room only 1-2 persons A$116

Park Royal on St. Kilda Road
562 St. Kilda Road, Melbourne 3004
Tel: 03-529 8888
Two kilometres from downtown
Room only 1-2 persons A$163

Regent of Melbourne
25 Collins St., Melbourne 3000
Tel: 03-630 321
Central
Room only 1-2 persons A$215

Rockman's Regency
Corner of Exhibition & Lonsdale streets. Melbourne 3000
Tel: 03-662 3900
Central
Room only 1-2 persons A$135-A$215

Settlers Old Melbourne
5-17 Flemington Road, North Melbourne 3051

Tel: 03-329 9344
One kilometre from downtown
Room only 1 person A$140, 2 persons A$150

Southern Cross
131 Exhibition St., Melbourne 3000
Tel: 03-653 0221
Central
Room only 1 person A$155, 2 persons A$175

Travelodge
St. Kilda, corner of St. Kilda Road & Park Street. South Melbourne 3000
Tel: 03-699 4833
Two kilometres from downtown
Room only 1-2 persons A$135

The Winsdor
Corner of Spring and Little Collins streets. Melbourne 3000
Tel: 03-653 0653
Central
Room only 1-2 persons A$185-A$245

Moderate

Victoria
215 Little Collins St., Melbourne 3000
Tel: 03-653 0441
Central
Room only 1-2 persons A$58-A$65

Budget

Kingsgate
131 King St., Melbourne 3000
Tel: 03-629 4171
Central
Room only 1-2 persons A$34-A$46

MOTELS

Superior

Melbourne Airport Travelodge
Melbourne Airport. Melbourne 3045
Tel: 03-338 2322
18 kilometres (11 miles) from downtown
Room only 1-2 persons A$124

Royal Parade Travelodge
441 Royal Parade, Parkville 3052
Tel: 03-380 9221
Two kilometres from downtown
Room only 1-2 persons A$90

Town House
701 Swanston St., Carlton 3000
Tel: 03-347 7811
Central
Room only 1-2 persons A$88-A$95

Moderate

City Park
308 Kingsway, South Melbourne 3205
Tel: 03-699 9811
Three kilometres from downtown
Room only 1-2 persons A$85-A$95

Elizabeth Tower
792 Elizabeth St., Melbourne 3000
Tel: 03-347 9211
Central
Room only 1-2 persons A$80-A$88

Lygon Lodge
220 Lygon St., Carlton 3053
Tel: 03-663 6633
One kilometre from downtown
Room only 1-2 persons A$66

Treasury Motor Lodge
Corner Albert & Powlett streets, East Melbourne 3002
Tel: 03-417 5281
Two kilometres from downtown
Room only 1-2 persons A$52-A$57

Budget

Domain Motel
52 Darling St., South Yarra 3141
Tel: 03-266 3701
Five kilometres (three miles) from downtown
Room only 1-2 persons A$49-A$65

Spencer Motel/Hotel
44 Spencer St., Melbourne 3000
Tel: 03-626 991
One kilometre from downtown
Room only 1-2 persons A$44-A$56

APARTMENTS

Superior (serviced)

Gordon
24-32 Little Bourke St., Melbourne 3000
Tel: 03-663 5355
Central
Room only 1-2 persons A$160-A$210

South Yarra Hill Suites
14 Murphy St., South Yarra 3141
Tel: 03-268 8222
Five kilometres (three miles) from downtown
Room only 1-2 persons A$100-A$140

Moderate (serviced)

Albert Heights
83 Albert St., East Melbourne 3002
Tel: 03-419 0955
One kilometre from downtown
Room only 1-2 persons A$60-A$65

Aston Apartments
42 Powell St., South Yarra 3141
Tel: 03-266 2953
Four kilometres (2.5 miles) from downtown
Room only 1-2 persons A$56

City Gardens Holiday Apartments
335 Abbotsford St., North Melbourne 3051
Tel: 03-320 6600
Two kilometres from downtown
Room only 1-2 persons A$80-A$90

South Yarra Place
41 Margaret St., South Yarra 3141
Tel: 03-267 6595
Three kilometres from downtown
Room only 1-2 persons A$48-A$61

Budget

Da Vinci Backpackers Flats
12 Burnett St., St. Kilda 3182
Tel: 03-534 2888
Three kilometres from downtown

CAMPGROUNDS

Melbourne has a dozen or so campsites but none of them are close to the city. The most centrally situated:

Footscray Caravan Park
163 Somerville Rd
Footscray 3011
Tel: 03-314 6646
No camping, on-site vans
A$14 for 2 persons

Melbourne Caravan Park
265 Elizabeth St
Coburg East 3058
Tel: 03-354 3533
10 km north of city
camping from A$5
on-site vans from A$7

INNS

Moderate

City Limits Inn
20 Little Bourke St.
Melbourne 3000
Tel: 03-662 2544
Central
Room only 1-2 persons A$64-A$76

Flagstaff City Motor Inn
45 Dudley St
Melbourne 3000
Tel: 03-329 5788
Central
Room only 1-2 persons A$56-A$62

Ramada Inn
539 Royal Pde
Parkville 3052
Tel: 03-380 8131
3 km from downtown
Room only 1-2 persons A$52-A$57

Travel Inn
Corner of Grattan & Drummond streets.
Carlton 3053
Tel: 03-347 7922

2 km from downtown
Room only 1-2 persons A$58-A$63

Budget

Backpackers City Inn
197 Bourke St.
Melbourne 3000
Tel: 03-650 5160
Dormitory/rooms available

Centre City Travel Inn
500 Flinders St.
Melbourne 3000
Tel: 03-625 015
1 km from downtown
Room 1-2 persons A$52-A$62
Extra persons A$6

Melbourne Travellers' Inn & Backpackers Centre
2 Enfield St.
St. Kilda 3182
Tel: 03-534 8159
3 km from downtown
Dormitory A$10
Room 1-2 persons A$14-A$24

Park Squire Motor Inn
94 Flemington Rd.
Parkville 3052
Tel: 03-329 6077
3 km from downtown
Room 1-2 persons A$50-A$55

YOUTH HOSTELS

Budget

Melbourne Youth Hostel
500 Abbotsford St.
North Melbourne 3051
Tel: 03-328 2880
Room 1 person $A11 YHA Members

Travel Lodges

City Lodge
235 King St.
Melbourne 3000
Tel: 03-670 6679
Central. Basic and cheap.

HOST FARMS

Various in Countryside Victoria, contact:
Host Farms Association
7 Abbott St.
North Balwyn 3104
Tel: 03-857 6767

This Association has a booklet describing country farm accommodation available in Victoria.

HOME STAYS

Various Australian Home Accommodation
Suite 4, 209 Toorak Road
South Yarra
Tel: 03-241 3694

Stay with an Australian Family

FOOD DIGEST

WHAT TO EAT

Melbourne is without a doubt Australia's culinary capital. The Melbourne Yellow Pages telephone directory has 26 pages of restaurants to prove it. The BYO (bring your own) licence system allows patrons to drink their own liquor with their meal. The result is a considerable saving in meal expenses, since it is rare to be charged corkage.

There are restaurants all around the city and there are some distinct national quarters such as:-

Acland Street, St. Kilda is famous for its decadent European cake and coffee shops some of which also serve goulashes and grills.

Lygon Street, Carlton is the place for Italian food.

Swan Street, Richmond and **Lonsdale Street** in the city for Greek food.

Victoria Street, Richmond for Vietnamese restaurants.

Brunswick Street, Fitzroy for Ethiopian, Indian and Afghani food.

Little Bourke Street for Chinese food. *Dim Sum* is a must.

The *Age Good Food Guide* is the most comprehensive guide to eating out in Melbourne and is available from bookshops. *Cheap Eats* is another good reference for the budget conscious.

Australian

Colonial Tramcar
254 Bay St.
Brighton
Tel:596 6500. Licensed.

A unique Melbourne experience: dine in an elegant tramcar (Expensive).

Jimmy Watson's
Lygon Street
Carlton
Tel: 347 3985

A Melbourne institution, informal and inexpensive eating near the University. Licensed Wine Bar.

Chinese

Flower Drum
103 Little Bourke St.
City.
Tel: 663 2531. Licensed.

Considered to be the best Chinese restaurant, and is also among the most expensive.

Taihu Restaurant
23-25 Tattersalls Lane
Tel: 663 6569.

Specialising in Szechuan, Beijing and Jiansu cuisine (Inexpensive).

Asian Food Plaza
196 Russell St.
Tel:663 3536. BYO.

Orchids Garden Restaurant
119 Little Bourke St.
Tel: 662 3591. Licensed.

Deli Eating

Bourke Street Diner
40 Bourke St.
City
Tel: 663 5030.

Old Paper Shop Deli
266 Clarendon St.
South Melbourne
Tel: 690 6702.

French

Fanny's
243 Lonsdale St.
City
Tel: 663 3017. Licensed.

Rated very highly.

Mietta's
7 Alfred Place
City
Tel: 654 2366. Licensed.

Considered by many to be Melbourne's finest restaurant. (Expensive).

Rogalsky's
442 Clarendon St.
South Melbourne
Tel: 690 1977. Licensed.

Stephanie's
405 Tooronga Road
Hawthorn East
Tel: 20 8944. Licensed.
Rated the BEST MELBOURNE RESTAURANT in 1988 by *The Age Good Food Guide*. A bit way out of the city, but worth it.

Greek

Jim's Greek Restaurant
32 Johnston St.
Collingwood
Tel: 419 3827.

Mandalis Taverna
1030 High St.
Armadale
Tel: 5097274.

The Greek Inn
105 Clarendon St.
South Melbourne
Tel: 90 5684. BYO.

Italian

Alfio's
164 Toorak Road
South Yarra
Tel: 241 8545. BYO.

Cafe Maximus and Rosati's
Acland Street
St. Kilda.

Society
23 Bourke St.
City
Tel: 654 5378. Licensed.
Moderately priced.

Indian

Rajah Sahib
23 Bank Place
City.
Tel: 670 5521. BYO.

The Empress of India
466 Swanson St.
Carlton
Tel: 347 8555. BYO.

Japanese

Kenzan
45 Collins St.
City.
Tel: 654 8933. Licensed.

The Shogun Japanese Restaurant
Coverlid Place
City.
Tel: 662 2471. Licensed.

Lebanese

Lebanese House Restaurant
268 Russell St.
City
Tel: 662 2230. BYO.

Alba's
109 Elgin St.
Carlton.
Tel: 347 0006

Malaysian
Malaya
30 Crossley St.
City.
Tel: 662 1305. Licensed.
A simple, inexpensive restaurant with a wide selection of excellent dishes.

Pub Food

Black Prince Hotel
99 Curzon St.
North Melbourne
Tel: 329 6120. Bistro Style.

The Palace Hotel
893 Burke Road
Camberwell
Tel: 813 3566
Regarded by locals as one of the best food bargains in Melbourne.

Victoria Hotel
123 Beaconsfield Parade

Albert Park
Tel: 690 3666

Seafood

Ilios
174 Lygon St.
Carlton
Tel: 663 6555. BYO.
Melbourne's premier Greek restaurant.

Melbourne Oyster Bar and Seafood Restaurant
209 King St.
City
Tel: 670 1881. Licensed.

Fish Exchange
349 Flinders Lane
City,
Tel: 62 7808. Licensed.

Jean-Jacques By The Sea
St. Kilda Seafront
Tel: 534 6528.
A La Carte and Take Away, BYO.

Steakhouse

Vlado's
61 Bridge Road
Richmond
Tel: 428 5833. BYO.
A unique restaurant for carnivores.

Theatre Restaurants

There are a number of these in Melbourne and its suburbs. Here are three worth a visit:

Bull'N Bush and Naughty Nineties
675 Glenferrie Road
Hawthorn
Tel: 818 7567. BYO.
Four-course meal and musical comedy.

Dirty Dick's Elizabethan Rooms
23 Queens Road
City
Tel: 267 4788.
Licensed Bawdy comedy with traditional English food.

Last Laugh
64 Smith St.
Collingwood
Tel: 419 8600.
Licensed. Good food and live comedy.

24-Hour Food

Fast Eddys Cafe
32-38 Bourke St.
City
Tel: 662 3551.
BYO. 24 hours a day and seven days a week with a full menu.

Vegetarian

The Wholemeal
52 Collins St.
City
Tel: 631 596. BYO.

Shakahari Vegetarian Restaurant
329 Lygon St.
Carlton
Tel: 347 3848. BYO.

Vietnamese

Que-Huong
176 Bridge Road
Richmond
Tel: 429 1213. BYO.

DRINKING NOTES

Licensing laws in Victoria have recently been relaxed to allow liquor to be served at times convenient to the license holder with the result that you can get a drink pretty well around the clock. Some pubs stay open through the night and close for the day while others cater to the morning drinker and keep shop hours. However most pubs close sometime between 10.30 p.m. and midnight and reopen in the morning.

The minimum age for the independent consumption of alcohol is 18 years, but people younger than this may drink if in the company of their parents or guardians.

Beer in pubs is sold in jugs, which contain over four glasses, "Pots" which are 10 oz glasses and glasses which contain 7 oz.

The larger hotels have comfortable and

expensive bars. Two worthy of note are:-

The Cricketers Bar in the Windsor Hotel, Spring Street which is decorated with mementos from cricketing history.

The News Bar at the Regent Hotel, Collins Street is an interesting place to drink beside the newsmakers.

Some pubs of note are:-

The Loaded Dog, 324 St. George's Road, North Carlton, where they serve a variety of ales that they brew on the premises. Live music (loud) is another feature of this interesting pub.

The Sherlock Holmes Inn at 415 Collins St. is a fun place to meet friends for a drink.

Young and Jacksons, opposite Flinders Street Station is a pub where you can take a drink upstairs while admiring the well-proportioned, naked form of Chloe, Melbourne's most famous painting.

The Red Eagle at 111 Victoria Ave., Albert Park is an interesting meeting place with good food available.

THINGS TO DO

The following lists are a selection of the better known tourist sites in and around Melbourne. Prices were correct at the time of publication but telephone numbers are supplied so that entry times and prices can be checked.

HISTORICAL LANDMARKS

Como House
Como Avenue, South Yarra
Tel: 241 2500
Hours: 10 a.m. - 5 p.m. Monday - Sunday
Cost: $4 Adults
$2 Child
$2.60 Concession
$9 Family
Closed: Good Friday and Christmas Day.

Built in 1855 and set in five acres of gardens. Como is an elegant colonial mansion classified by the National Trust.
How to get there: catch tram no. 8 from Swanston Street. Alight stop no. 30 (Toorak Road). Walk down Como Avenue.

Captain Cook's Cottage
Fitzroy Gardens, Melbourne
Tel: 419 8742
Hours: 9 a.m. - 5.15 p.m. daily
Cost: $1 Adult
$0.40 Child
Pensioners Free

Original house of the parents of the discoverer of the east coast of Australia. This cottage was brought from Great Ayton, Yorkshire, England in 1934.

How to get there: catch tram no. 75 along Flinders Street. Alight stop no. 14A. Walk through gardens.

Polly Woodside
Corner of Normanby & Phayer streets, South Melbourne
Tel: 699 9760
Hours: 10 a.m. - 4 p.m. Monday - Friday
noon - 5 p.m. Saturday - Sunday
Cost: $5 Adults
$2 Child
$3 Concession
$10 Family
Closed: Christmas Day and Good Friday.

The Polly Woodside is a deepwater commercial square-rigged sailing ship built in 1885 and is the last of its kind still afloat in Australia.

How to get there: Catch tram no. 10 along Collins Street, tram turns down Clarendon Street. Alight stop no. 15, walk west along Yarra Bank Road.

La Trobe's Cottage
Birdwood Avenue, South Yarra
Tel: 654 5528
Hours: 11 a.m. - 4.30 p.m.
Saturday - Thursday
Cost: $2.50 Adults
$1.50 Child/Pensioner
Closed: Friday

One of the earliest surviving timber portable houses, this is the restored residence of Victoria's first Lieutenant General.

How to get there: catch tram no. 8 from Swanston Street. Alight stop no. 19 in Toorak Road.

Old Melbourne Gaol
Russell Street, Melbourne
Tel: 663 7228
Hours: 10 a.m. - 4.30 p.m. daily
Cost: $3.50 Adults
$1.70 Child
$2.60 Pensioner
$9 Family

Built between 1841 and 1864, this gaol remained in use until 1929 and serves as a grim reminder of early convict days. Best known as the place where Ned Kelly was hanged in 1880.

How to get there: catch any tram along Swanston Street. Alight Latrobe Street. Walk one block to Russell Street.

Rippon Lea
192 Hotham St., Elsternwick
Tel: 523 9150
Hours: 10 a.m. - 5 p.m. daily (mid-June)
11.30 a.m. - 3 p.m. Wednesday - Friday (mid-August)
10 a.m. - 5 p.m. Weekends
Cost: $4 Adults
$2 Child
$2.60 Concession

Built in 1868 by Sir Fredrick Sargood, this 15-room Romanesque-style house still retains 5.26 hectares (13 acres) of beautiful gardens.

How to get there: catch Sandringham train from Flinders Street Station to Rippon Lea Station, walk east along Glen Eira Road to Hotham Street.

Shrine of Remembrance
Between Domain and St. Kilda roads, Melbourne.
Tel: 654 8415
Hours: 10 a.m. - 5 p.m. daily
Cost: Free

State of Victoria's war memorial built to honour Australia's war dead.

How to get there: catch any tram along Swanston Street. Alight stop no. 12 in St. Kilda Road.

Parliament House
Spring Street, Melbourne
Tel: 651 8911
Hours*: 10 a.m., 11 a.m., 2 p.m. (out of session)
11 a.m., 3 p.m. (in session)
*Guided Tours Only
Cost: Free

House of Victorian Legislative Council and Legislative Assembly. Built in 1856.

How to get there: Catch any tram along Bourke Street. Alight Spring Street.

PARKS AND GARDENS

Albert Park Lake
Albert Road, Albert Park
Tel: 51 5588
Hours: open 24 hours
Cost: Free

Great for biking, jogging and picnicking.

How to get there: catch tram no. 55 travelling north along William Street. Alight at stop no. 23.

Carlton Gardens
Bounded by Nicholson & Rathdowne streets & Victoria Parade.
Hours: open 24 hours
Cost: Free

Features superb trees and Royal Exhibition Buildings built in 1880.

How to get there: catch tram no. 96 along Bourke Street. Alight stop no. 10 in Nicholson Street.

Flagstaff Gardens
Bounded by King, Latrobe and William streets, Melbourne
Hours: open 24 hours
Cost: Free

Surrounded by historic buildings.

How to get there: catch tram no. 55/56 along William Street. Alight corner Latrobe & William streets.

Fitzroy & Treasury Gardens
Bounded by Spring, Wellington, Clarendon, Albert & Lansdown streets, Melbourne
Tel: 658 9800
Hours: open 24 hours
Cost: Free

This is where you will find Captain Cook's Cottage, J.F. Kennedy's memorial, the conservatory and Fairy Tree.

Kings Domain
Includes Alexandra & Queen
Victoria Gardens.
Hours: open 24 hours
Cost: Free

You will find the Floral Clock and Pioneer Woman's Memorial Garden, also the home to the Sidney Myer Music Bowl.

How to get there: catch tram no.15 along St. Kilda Road (Swanston Street). Alight stop no. 12.

Royal Botanic Gardens
Between Alexandra & Domain Roads, South Yarra.
Tel: 63 9424
Hours: 7 a.m. - Dusk, Monday - Saturday
8.30 a.m. - Dusk, Sunday (Summer Months)
7.30 a.m. - Dusk, Monday - Saturday
9 a.m. - Dusk, Sunday (Winter Months)

How to get there: catch tram no. 8 along St. Kilda Road (Swanston Street). Alight stop no. 21.

Craft Cottage (Botanic Gardens)
Hours: 10 a.m. - 3 p.m. daily
Cost: Free
Closed: Public Holidays

Covering 41 hectares (101 acres) of gardens. Over 12,000 species of native and exotic plants. Recognised as one of the best botanic gardens in the world.

OTHER ATTRACTIONS

Royal Melbourne Zoo
Elliot Street, Parkville
Tel: 347 1522
Hours: 10 a.m. - 5 p.m. daily
Cost: $5.50 Adults
$2.65 Child/Pensioner

Melbourne's zoo rates third in the world. More than 300 species of native and exotic animals in a beautiful 24-hectare (60-acre) garden setting. How to get there: catch tram No. 55 along William Street. Alight stop No. 23 behind zoo.

Victorian Arts Centre
100 St. Kilda Road, Melbourne
Tel: 617 8211

TOURS

Arts Centre/Concert Hall:
Hours: 10.30 a.m. onwards - daily
Cost: $3 Adult
$2 Child/Pensioner

Backstage:
Hours: Sunday only - ring for tour time
Tel: 617 8151
Cost: $7 per person (no concession)

Tour runs for 1.5 hours.

Works of Art:
Hours: ring for tour time Tel: 617 8151
Cost: $5 Adults (includes refreshments)
$3.50 Concession.

Special Package Tours:
Hours: tours run every day - ring for tour time.

Tel: 617 8211
Cost: $59 - $75 (depending on show)
Tour includes:- Tour, Dinner, Show.

MARKETS

Camberwell Market
Located in the car park opposite Target, Union Street, Camberwell.
Hours: 6 a.m. - 1.30 p.m. Sundays
A popular Sunday market selling a variety of arts/crafts and second-hand goods.

Dandenong Market
Corner of Cleeland & Clow streets, Dandenong
Tel: 791 6500
Hours: Tuesday, Friday, Saturday mornings
Historic general produce market—also wide range of consumer goods, Trash & Treasure type auction every Tuesday.

Dingley Village Craft Market
Marcus Road, Dingley
Tel: 551 6275
Hours: First Sunday of every month 9 a.m. - 2 p.m.
Attracts the best of Victoria's craft people and displays of their work.

Melbourne West End Market
47 McIntyre Road, Sunshine
Tel: 312 3366
Hours: Saturday & Sunday 8.30 a.m. - 5.30 p.m.
600 stalls undercover, and food halls. Bargains, food, fun and wonderful multicultural atmosphere.

Moonee Ponds Market
Homer Street, Moonee Ponds
Hours: Thursday 8 a.m. - 6 p.m.
Friday 8 a.m. - 9 p.m.
Saturday 8 a.m. - 1 p.m.
Fabulous variety section, meat, deli's, fish, poultry, vegetables, fruit, etc.

Prahran Market
177 Commercial Road, Prahran
Tel: 522 3302
Hours: Tues & Thurs 7.30 a.m. - 5 p.m.
Friday 6.30 a.m. - 6 p.m.
Saturday 6 a.m. - 12.30 p.m.

Pipeworks Market and Leisure Complex
400 Mahoneys Road, Campbellfield
Tel: 357 1155
Hours: Saturday & Sunday 9 a.m. - 5 p.m.
Cost: $1 Adult
Free Child
One of Melbourne's premier entertainment attractions featuring over 600 variety stalls, 20 international take-aways, licensed bar and leisure complex.

Preston Market
30A Centreway, Preston
Tel: 478 1088
Hours: Thurs 8 a.m. - 6 p.m.
Fri 8 a.m. - 9 p.m.
Sat 8 a.m. - 1 p.m.
Fruit, vegetables, leathergoods, footwear and jewellery.

St. Kilda Sunday Art Bank
Upper Esplanade, St. Kilda
Tel: 536 1333
Hours: Sunday 9 a.m. - 6 p.m.
Stalls selling handcrafted leather, jewellery, pottery, glass, toys, cottage crafts, hand painted/appliquéd windcheaters—paintings, etc.

Queen Victoria Market
Elizabeth Street, Melbourne
Tel: 658 9800
Hours: Tuesday - Thursday 6 a.m. - 2 p.m.
Friday 6 a.m. - 6 p.m.
Saturday 6 a.m. - 1 p.m.
Sunday 9 a.m. - 4 p.m.
Six hectares (15 acres) in the city with over 600 stalls. A crowded colourful market with everything from vegetables to clothing available. One of Melbourne's most famous tourist attractions.

South Melbourne Market
Corner of Coventry and Cecil streets, South Melbourne
Tel: 699 4077
Hours: Wed 6 a.m. - 2 p.m.
Fri 6 a.m. - 6 p.m.
Sat 6 a.m. - noon
Sun 9 a.m. - 4 p.m.
A historic, friendly market located in nearby South Melbourne.

OUTSIDE MELBOURNE

There are numerous places of interest to visit from Melbourne and they can be reached by car, train or coach.

Dandenong Ranges (35 kilometres or 22 miles east of the city)
Very pretty hills with pockets of rainforest. Attractions: Puffing Billy (870 8411) steam train between Belgrave and Emerald; William Ricketts Sanctuary (751 1300). Clay sculptures of Aboriginal mythology and Ricketts' own philosophy.

Healesville Sanctuary (63 kilometres or 39 miles east of the city)
The place to see much of Australia's wildlife including the elusive platypus.

Mornington Peninsula (60 kilometres or 37 miles south of the city)
Pretty coastline and beaches with small resort towns such as Portsea and Sorrento.

Phillip Island (129 kilometres or 80 miles south of the city)
The place to see koalas, seals and mutton birds but the creature that makes the island famous is the fairy penguin which parades up the beach at dusk each night.

The Grampian Mountains (260 kilometres west of Melbourne)
Spectacular views, bushland and Spring wildflowers.

Ballarat (112 kilometres or 67 miles northwest of Melbourne)
Sovereign Hill is an authentic recreation of an 1850s goldmining town. Ballarat town is also well worth a visit in its own right.

Bendigo (115 kilometres or 71 miles northwest of Melbourne)
Another goldmining town, with a famous pottery and talking tram.

Great Ocean Road
(southwest of Melbourne)
Spectacular coastal scenery with some good beaches and excellent photographic possibilities.

The Murray River forms a large part of the border with New South Wales. Cruising on houseboats or paddle steamers. Towns of interest are: Mildura, Swan Hill and Echuca.

Wilson's Promontory (southeast of Melbourne)
A wonderful mix of rugged mountains and spectacular coastline.

Gippsland Lakes (391 kilometres or 242 miles east of Melbourne)
Delightful environment for sailing, fishing and swimming. The district's town is Lakes Entrance.

The Victorian Alps
(northeast of Melbourne)
Contains several ski resorts with facilities for cross-country and downhill skiing: Falls Creek, Mount Buller, Mount Buffalo, Mount Hotham. The Bogong High Plains provide a wonderland for cross-country skiers in the winter and for horse riders in the summer. Other towns worth a visit in the mountains are Bright and Mount Beauty. On the way a visit to historic Beechworth will prove rewarding.

Rutherglen (235 kilometres or 146 miles northeast of Melbourne)
This is the centre of winegrowing in the area, where visitors are made welcome at cellar tastings.

For bookings and full details on tours, departures and costs contact: Victour Travel Centre, 230 Collins St., Melbourne, VIC, 3000. 03-619 9444 or:

TRAVEL PACKAGES

The following companies offer morning, afternoon and full day trips of Melbourne and Victoria. Buses will pick up from various hotels around the city.

AAT Kings
108 Ireland St.
West Melbourne
Tel: 666 3363

Ansett Pioneer
489 Swanston St.
Melbourne.
Tel: 668 3144

Australian Pacific Tour Centre
181 Flinders St.
Melbourne 3000
Tel: 650 1511

The tours listed below are a selection of tours available through the companies listed above:-

City, Blue Dandenongs and Fairy Penguins. Daily 9 a.m. Full Day.
City & Blue Dandenongs. Daily 9 a.m. Half & Full Day.
City Sights. Daily 2 p.m. Half Day.
Fairy Penguins. Daily 2 p.m. Half Day/ Evening.
Sovereign Hill, Ballarat 9 a.m. Full Day.
Bendigo, Castlemaine, Mineral Springs, Maldon. Fri days 9 a.m. Full Day.
Puffing Billy Steam. Tues., Thurs., 9 a.m. Full Day Train, Sat.
Melbourne Heritage. Wed, Sat., 9.15 a.m. Half Day.
Wallan Woolshed. Wed., Sat., 12.15 p.m. Half Day (Oct-Apr).
City Sights & Wallan. Wed., Sat., 1215 p.m. Full Day.
Woolshed. Grand Tour Melbourne. Daily 9.15 a.m. Full Day.
Lorne & Great Ocean Road. Fri., 9.15 a.m. Full Day.
Wilsons Promontory, various, 8.55 a.m. Full Day National Park.
Echuca Paddle Steamer. Wed 8.55 a.m. Full Day.
The average cost of a half day tour is approximately $20 and for a full day tour $40.

Aussie Football Tours
Suite 3, 36 Jollimont Terrace
Melbourne 3002
Tel: 650 1279
A unique Melbourne experience for those interested in high-flying, bone-crunching and electrifying sport.

Cobb & Co Horse Drawn Carriages
318 Melrose Drive
Tullamarine, 3040
Tel: 338 7050
Year round four-hour tours by horse-drawn carriages by day.

Jayrow helicopters
Hanger 59 Moorabin Airport
Tel: 587 1833
Specialising in scenic helicopter flights over Melbourne.

Moloney Aviation
Terminal Building, Essendon Airport
Tel: 379 2122
Air charter direct flights to the Penguin Parade, 12 Apostles, Sovereign Hill gold mining township, the Grampian Mountains and scenic air tours of Melbourne.

Outdoor Travel Centre
1st Floor, 377 Little Bourke St.
Melbourne 3000
Tel: 670 7252
Adventure days and weekend specialist offering: climbing, whitewater rafting, cross-country skiing, horse riding, ballooning and cycling trips.

Wheel Drive Oz Trek Tours
15 Frances Ave.
Greensborough
Victoria 3088
Tel: 819 6167
Two- and three-day tours to remote and scenic Victoria. Rafting included in the three-day tour.

Melbourne Heritage Walks
22/382 Toorak Road
South Yarra 3141
Tel: 241 1085
In-depth walking tours guided by knowledgable devotees of Melbourne.

Pamm's Shopping Tours
PO Box 38
Brighton North 3186
Tel: 592 6911
Shopping tours by the lady who wrote a book on discount shopping in Melbourne.

Steam Tug Wattle
11 North Wharf, Melbourne
Tel: 328 2739
Cost: $8 Adults
$5 Child pensioner

Two hour cruises of the Port of Melbourne in an authentically restored historic steamer.

Tourist Tram
Corner of Swanston & Victoria streets, Melbourne.
Tel: 617 0900
Hours: Departure Return Journey (St. Kilda Beach Terminus)
10.40 a.m., 11.50 a.m., 1 p.m., 11.15 a.m., 12.25 p.m., 1.35 p.m., 2.10 p.m., 3.20 p.m., 4.30 p.m., 2.45 p.m., 3.55 p.m.

Experience the old world charm of the tram's refurbished interior as it travels along Swanston Street and St. Kilda Road to St. Kilda Beach.

Vintage Omnibus Tours
6 Nevada St.,
North Balwyn
3104
Tel: 857 9417

Daily short charabanc tours of the city (cost $20).

Vintage Train Day Tours
Box 4870
Melbourne 3001
Tel: 62 4806

This is an infrequently-operated tour by steam locomotive.

V/Line
Spencer Street Station
Spencer Street
Melbourne 3000
Tel: 619 1500

V/line (the State Transport Authority) operate a large number of tours into country Victoria.

Air Adventure Australia Pty Ltd
P.O Box 339
Hamilton
Vic 3300
Tel: (055) 72 1371
Fax: (055) 725979

Guided tours through the outback in twin-engined, luxury aircraft. Individual itineraries for special interest groups.

Australian Japan Tourist Service
120 Exhibition St.
Melbourne 3000
Tel: (03) 650 9685
Fax: (03) 654 7078

Japanese-speaking tour guides.

Australian Hospitality Services
610 Glenferrie Road
Hawthorn 3122
Tel: 819 3791

Guiding service for two to four people.

Guideline
179 Grattan St.
Melbourne 3053
Tel: (03) 347 7483
Fax: (03) 347 0182

Multi-lingual guides lead half-day city sights to fully escorted tours.

Tour Design
51 Park St.
South Yarra 3141
Tel: (03) 266 4572
Fax: (03) 427 1936

Creative itineraries, individually tailored to specific interests.

CULTURE PLUS

Melbourne offers much to feed and stimulate both the mind and the spirit. The lists that follow will facilitate access to the city's cultural offerings.

MUSEUMS

Australian Gallery of Sport
Melbourne Cricket Ground, Jolimont
Tel: 654 8922
Hours: Wednesday - Sunday 10 a.m. - 4 p.m.
Cost: $3 Adults
$1 Child/Pensioner
Guided tours of cricket ground (not gallery), duration 2 hours.
Cost of Tour: $0.50 per person
Hour of Tour: Wednesday 10 a.m. only

How to get there: catch tram no. 70, 77 along Swan Street. Alight at stop no. 6.

Museum of Chinese Australian History
22 Cohen Place, Melbourne
Tel: 662 288
Hours: Mon, Wed, Thurs, Fri 10 a.m. - 5 p.m.
Sat & Sun noon - 5 p.m.
Cost: $2 Adults
$1 Child
$5 Family

How to get there: catch any tram along Bourke Street. Alight at Exhibition Street, walk down Little Bourke Street to Cohen Place.

Museum of Victoria
322-328 Swanston Street, Melbourne
Tel: 669 9884
Hours: Monday - Sunday 10 a.m. - 5 p.m.
Cost: Free
Closed: Christmas, Anzac Day and Good Friday.

How to get there: Catch any tram along Swanston St. Alight at Latrobe Street.

Melbourne Fire Museum
48 Gisborne St., East Melbourne
Tel: 66 2907
Hours: 10 a.m. - 4 p.m. Sunday
Cost: $2 Adults
$1 Child/Pensioner

Preservation and public display of all forms of the fire fighting equipment, photographs, uniforms and memorabilia.

How to get there: Catch any tram along Collins Street. Alight at corner of Albert & Gisborne streets.

Railway Museum
Champion Road, North Williamstown
Tel: 51 6146
Hours: Wednesday 1 p.m. - 4 p.m.
Weekends/Public Holidays 1 p.m. - 5 p.m.
Cost: $1.50 Adult
$0.70 Child/Pensioner

Museum display of locomotives, carriages, wagons, trolleys, photographic material and railway memorabilia displays.

How to get there: travel to Williamstown North by train from Flinders Street. Museum next door.

ANZ Banking Museum
380 Collins St., Melbourne
Tel: 607 4301
Hours: Monday - Friday 9.30 a.m. - 4 p.m.
Cost: Free.

History of Australia banking and services from the ANZ banking archives.

How to get there: catch any tram along Collins Street.

Victoria Racing Museum
Caulfield Race Course, Station Street, Caulfield
Tel: 572 1111
Hours: 10 a.m. - 4 p.m. Tuesday and Thursday
Cost: Free

Displays of racing memorabilia. How to get there: catch Glen Waverly from Flinders Street. Alight at Caulfield.

The Jewish Museum of Australia
Corner of Toorak Road & Arnold Street, Toorak
Tel: 266 1922
Hours: 11 a.m. - 4 p.m. Wednesday
& Thursday
2 p.m. - 5 p.m. Sunday
Cost: $2 Adults
$1 Child/Pensioner

Exhibitions displaying Jewish history, culture, religion and lifestyle.

How to get there: Catch tram no. 3, 5, 6 from Swanston Street. Alight at stop no. 19.

Performing Arts Museum
100 St. Kilda Road, Melbourne
Tel: 617 8211
Hours: 11 a.m. - 5 p.m.
Cost: $2 Adults
$1.10 Child

Located in the Concert Hall. Unique in Australia, presenting a cavalcade of colourful exhibitions on all aspects of past and present performing arts.

ART GALLERIES

Aboriginal Artists Gallery
50 Bourke St., Melbourne
Tel: 663 5716
Hours: 9 a.m. - 5 p.m. Mon - Fri
9 a.m. - 1 p.m. Saturday
Closed: Sunday

Fine selection of traditional and contemporary Aboriginal art and artifacts. Continuous exhibition of art and craft.

How to get there: catch any tram along Bourke Street. Alight at Exhibition Street.

Aboriginal Handicrafts
9th Floor, 125-133 Swanston St., Melbourne
Tel: 650 4717
Hours: 10 a.m. - 4 p.m. Mon - Thurs.
10 a.m. - 5 p.m. Fridays
Closed: Weekends

Genuine handcrafted artifacts from Aboriginal communities—boomerangs, didgeridoos, bark paintings, carvings, weapons, reference material, books, cassettes.

How to get there: catch any tram along Collins Street. Alight at corner of Swanston & Collins streets, walk north along Swanston Street.

Graphic Illusion Gallery
69 Davis Ave., South Yarra
Tel: 266 2342
Hours: 11 a.m. - 5 p.m. Wed - Sat
2 p.m. - 5 p.m. Sunday

Specialising in fine art and craftwork by leading contemporary Australian artists. Displays including jewellery, ceramic sculpture, paintings, drawings & prints.

How to get there: catch tram no. 8 from Swanston Street. Alight at stop no. 26 in Toorak Road, walk back to Davis Avenue.

Meat Market Craft Centre
42 Courtney St., North Melbourne
Tel: 329 9966
Hours: 10 a.m. - 5 p.m. Daily

State craft centre, in a superbly restored former meat market, changing exhibitions, resources and information centre.

How to get there: catch tram no. 51 along Elizabeth Street. Alight at stop no. 15, walk down Blackwood Street. See Australian artists at work.

Pottage Original Crafts
1137 High St., Armadale
Tel: 20 8800
Hours: 10 a.m. - 5 p.m. Mon - Fri
9.30 a.m. - 1 m Saturday
2 p.m. - 5 p.m. Sunday

An excellent range of Australian crafts and interesting handwork, pottery, jewellery, leather goods, woodwork, glassware, handspun wools, etc.

How to get there: catch tram no. 6, 7, 38 along High Street. Alight at stop no. 39.

Thingummybob
58 Ross St., Toorak
Tel: 241 6719
Hours: 9.30 a.m. - 5.30 p.m. Mon - Fri
9.30 a.m. - 1 p.m. Saturday

Unique Australian-made goods handcrafted and manufactured.

How to get there: catch tram no. 8 along St. Kilda Road. Alight at stop no. 33 in Toorak Road.

Wondoflex Yarn Craft Cottage
1353 Malvern Road, Malvern
Tel: 20 6231

Hours: 9 a.m. - 5.30 p.m. Mon - Fri
9 a.m. - noon Saturday

Everything for the handspinner, weaver and knitter.

How to get there: catch tram no. 72, 73 along St. Kilda Road. Alight at stop no. 43.

Queen Victoria Antique Arts and Craft Centre
120 Franklin St., Melbourne
Tel: 328 2266
Hours: 10 a.m. - 5.30 p.m. Mon - Fri
9 a.m. - 5.30 p.m. Sat - Sun

Largest antique art and craft centre in the southern hemisphere.

How to get there: catch any tram along Elizabeth Street. Alight at corner of Victoria & Elizabeth streets.

National Gallery of Victoria
180 St. Kilda Rd., Melbourne
Tel: 618 0222
Hours: 10 a.m. - 5 p.m. Tues - Sun
Cost: $1.20 Adult
$0.60 Child

Part of the Victorian Arts Centre complex, the Sir Roy Ground building houses the State of Victoria's Art collection. Exhibitions of European, American, Asian, and Australian art including paintings, sculpture, glass, ceramics.

THEATRES

Cultural life in Melbourne is rich indeed. It is a city with style and grace. The Arts Centre is the focal point for live performance in the city, with its Melbourne Concert Hall, State Theatre (mostly dance and opera), and two drama theatres, The Studio and The Playhouse.

Details of live performances at The Victorian Arts Centre can be obtained by telephoning 617 8211 or found in the Entertainment Guide in Friday's *Age*, or in its own poster size "Diary," available from the Arts Centre or Victour's office in Collins Street.

Other Theatre venues include:-

Athenaeum Theatre
118 Collins St.
Tel: 633 831

Comedy Theatre
240 Exhibition St.
Tel: 662 2222

Her Majesty's Theatre
219 Exhibition St.
Tel: 663 3211

Princess Theatre
163 Spring St.
Tel: 662 2911

Russell Street Theatre
19 Russell St.
Tel: 654 400

St. Martins Theatre
South Yarra
Tel: 267 2551

CONCERTS

Orchestral concerts, other than those performed at the Concert Hall of The Victorian Arts Centre (Tel: 617 8211) are given at:-

Dallas Brooks Hall
Victoria Parade, East Melbourne
Tel: 419 2288

Robert Blackwood Hall
Monash University
Wellington Parade
Clayton.
Tel: 565 3091

Orchestral performances are given outdoors in the summer months at:-
Sidney Myer Music Bowl, Tel: 617 8332, Domain Park.

Tickets can be booked through Bass Booking Service (who have offices in large stores and other points around the city) by telephoning 11500.

Half Tix sell half priced tickets on the day of the performance of live shows....for cash. It is situated in Bourke Street Mall and can be telephoned on 65 0940.

MOVIES

Melbourne has dozens of cinemas in and around the city, including some complexes with two or more cinemas. They are generally modern, air-conditioned and comfortable establishments.

Information about programs can be found in *The Herald* each day or the Entertainment Guide section of *The Age* on a Friday. A cinema that is worth a special mention because of its distinctive atmosphere is:

The Astor
Corner of Chapel Street and Dandenong Road
St. Kilda
Tel: 511 414

The Astor shows the best of new and old with a different film each night.

DIARY OF EVENTS

The following is a list of major events through the year in Melbourne. More information is available through tourist literature such as *This Week in Melbourne* and by telephoning Leisureline: 11 671.

See also Public Holidays earlier in the Travel Tips.

January
Cricket International Series
Summer in the city—music and entertainment
February
Golf Championship Series
Cricket International Series
Chinese New Year Festival, Chinatown
March
Water Skiing Competition
Moomba Festival (10 days of fun and Grand Float Parade). Information: 654 7111
Comedy Festival
Greek Antipodes Festival
Melbourne International Motor Show
April
National Trust Heritage Week
Anzac Day March (25th April)
May
Caravan and Camping Show
June
Melbourne Film Festival (10 days). Information 663 2954
Winter Ballet Season
July
National Boat Show
Sheep and Woolcraft Show
August
Sun-News Pictorial Home Show
Italian Week
September
V.F.L. Grand Final
Royal Melbourne Show
Spoleto Melbourne—Festival of Three Worlds
Fringe Spoleto—avant-garde, alternative festival
Chinese Moon Lantern Festival
October
Melbourne Marathon
International Wine and Food Fair
Italian Arts Festival
Caulfield Cup—Horse Racing
Hispanic Festival—Fitzroy
November
Melbourne Cup Carnival—Horse Racing
Lygon Street Fiesta—Carlton
December
Cricket—International Series
Melbourne to Hobart Yacht Race
Carols by Candlelight

ARCHITECTURE

Some buildings of architectural merit are:-

General Post Office
corner of Elizabeth and Bourke streets.
Cathedral Room
380 Collins St.

Vaulted ceiling and stained glass. This was the Stock Exchange.

ANZ Bank Building
386-388 Collins St.

The exterior is a mixture of sandstone and granite, while the interior is a study in green beauty.

Stock Exchange
351 Collins St.

A building with a lot of style. The public gallery is open Monday to Friday 10 a.m. to 3 p.m.

Bank of New Zealand
395 Collins St.

The Rialto Building is Melbourne's tallest and is a modern building attached to the Menzies at Rialto. It is a good example of a building of distinction being restored beautifully while fulfilling the functions of a modern hotel.

The Council Chamber of the State Parliament, facing the Eastern end of Collins Street has been described as "A work of Art. The best Corinthian room in the World."

Customs House building, 426 Flinders St. is an interesting building with an equally interesting sign set in the pavement outside.

NIGHTLIFE

When the lights go off in Melbourne's offices, and the shops close their doors, the entertainment lights go on. The three major newspapers, *The Age*, *The Herald* and *Sun News* together with *This Week in Melbourne* have up-to-date listings of night spots.

NIGHTCLUBS & DISCOS

Baden Powell Cub Club
61 Victoria Parade, Collingwood.
Tel: 417 2626
Jazz.

Barbarella's
135 Smith St., Fitzroy.
Tel: 417 2306
Dance music from the 60s onwards. Wednesday-Saturday from 9 p.m.

Disco River Cruise on the ferry "Spirit of Victoria."
Tel: 820 1533
Departs Station Pier 8.30 p.m. BYO.

Hippodrome
14-20 King St., City.
Tel: 614 5022
New three-level disco.

Impression
536 Swanston St., Carlton.
Tel: 347 4722
Disco for the young.

Inflation
60 King St., City.
Tel: 614 6122
Gay night: Wednesday.

Juliana's Supper-Club
Hilton Hotel,
192 Wellington Parade, East Melbourne.
Tel: 419 3311.

Melbourne Metro
20 Bourke St., City.
Tel: 663 4288
Sophisticated light and sound systems.

Melbourne Underground
22 King St.
Tel: 614 7677
Open till 7 a.m. Tuesday-Saturday.
One of Melbourne's best.

Zuzu's Nightclub
186 Exhibition St.
Tel: 662 0511
Special laser light effects.

PUBS

Armadale Hotel
1068 High St.
Armadale.
Tel: 509 0277
Live Rock.

Limerick Arms Hotel
36 Clarendon St.
South Melbourne.
Tel: 690 2626
Live Jazz.

Loaded Dog
324 St. George's Rd.
North Fitzroy.
Own brew and imported beers, live music.
Tel: 489 8222.

Museum Hotel
293 Latrobe St.
City.
Tel: 670 0128
Home to the Victorian Jazz Club.

CABARETS

Crystal T's
672 Sydney Road
Brunswick.
Adult cabaret
Tel: 383 2944

Industry Restaurant & Cabaret
453 Swanston St.
City
Tel: 663 6471
Full size video screen and latest facilities.

The Palace
Lower Esplanade
St. Kilda.
Tel: 534 5801
Rock venue, Thursday-Saturday.

GAMBLING

TAB (Totalizator Agency Board) shops exist in the city at 1 Queen St., Tel: 268 2100 and most suburbs. Bets can be placed on races on the totalizator system. This is the only form of off-course betting on races allowed in Victoria.

There are no casinos in conservative Victoria, and as Australians are inveterate gamblers, it seems unlikely that the State Government will change this in the near future.

Keno, Tattslotto are two numbers games that have a huge following to match their sometimes huge money prizes. These two games together with scratchcards are available from newsagents and some pharmacies.

BORDELLOS

There are licensed (legal) bordellos in the State of Victoria. Two that advertise prominently are:-

The Palace
8-16 Palmerston Crescent
South Melbourne.
Tel: 699 9974

Romantics
71-73 Colebrook St.
Brunswick
Tel: 383 6682

SHOPPING

Melbourne is Australia's shopping capital, and the reason that it holds this exalted position is because of the way that shopping is organised into streets that have a speciality or particular character. There are exciting markets of every type and they are listed later in this section.

WHAT TO BUY

Australia's duty free industry is among the most competitive in the world, so if you are an overseas visitor take a close look at the prices and remember that Australia, unlike some duty free ports, is not used as a dumping ground for superceded goods.

Opal, diamond and sapphire are good buys, as are all crafts.

SPECIALITY AREAS

Street Speciality	**Area**
Acland Street Continental Cake Shops	**St. Kilda**
Bay Street Good browsing street	**Port Melbourne**
Block Arcade Atmosphere shopping off Elizabeth Street	**City**
Bourke Street Department stores e.g. Myers, David Jones	**Mall City**

Chapel Street — **South Yarra**
designer boutiques
Jam Factory (No. 500)

Collins Street — **City**
Luxury goods/boutiques
Georges Australia is THE store
Gold and silver at Makers Mark (No. 85)

High Street — **Armadale**
Antique and furniture shops
Australiana General Store (No. 114)

Lygon Street — **Carlton**
Australia's Via Veneto

Swan Street — **Richmond**
Designer clothes seconds shops—fashion bargains.

Victoria Street — **Richmond**
Little Vietnam - restaurants and shops

DUTY FREE SHOPS

Here are three of the many Duty Free shops in Melbourne:-

International Duty Free
189 Collins St.
Tel: 654 4771

Downtown Duty Free
129 Exhibition St.
Tel: 63 3258

City International
185 Swanston St.
Tel: 663 4437

SOUVENIRS

Souvenir shoppers should visit one or more of the following shops:-

Aboriginal Handcrafts
125 Swanston St.
Tel: 650 4717

Antipodes Authentic Australian Arts
22 Toorak Road
South Yarra
Tel: 266 5749

Australiana General Store
114 High St.
Armadale
Tel: 509 3795

Queen Victoria Arts and Crafts Centre
114 Franklin St.
City
Tel: 328 1461

Yarrandoo
Shop 8, Collins Place
45 Collins St.
City
Tel: 650 2050

MARKETS

Melbourne markets are fun and interesting, but there is not time to visit them all, so try to get to Melbourne's biggest: Victoria Markets, and the best craft market at the old Meat Markets.

Camberwell Market
Located in the car park opposite Target, Union Street, Camberwell.
Hours: 6 a.m. - 1.30 p.m. Sundays

A popular Sunday market selling a variety of arts/crafts and second hand goods.

Dandenong Market
Corner of Cleeland Street & Clow Street, Dandenong
Tel: 791 6500
Hours: Tues, Fri, Saturday mornings

Historic general produce market—also wide range of consumer goods, Trash & Treasure type auction every Tuesday.

Dingley Village Craft Market
Marcus Road, Dingley
Tel: 551 6275
Hours: First Sunday of every month 9 a.m. - 2 p.m.

Attracts the best of Victoria's craft people and displays of their work.

Melbourne West End Market
47 McIntyre Road, Sunshine
Tel: 312 3366
Hours: Sat & Sun 8.30 a.m. - 5.30 p.m.

600 stalls undercover, and foodhalls. Bargains, food, fun and wonderful multicultural atmosphere.

Moonee Ponds Market
Homer Street, Moonee Ponds
Hours: Thur 8 a.m. - 6 p.m.
Fri 8 a.m. - 9 p.m.
Sat 8 a.m. - 1 p.m.

Fabulous variety section, meat, deli's, fish, poultry, vegetables, fruit, etc.

Prahran Market
177 Commercial Road, Prahran
Tel: 522 3302
Hours: Tues & Thurs 7.30 a.m. - 5 p.m.
Friday 6.30 a.m. - 6 p.m.
Saturday 6 a.m. - 12.30 p.m.

Pipeworks Market and Leisure Complex
400 Mahoneys Road, Campbellfield
Tel: 357 1155
Hours: Sat & Sun 9 a.m. - 5 p.m.
Cost: $1 Adult
Free Child

One of Melbourne's premier entertainment attractions, featuring over 600 variety stalls, 20 international take-aways, licensed bar and leisure complex.

Preston Market
30A Centreway, Preston
Tel: 478 1088
Hours: Thurs 8 a.m. - 6 p.m.
Fri 8 a.m. - 9 p.m.
Sat 8 a.m. - 1 p.m.

Fruit, vegetables, leathergoods, footwear and jewellery.

St. Kilda Sunday Art Bank
Upper Esplanade, St. Kilda
Tel: 536 1333
Hours: Sunday 9 a.m. - 6 p.m.

Stalls selling handcrafted leather, jewellery, pottery, glass, toys, cottage crafts, hand painted/appliquéd windcheaters - paintings, etc.

Queen Victoria Market
Elizabeth Street, Melbourne
Tel: 658 9800
Hours: Tues - Thur 6 a.m. - 2 p.m.
Friday 6 a.m. - 6 p.m.
Saturday 6 a.m. - 1 p.m.
Sunday 9 a.m. - 4 p.m.

Six hectares in the city with over 600 stalls. A crowded colourful market with everything from vegetables to clothing available. One of Melbourne's famous tourist attractions.

South Melbourne Market
Corner of Coventry and Cecil streets, South Melbourne
Tel: 699 4077
Hours: Wed 6 a.m. - 2 p.m.
Fri 6 a.m. - 6 p.m.
Sat 6 a.m. - noon
Sun 9 a.m. - 4 p.m.

A historic, friendly market located in nearby South Melbourne.

BOOKSHOPS

Bookshops are listed in The Yellow Pages telephone directory and include the following of particular interest to the traveller:-

A-Roving Travel Things, 42, Toorak Road, Toorak, Tel: 267 3395
Bowyangs, 259 High St., Kew, Tel: 862 3526.
Travel Guides, 90 Burwood Road, Hawthorn, Tel: 819 2322.
Travelbooks, 295 Wattletree Road, Malvern East, Tel: 500 0454.

For government publications go to:-

The Victorian Government Bookshop, 318 Little Bourke St., Melbourne. Tel: 663 3760. This is also the home of Information Victoria Centre which is the ultimate source of information on things Victorian.

COMPLAINTS

In the event of your having a complaint, talk first with the proprietor/manager of the offending establishment and if you are not satisfied with the actions taken to remedy the situation, make it known that you will contact the:

Ministry of Consumer Affairs
500 Bourke St.
Melbourne 3000
Tel: 602 8123

Your first contact can be by telephone, but you will need to put your case in writing. If the store is a member of the Melbourne Tourism Authority, it may be worth asking the authority to negotiate on your behalf.

SPORTS

PARTICIPANT

The city has much to offer those people who look for physical recreation. The beach at St. Kilda offers swimming, sailboard hire and cycle hire.

The City Baths at 438 Swanston St., City. Tel: 663 5888, offer sauna, spa, massage, Turkish baths, squash courts, gymnasium and pool.

Cycles can also be hired for the delightful 11 km ride along the Yarra River from Princes Bridge Tel: 288 5177.

Ice skating is possible at Sidney Myer Music Bowl, Kings Domain. Tel: 617 8360. Skates can be hired. Open daily 10 a.m. - 9 p.m.

Jogging tracks include: The Yarra River, The Tan (around the Botanical Gardens), Albert Park Lake, Princes Park, Carlton and The Promenade, St. Kilda.

Sailing and rowing is on offer at Albert Park Lake.

There is a well-equipped **gymnasium** at the Hyatt Hotel, 123 Collins St., City. Tel: 657 1234.

Public **golf** links are to be found at:-
Albert Park, Aughtie Drive, South Melbourne. Tel: 690 1607 and Richmond, corner of Madden Grove and Loyola Grove, Burnley. Tel: 42 3133.

Tenpin **bowling** can be played at Southern Cross Bowl, 95 Bourke St., City. Tel: 623 2543.

Squash courts can be hired at The City Baths, 420 Swanston St., City. Tel: 663 5888.

Tennis courts can be hired at one of the world's leading tennis venues: The National Tennis Centre, Flinders Park, East Melbourne. Tel: 267 7211

SPECTATOR

Visitors to Melbourne may enjoy a visit to M.C.G. (Melbourne Cricket Ground) for Aussie Rules Football in the winter and cricket in the summer. The VFL Grand Final which is played in September is the sporting event of the year and the visitor would have to be well connected to obtain a ticket at short notice.

The Australian Gallery of Sport (Tel: 654 8922) is also situated here and between 10 a.m. and 4 p.m. Wed-Sat displays sporting memorabilia.

Nearby is the National Tennis Centre which hosts the Victorian Open Tennis Championship in December and the Australian Open in January.

Racing enthusiasts will find horse or harness racing at Mooney Valley Racecourse or Caulfield Racecourse.

SPECIAL INFORMATION

DOING BUSINESS

Melbourne is the financial capital of Australia as well as the major manufacturing centre.

The first point of contact for business people arriving in Melbourne for the first time should be:

The Chamber of Commerce
World Trade Centre
Melbourne 3000
Tel: (03) 611 2233

This organisation is well versed in advising and assisting business people and provide the following services:-

* Introductions to Government and private enterprise organisations
*Office accommodation
*Office services
*Trade information service/library
*Advice and assistance
*Lobbying

CHILDREN

Melbourne Zoological Gardens, Parkville, four kilometres north of the city, is open daily from 9 a.m. to 5 p.m. Over 3,000 animals are housed in natural settings. Tel: 347 1522.

Luna Park is a fun fair on the Esplanade in St. Kilda. There are many amusements and rides available. For information, call: 534 0812.

The Museum of Victoria at 328 Swanston St., city contains a Children's Museum. It is open daily 10 a.m. to 5 p.m. For information call: 669 9888.

In most of the parks and gardens, listed earlier in the book, there are play areas for children.

GAYS

Meeting places for gays are numerous; here are a few:

Inflation nightclub (Tel: 614 6122) has a Gay Night on Wednesday from 9 p.m.

Club 397 at 397 Swanston St. (Tel: 663 5348) is a mixed gay disco open from 10 p.m. on Thursday, Friday and Saturday.

Stilettoe's, Anglers Club, 229 Queensberry St., Carlton (Tel:347 2666) Women only. Open alternate Saturdays.

The Exchange, 119 Commercial Road, South Yarra (Tel: 267 5144). Open from 7 p.m. daily. Men only.

DISABLED

Many of Melbourne's facilities make provision for the needs of the disabled, this is particularly true of public buildings and the newer hotels. Advice and assistance is offered by:-

The Australian Council for the Rehabilitation of the Disabled (ACROD)
7 Mair St., Brighton Beach, VIC 3186
Tel: 598 8555.

The Met offers a telephone typewriter service for the hearing impaired.
Tel: 618 2208 Monday - Friday 8.15 a.m. - 5.00 p.m.
Wheelchair assistance is also available to Met users.
Tel: 619 7482.

STUDENTS

Students visiting Melbourne are advised to contact the Students' Union of one of the three universities in the city or of the many Colleges of Advanced Education. The union will be able to advise on student happenings and on the availability of facilities to visiting students.

Here are some contact numbers:

Melbourne University Union
Tel: 341 6973
After hours: 347 3532
Latrobe University Union
Tel: 347 2319
Monash University Union
Tel: 565 4000

PILGRIMAGES

As the home of Aussie Rules Football and cricket, a visit to Melbourne's Australian Gallery of Sport at the Melbourne Cricket Ground (off Wellington Parade), by followers of these sports could approach a religious experience.

The Australian Gallery of Sport is open Wednesday to Sunday from 10 a.m. to 4 p.m. Further information can be sought by telephoning 654 8922.

Photography

All film types are readily available and developing of colour film can take as little as an hour, black and white could take a few days. Care should be taken not to expose film to the X-rays of security devices at airports.

Some of the best views of Melbourne can be seen from the following locations and photographers visiting Melbourne are advised to go to at least one of them:

AMP Building
535 Bourke St.
Lookout Tour at 1.40 p.m. Monday-Friday.

Shrine of Remembrance
St. Kilda Road,
Regent Hotel, 25 Collins St., 35th Floor restaurant.

The Westgate Bridge has spectacular views, although stopping on the bridge is not permitted.

Photographers wishing to make contact with others in Melbourne could contact :

The Melbourne Camera Club
13 Bruce St., Mount Waverley
Tel: 807 3701 or

The Swinburne Institute of Technology
John Street, Hawthorn
Tel: 819 8911.

Language

ABC
Australian Broadcasting Commission
ACT
Australian Capital Territory (Canberra)
ACTU
Australian Council of Trade Unions
ALP
Australian Labor Party
ASIO
Aussie CIA
Abo
Aborigine (impolite, and usually racist)
Alice, The
Alice Springs
Anzac
Member of the Australian and New Zealand Army Corps in World War I
Arvo
Afternoon
BHP
Broken Hill Proprietary, a large mining multinational
Back of beyond
The Outback
Back of Bourke
Far Outback
Banana bender
Queenslander
Barbie
Barbecue
Barrack
To cheer at a sporting event
Bastard
Term of endearment (when it's not a term of abuse)
Battler
Person who struggles hard for a living
Beaut
Short for "beautiful" (very good, great)
Beergut
Self explanatory
Beg yoursf
I beg your pardon

Bell
(give someone a)Telephone someone
Bible basher
Minister
Bikies
Outlaw motorcyclists (other motorcyclists are "bikers")
Billabong
Water hole in semi-dry river
Billy
Container used for boiling water for tea
Bitumen
Surfaced road
Black Stump, The
Where the back of Bourke begins
Bloke
Man—used like "guy" in the U.S.
Bloody
Universally undeleted expletive, as in "up at Tumba-bloody-rumba shootin' kanga-bloody-roos"
Blowie
Blowfly
Bludger
Sponger, ne'er do well
Blue
A fight. Also a redhead
Bonzer
Terrific
Bookie
Bookmaker
Boot
Trunk of a car
Booze
Any alcohol
Bottle shop
Liquor shop, off licence
Buckley's Chance
One chance in a million
Bunch of fives
A fist
Bush
Countryside outside cities and towns
Bushranger
Highwayman
Chemist
Pharmacist
Chiko Roll
Former spring roll/junk food
Chips
French fried potatoes
Chook
Chicken
Chuck a Uey
Do a U-turn (very popular manoeuvre by Australian politicians)
Corroboree
Aboriginal ceremonial gathering
Cossies
swimsuit (also "trunks," "togs," "swimmers")
Cowcockycattle
farmer
Crissie
Christmas
Crook
Broken, sick or no good
Cuppa
Cup of tea
Dag/daggy
Dreadful looking
Daks
Trousers
Deli
Delicatessen
Demo
Demonstration (political or practical)
Dero
Derelict; drunkard
Didgeridoo
Aboriginal droning instrument
Digger
Australian soldier, but used by foreigners meaning Australian.
Dill
Idiot
Dingo
Wild Australian native dog
Dinkie die
The whole truth
Donk
Car engine
Drongo
Worthless person
Duco
Car paint
Dunny
Toilet ("Useless as a glass door on a dunny" or "Couldn't run a two door dunny")
Fair dinkum
Same as "Dinkie die" above
Flake
Sharkmeat by another name, tastes as sweet
Flat out
As fast as one can go
Floater
Meat pie floating in horribly overcooked tinned peas (South Australian dish)

Flog
Sell or hock
Footpath
Pavement or sidewalk
Footy
Football
Fossicking
Hunting for gems or semi-precious stones.
Funnel web
Poisonous spider
G'day
Good day: standard greeting
Garbo
Garbage man
Gong, The
Wollongong
Grazier
Large scale cattle or sheep farmer
Greenie
A conservationist
Grog
Any alcoholic drink
Heart starter
First drink of the day
Hoon
Hooligan
Humpy
Aboriginal shack
Interstate
To be in another state
Joey
Baby kangaroo (in the pouch)
Journo
Journalist
Kangaroos in his top paddock
A bit crazy
Kiwi
New Zealander
Knock
To criticise
Lamington
Square sponge cake covered in chocolate icing and coconut
Lay-by
Put a deposit on an article so the shop will hold it for you
Lollies
Sweets, candy
Loo
British/Australian slang for toilet
Manchester
Household linen, sheets
Mate
Your best buddy or comrade (does not mean spouse)
Middy
Ten-ounce beer glass (in NSW)
Milk bar
Corner shop, Ma and Pa store
Mob
A group of persons or things (not necessarily unruly)
Mozzie
Mosquito
Mug
A gullible fool
New Australian
Recent immigrant
No worries
She'll be right
O.S.
Overseas
Ocker
Quintessential Aussie bumpkin-loudmouth
Outback
The bush; uncivilised, uninhabited country
Oz
Australia
Pavlova
Meringue and cream dessert, once considered the pinnacle of puddings.
Perve
To watch a member of opposite sex with admiration (does not mean "perverted")
Pinch
Arrest, as in "you'll get pinched for that mate."
Pissed
Drunk
Plonk
Cheap wine
Poker machine
Slot machine
Pom or Pommy
English person
Poof, poofter
Male homosexual (impolite)
Postie
Mailman
Prang
Accident, crash
Pub
"Public house," bar, drinking establishment
RSL
Abbreviation for Returned Servicemen's League
Ratbag
Eccentric character (also a friendly term of abuse)

Ratshit
Lousy, ruined
Red-back
Poisonous spider
Road train
Semi-trailer with additional trailer
Roo
Kangaroo
Rubbish
Deride
Rug rat
Baby (also "ankle-biter")
Schooner
Large beer glass
Scrub
Bushland
'Scuse I
Excuse me
Sea wasp
Box jellyfish, highly poisonous
Sealed (road)
Surfaced road, as opposed to dirt road
Semi-trailer
Articulated truck
Septic, Seppo
American (= Yank = septic tank)
She'll be apples/right
It'll be all right
She's sweet
Everything is all right
Sheila
Young woman
Shout
Buy round of drinks (as in "it's your shout")
Sickie
Day off work ostensibly due to illness
Silvertail
Member of high society
Smoke-o
Tea break
Snags
Sausages
Speedos
Gents nylon swimming trunks
Sprog
Baby
Spunky
Good-looking
Squatter
Large landholder
Squattocracy
Australian "old money,"made by grabbing land when the country was first settled.
Station
Large farm or ranch
Stickybeak
Busy body
Stockman
Cowboy, station hand
Strides
Trousers
Strine
Vernacular Australian
Stubby
Small bottle of beer
TAB
Abbreviation for Totalizator Agency Board, legal offtrack betting shop
Tazzie
Tasmania
Tea
Evening meal
Telly
The TV, also the Sydney Daily Telegraph
Tinny
Can of beer
Togs
Swimming suit (sometimes called a "bathing costume," too)
Trendy
Middle-class trend follower
Tube
Can of beer
Tucker
Food
Turps
Any form of alcohol. ("On the turps"— to be drinking)
Two up
Popular gambling game involving two pennies thrown in the air
Uni
University
Ute
Short for utility truck—a pickup truck
Vegemite
A brown yeast sandwich spread, on which Australians grow up, it's an acquired taste
Walkabout
Travelling on foot for long distances, believed to be an Aboriginal tradition
Wet (the)
Rainy season in the tropical part of Australia
Wharfie
Docker, waterside worker
Whinge
Complain
Wog
Minor disease; also (impolite) a foreigner

from anywhere around the Mediterranean
Wop
Southern European (again impolite)
Wowser
Bluenose, prude, killjoy
Yabber
Chatter
Yabby
Small freshwater crayfish
Yack
To talk
Yahoo
An unruly type
Yakka
Work
Yobbo
Hoon, loudmouth
Youse
Plural of you

FURTHER READING

The Heritage of Australia: The Illustrated Register of the National Estate. Melbourne: Macmillan, 1981

Wilson, Robert. *The Book of Australia*. Sydney: Lansdowne Press, 1982.

Cameron, Roderick. *Australia: History and Horizons*. London: Weidenfeld and Nicolson/Hicks Smith, 1971

McGonigal, David. *Wilderness Australia*. Reed Books, 1987.

Worrell, Eric. *Australian Wildlife: Best-Known Birds, Mammals, Reptiles, Plants of Australia and New Guinea*. Sydney: Angus and Robertson, 1966

Kepert, L. *History As It Happened*. Melbourne: Nelson, 1981.

Lauder, Afferbeck. *Strine*. Sydney: Lansdowne Press, 1982.

A Pedestrian Guide to Melbourne, Available Melbourne Town Hall, corner of Collins & Swanston streets.

Melbourne Bike Tours, published by The State Bicycle Committee.

Forell, Claude and Erlich, Rita. *The Age Good Food Guide*.1988.

USEFUL ADDRESSES

TRANSPORTATION

Ansett Airlines
489 Swanston St.
668 1211
Australian Airlines
294 Collins St.
665 3333
Qantas Airways
114 William St.
602 6111
TT Lines
Station Pier
645 2766
Interstate Bus Services
Corner of Swanston & Flinders streets
654 8477
V/Line
Spencer Street Station
619 1500
Metrail (suburban Rail Services)
619 8888
Royal Automobile Club of Victoria
123 Queen St.
790 2211
Skybus Coach Service
58 Franklin St.
663 1400

GENERAL INFORMATION

Post Office
Bourke Street Mall
609 4562
Victour Tourist Info
230 Collins St.
619 9444
Melbourne Tourism Authority
80 Collins St.
654 2288
Travellers Aid Society
169 Swanston St.
654 2600
Interpreter Service
662 3000
Police, Fire and Ambulance
000
Public Transport Information
619 0900
Taxi (Combined)
810 022

CONSULATES

Most countries maintain an embassy in Australia's capital, Canberra, and many countries also provide consular services in and around Melbourne.

American Consulate-General
24 Albert Road
South Melbourne 3205
(03) 697 7900

Austrian Consulate-General
897 High St.
Armadale 3143
(03) 509 0360

Barbados Consulate-General
5 Collins St.
Melbourne 3000
(03) 654 1944

Belgian Consulate
422 Collins St.
Melbourne 3000
(03) 602 4737

British Consulate-General
330 Collins St.
Melbourne. 3000
(03) 602 1877

Canadian Consulate-General
1 Collins St.
Melbourne 3000
(03) 654 1433

Chilean Consulate
180 Collins St.
Melbourne 3000
(03) 654 4479

Chinese Consulate-General of the People's Republic of China
82 Queens Road
Melbourne 3000
(03) 529 2282

Danish Consulate-General
865 Nepean Highway
Moorabbin 3189
(03) 557 7616

Dominican Republic Consulate
242A Kooyong Road
Toorak 3142
(03) 20 5917

Ecuador Consulate
2 Glen St.
Hawthorn 3122
(03) 819 1185

Federal Republic of Germany Consulate-General
480 Punt Road
South Yarra 3141
(03) 266 1261

Finnish Consulate
313 Montagues St.
Albert Park 3206
(03) 699 1388

French Consulate-General
492 St. Kilda Road
Melbourne 3004
(03) 820 0944

German Democratic Republic Consulate-General
96 Albert St.
South Melbourne 3205
(03) 699 9966

Greek Consulate-General
34 Queens Road
Melbourne. 3000
(03) 266 4524

Honduras Consulate
9 St. George Court
East Brighton 3187
(03) 592 3772

Icelandic Consulate-General
2 Montalto Ave.
Toorak 3142
(03) 241 3546

Indonesian Consulate
52 Albert Road
South Melbourne 3205
(03) 690 7811

Italian Consulate-General
34 Anderson St.
South Yarra 3141
(03) 267 5744

Japanese Consulate-General
492 St. Kilda Road
Melbourne 3004
(03) 267 3244

Latvian Consulate
38 Longstaff St.
Ivanhoe East 3079
(03) 49 6920

Lebanese Consulate-General
84 Wellington St.
Windsor 3181
(03) 529 4498

Malaysian Consulate
434 St. Kilda Road
Melbourne 3004
(03) 267 5339

Maltese Consulate
343 Little Collins St.
Melbourne 3000
(03) 670 8427

Mauritius Consulate
11 St. Georges Road
Toorak 3142
(03) 241 4112

Monaco Consulate
National Bank House
500 Bourke St.
Melbourne 3000
(03) 602 3088

Nauru Consulate-General
80 Collins St.

Melbourne 3000
(03) 653 5709

Nepal Consulate-General (Royal)
Suite 601, 126 Wellington Parade
East Melbourne 3002
(03) 419 8783

Netherlands Consulate-General
499 St. Kilda Road
Melbourne 3004
(03) 267 7933

New Zealand Consulate-General
330 Collins St.
Melbourne 3000
(03) 670 8111

Nicaraguan Consuls
24 Centreway St.
Keilor East 3036
(03) 336 2411

Norwegian Consulate-General (Royal)
1 Collins St.
Melbourne 3000
(03) 650 4983
(03) 645 1879

Peruvian Consulate
Building B
World Trade Centre
Melbourne 3000
(03) 611 2636

Portugal Consulate
114 Albert St.
South Melbourne 3205
(03) 699 2122

Republic of San Marino
Consulate-General
38 Royena Road
Moorabbin 3189
(03) 555 9963

Senegal Consulate
15 Fenwick St.
Kew 3101
(03) 862 1239

Switzerland Consulate-General
3 Bowen Crescent
Melbourne 3000
(03) 267 2266

Thailand Consulate-General (Royal)
55 Elizabeth St.
Melbourne 3000
(03) 62 7668

Turkish Consulate-General
180 Brunswick Road
Brunswick. 3056
(03) 388 0178

United States Consulate-General
24 Albert Road
South Melbourne 3205
(03) 697 7900

Venezuela Consulate
8 Lisson Grove
Hawthorn 3122
(03) 818 5162

Yugoslavia Consulate
58 Lisson Grove
Hawthorn 3122
(03) 818 2254

ART/PHOTO CREDITS

Borthwick, John	40L, 59, 157
Bowden, David	112R, 148, 163, 166, 176, 177, 180
Brooke, Marcus	18-19, 31, 34, 40L, 40R, 82, 94, 99L, 131, 170-171
Gottschalk, Manfred	169
Heaton, D.J.	51, 93, 114, 142-143
Hendrie, Peter/The Image Bank	50, 102, 103, 149
La Trobe Collection	26-27, 28, 29, 30, 32, 33, 46L,46R, 52, 56, 150, 172-173
McGonigal, David	70, 107, 109R, 110, 111
Messent, David	156
Newman, Robbi	35, 49, 60, 89, 95, 99R, 106, 109L, 121, 122, 154
Photobank	62
Photo Library Sydney	83
Photographers International	54
Sattlberger, Chris	61, 63, 184
Santos, Emmanuel	116, 132, 134, 137, 138
Steel, Paul	1, 3, 9, 14-15, 17, 20-21, 22, 24 25, 36-37, 38-39, 41L, 41R, 43, 44-45, 47, 48, 58, 65, 66-67, 73, 76, 77L, 77R, 78, 79, 80, 81, 86, 87, 88, 90, 91, 92, 96-97, 100, 101, 104, 105, 108, 112L, 113, 117, 118-119, 123, 124, 125, 126, 127, 128, 129, 130L, 130R, 133, 140-141, 146, 147, 151, 152L, 153, 155, 158-159, 160, 161, 162, 164, 165, 167, 178, 179, 182, 183
Sipa Press	55
Victorian Tourism Commission	115

The photographs on pages 110 and 111
appear courtesy of the National Trust of Australia (Victoria).

INDEX

A

B

C

D

E

F

G

H

I - K

L

M

N

O

P

Q - R

S

T

U - V

W